Sins of My Brothers

Sins of My Brothers

PHILLIP ANTHONY PERRY

Fork in the Road Press

Franklin, Tennessee

Copyright © 2023

All rights reserved.

Sins of My Brothers

Printed in the United States of America

No part of this publication may be reproduced, distributed, or transmitted in any form or by any means, including photocopying, recording, or other electronic or mechanical methods, or by any information storage and retrieval system without the prior written permission of the publisher, except in the case of very brief quotations embodied in critical reviews and certain other noncommercial uses permitted by copyright law.

ISBN: 979-8-9889759-0-8

Library of Congress Control Number: 2023916006

Dedication

For Lesa and Alex

Contents

Introduction		ix
A Brief Note About The Geneva Bible & The Soldier's Pocket Bible		xiii
Prologue		xvi

PART I. ANDERSONVILLE, GEORGIA CAPTIVI IN INFERNO

1.	"Captured"	2
2.	"In Bonds"	8
3.	"In the pit"	18
4.	"Drenched in blood"	24
5.	"New tenant"	31
6.	"The drummer boy"	39
7.	"The Angel of Andersonville"	46
8.	"Mad as a hatter"	52
9.	"The Reckoning"	57
10.	"Running the gauntlet"	61
11.	"Time's up!"	66
12.	"Skeletons in rags"	72
13.	"Is that scarecrow really a provost?"	79

14.	"Found alive"	*88*

PART II. CONSPIRACY AND SURRENDER

15.	"Inauguration Day"	*96*
16.	"Starstruck"	*101*
17.	"Reconnaissance"	*108*
18.	"One of the largest and best steamers ever constructed..."	*117*
19.	City Point	*124*
20.	"Options"	*128*
21.	"...and I would rather die a thousand deaths."	*133*
22.	April 9, 1865	*138*
23.	"We are all Americans."	*143*
24.	"My heart is too full to say more."	*148*
25.	"I'm done playing."	*154*
26.	"Now, by God, I will put him through."	*159*

PART III. SICARIUS

27.	"Disturbing Dreams"	*165*
28.	April 14, 1865 - Good Friday	*170*
29.	"...and your old men shall dream dreams."	*181*
30.	"Hail to the Chief"	*188*
31.	"Sic Semper Tyrannis!"	*193*
32.	"Oh! My husband's blood!"	*198*

33.	"Murder! Murder!"	*203*
34.	"Now he belongs to the ages."	*210*

PART IV. THE JOURNEY HOME

35.	Easter Sunday Photos	*215*
36.	"I was a stranger..."	*220*
37.	"Darkness favors us."	*230*
38.	Camp Fisk	*236*
39.	"Windfall Profits"	*242*
40.	"No, they can all go on one boat."	*246*
41.	"Boots and Saddles"	*251*
42.	"JWB"	*254*
43.	"...the greatest trip ever made on the western waters."	*264*
44.	"missed the boat"	*270*
45.	"Trapped"	*278*
46.	"Useless, useless!"	*286*
47.	April 27, 1865	*292*

PART V. THE AFTERMATH

48.	"We cannot hold out any longer!"	*300*
49.	"Gruesome Cargo"	*305*
50.	"I want you to die quick."	*310*
51.	"It Was Murder!"	*319*
52.	Change	*326*

53.	Epidemic and Extradition	*331*
54.	Madness	*337*
55.	The Angel and the Bad Men	*342*
	Epilogue	*349*
	Acknowledgements	*354*
	References	*357*
	Notes and Resources	*366*
	Index	*417*
	About the Author	*425*

33.	"Murder! Murder!"	*203*
34.	"Now he belongs to the ages."	*210*

PART IV. THE JOURNEY HOME

35.	Easter Sunday Photos	*215*
36.	"I was a stranger..."	*220*
37.	"Darkness favors us."	*230*
38.	Camp Fisk	*236*
39.	"Windfall Profits"	*242*
40.	"No, they can all go on one boat."	*246*
41.	"Boots and Saddles"	*251*
42.	"JWB"	*254*
43.	"...the greatest trip ever made on the western waters."	*264*
44.	"missed the boat"	*270*
45.	"Trapped"	*278*
46.	"Useless, useless!"	*286*
47.	April 27, 1865	*292*

PART V. THE AFTERMATH

48.	"We cannot hold out any longer!"	*300*
49.	"Gruesome Cargo"	*305*
50.	"I want you to die quick."	*310*
51.	"It Was Murder!"	*319*
52.	Change	*326*

53.	Epidemic and Extradition	*331*
54.	Madness	*337*
55.	The Angel and the Bad Men	*342*
	Epilogue	*349*
	Acknowledgements	*354*
	References	*357*
	Notes and Resources	*366*
	Index	*417*
	About the Author	*425*

Introduction

Growing up in Franklin, Tennessee during the '60s and '70s was a special time. A simpler time when kids could be kids. Franklin was a small town then. Today it's still a charming old town, teeming with Civil War history in practically every place you look. As kids, we didn't give much thought to the street names downtown—names that rang out during the Battle of Franklin in November 1864. Historically significant names such as Cleburne (Patrick R.), Stewart (A. P.), Gist (States Rights), Adams (John), Hood (John Bell), Strahl (Otho French), Granbury (Hiram B.), Carter (John C.), and Forrest (Nathan Bedford) label these scenic streets clustered along the main artery through Franklin. Columbia Avenue, the path taken by Hood's Confederate army to engage Federal breastworks in Union held Franklin also hosts the Carter House and the Lotz Museum.

I never gave much thought to the gravity of our chosen playground near our old neighborhood, Hill Estates. We knew Fort Granger was an old Civil War Union camp, but more importantly, we knew it was our secret place. I don't think any of us thought of it as historically sacred ground. We just thought it was a cool place to ride our bicycles and dirt bikes. We kept the secret playground just between us. For that day and all the others spent in Fort Granger, we would stake our claim there—share camaraderie and bond—perhaps the way the soldiers did one hundred years before.

Fort Granger would remain ours until we abandoned the camp, prompted by the monumental milestone of acquiring a driver's license. Still, I was surrounded and imbued with the relics of a Civil War battlefield.

The first time that I read anything memorable about the *Sultana* disaster was many years later, in 1992, the year of my son's birth. I had often traded books with co-workers who enjoyed reading as much as I did, and one of the books that came my way at the time was something new written by Jerry Potter. That inspiring book is titled, *"The Sultana Tragedy: America's Greatest Maritime Disaster"*. After reading the book, I was not only captured by the story but was also stunned that I had never heard of it before. I considered myself well-read and historically informed but somehow, this story had eluded me. How was that possible? The worst maritime disaster in U.S. history was virtually unknown.

After reading Potter's book, I asked around. It seemed that practically everyone I queried about the *Sultana* would shrug their shoulders and give me a blank stare. My well-read friends had never heard the story either. And when I would tell them about it, they were likewise befuddled and embarrassed. They had no knowledge of the event. The scant few that were familiar with the story were almost exclusively avid Civil War enthusiasts.

A few years later, Gene Eric Salecker followed the story and wrote a wonderful account titled, *"Disaster on the Mississippi: The Sultana Explosion, April 27, 1865"*. After reading those two books on the subject, I was hooked.

Before writing this text that you now hold, I had a lot of questions.

How could this tragedy that killed more people than the infamous *Titanic* be forgotten or relegated to the back pages of newspapers? How did all those victims wind up getting on this particular boat? Weren't there other transports available? Who was responsible? How could it have been prevented? What else was going on at that time? Was I absent from history class the day they taught about the *Sultana*?

I am pressed to recall anything being taught about the *Sultana* disaster in school. If the subject was covered, it probably wasn't enough to pique my interest. It was likely a half-page or less—if there was any mention of it at all.

To make sense of it in my mind, I began to put together a timeline. As my research expanded, my wall became filled with post-it notes filled with little snippets of events, names, and dates. These post-it notes became pages scattered on the floor. On this relatively short timeline, I noted several major historical events that occurred during this period, and down the rabbit hole I went. My wife thought I had succumbed to madness, but she humored me anyway. I allowed the research to take me wherever it led—to Andersonville, to Shiloh, to D.C., or a dozen other places.

The timeline revealed that in the span of just weeks (primarily the month of April 1865), Lincoln was sworn in for his second term, Lee (and Johnston) surrendered, Lincoln was assassinated, the manhunt and killing of John Wilkes Booth occurred, and then the *Sultana* disaster. Any one of these events would singularly be considered front-page news—and they were, but only fleetingly so for the *Sultana*. The public's fascination with the dark conspiracy, manhunt, and killing of Booth had somehow overshadowed the explosion of a boat filled with Union soldiers south of the Mason-Dixon line. It was as if the tragic past was murmuring out of the side of its mouth—like a jaded beat cop, "Nothing to see here—move along." The war was finally over and the public had obviously lost their stomach for yet another disturbing body count.

But I still wanted to know what happened. I wanted more details. I wanted *the story*. Not just the basic names and dates we were habitually forced to memorize in school—I wanted to hear the asides and innuendos. I wanted the dirt. I've tried to answer some of those nagging questions. Through it all, I felt there was a story here and I wanted to tell it. Based on my research and the resources available, I've tried to tell it truthfully as best I can.

A Brief Note About The Geneva Bible & The Soldier's Pocket Bible

All but forgotten today, the Geneva Bible (GNV) was the most widely read and influential English Bible of the 16th and 17th centuries. It was the Bible taken to America by Pilgrims and Puritans on the *Mayflower*. The Geneva Bible followed the Great Bible of 1539, the first Bible in the English language authorized by the Church of England.

Mary I was Queen of England and Ireland from 1553 until her death in 1558. Her execution of Protestants prompted her opponents to give her the moniker "Bloody Mary." Her persecution caused the Marian Exile, which drove 800 English scholars to the European continent, where a number of them gathered in Geneva, Switzerland.

There, a team of scholars led by William Whittingham, and assisted by Miles Coverdale, Christopher Goodman, Anthony Gilby, John Knox, and Thomas Sampson, produced The Geneva Bible, based on Greek and Hebrew manuscripts and a revision of William Tyndale's New Testament, which first appeared in 1526. The Geneva Bible New Testament was published in 1557, with the complete Bible appearing in 1560.

The Geneva Bible is unique among all other Bibles. It was the first Bible to use chapters and numbered verses and became the most popular version of its time because of its extensive marginal notes. These notes, written by Reformation leaders including John Calvin and others, were intended to help explain and interpret the Scriptures for the average reader.

For three generations, this Bible held sway in the homes of the English people. While Great Bibles and Bishops' Bibles were read out in the churches, Geneva Bibles were read by the firesides, well before and after the King James version was issued. A superb translation, it was the product of the best Protestant scholars of the day and became the Bible of choice for many of the greatest writers and thinkers of that time. The Geneva Bible was the Bible of William Shakespeare, John Bunyan, and Oliver Cromwell and was used exclusively in their writings. Because the language of the Geneva Bible was more forceful and vigorous, most readers strongly preferred this version to the Great Bible. In the words of theologian Cleland Boyd McAfee, "it drove the Great Bible off the field by sheer power of excellence."

With its variety of scriptural study guides and aids—which included cross-reference verse citations, introductions to each book of the Bible, maps, tables, woodcut illustrations, indexes, and other features—the Geneva Bible is regarded as history's first study Bible.

This version of the Bible is significant because, for the first time, a mechanically printed, mass-produced Bible was made available directly to the general public which came with a variety of scriptural study guides and aids (collectively called an apparatus), which included verse citations that allow the reader to cross-reference one verse with numerous relevant verses in the rest of the Bible. Scriptural study guides also included introductions to each book of the Bible that acted to summarize all the material that each book would cover.

The *Soldier's Pocket Bible* was issued in 1861 at the very beginning of the American Civil War. It is an exact reproduction of one issued in 1643 during the English Civil War. The quote on the title page, "Trust in the Lord and keep your powder dry," was Oliver Cromwell's famous battle cry to his troops. The little book consists of Bible passages, which might be of most help to a soldier.

The Soldier's Pocket Bible has a fascinating history connecting the American and English Civil Wars. Originally published in 1643 during the English Civil war, the booklet is a collection of 125 verses from the Geneva Bible translation to encourage soldiers in Oliver Cromwell's army. Only three original copies of this pamphlet are known. Antiquarian George Livermore discovered one in 1854; he later reprinted it for use by soldiers in the American Civil War. This was the Bible predominately carried by both the Yankee and the Rebel soldier. There are numerous stories about how this little book lifted spirits from despair and miraculously stopped Minié balls from penetrating the flesh.

PHILLIP ANTHONY PERRY

Prologue

*"Behold our God whom we serve
is able to deliver us from the hot fiery furnace,
and he will deliver us out of thine hand O King."*
—Daniel 3:17, The Soldier's Pocket Bible

April 27, 1865

A few hours before dawn, men in steamboats, flatboats, and makeshift rafts struggled to pull the wounded and emaciated bodies from the Mississippi River seven miles north of Memphis. They transferred scalded and burnt survivors to the steamers. The southbound *Bostonia II* was one of the first rescue boats to come upon the disaster close to an hour after the explosion.

Burning debris floated swiftly by on the surface of the river, lighting up the eerie scene. Men wailed and cried. Some begged God for relief, while others cursed Him. More than a thousand victims floundered about in the water, and close to that many flailed in agony on the burning ship.

The stench rising from the smoke was a combination of the burning vessel and its contents—livestock, painted wood, coal, carpets, and human corpses. In a thick fog and steady rain, the few recovery volunteers responding at a little past three in the morning had to shout to be heard above the din. Low visibility, less than twenty feet in the smoke and mist, forced rescuers to rely on hearing the victims' cries to locate survivors.

Many aboard the burning vessel were already dead, charred beyond recognition. Sounds of the living filled the air—pleading, screaming, and moaning. Croaks and gurgles accompanied their desperate cries.

Most of the victims, recently freed Union soldiers, had endured prisoner-of-war camps at Andersonville in Georgia and Cahaba in Alabama. The former POWs, released just days ago, were already in bad shape before they boarded the boat transporting them home. Many existed as little more than skin and bones, suffering from long-term captivity.

The Mississippi River had been at flood stage for the past week or more. Ongoing spring showers had become downpours, coupled with winter melts, raising the water level until swelling the river out of its banks. A small group of islands known as Paddy's Hen and Chickens disrupted the flow of the river enough to make it a swirling eddy. The brown water was more than three miles wide at this bend in the river and ice cold. Some of the flotsam had the lucky ones clinging to it. Horses and mules frantically swam with men hanging onto them, mane and tail.

The remainder of the sidewheel paddleboat had separated in the center, about where the pilothouse was. Smoke and steam belched from the gaping hole—the location of the boilers before the blast. The twin smokestacks fell akimbo across the hurricane deck, with an odd ornament fastened there on the cross-brace between the tumbled smokestacks—a huge rack of elk antlers.

The vessel, rudderless and swirling out of control in the swift current, listed and began to sink with the rest of the passengers still debating which would be worse—burning alive, drowning, or hypothermia. Most chose the water. Later, the others lost the option.

The drummer boy from Springfield, panting and gasping for air, clung to a sapling protruding from a sandbar. He clenched the young tree in both hands and struggled to hang on while keeping his head above the surface. The fierce river current proved to be a challenge, definitely more than his frail body could swim against. Nearly horizontal in the powerful current, he watched the horror of the catastrophe play out before his eyes—desperate men drowning and taking others down with them in a maniacal attempt to stay topside.

Liberating himself from the weight of the wool uniform, the drummer stripped himself of all his clothes, swam away from the wreckage and the others, and chose the Arkansas shore as his destination. He knew he had suffered serious burns, but the cold water numbed his pain. He decided if he could hold on long enough, he might regain enough strength to make it to the western bank. To conserve energy, he didn't scream like those around him—wailing and thrashing about.

People clung to whatever they could grab that floated. Pieces of gangplanks, shutters, doors, anything buoyant. Women and children flailed in the water too, crying and clutching each other. Some appeared briefly, submerged, then disappeared.

Later, bodies would be found in treetops on the Arkansas side of the Mississippi River. In the days and weeks that followed, bodies would be recovered from a ten-mile stretch of the waterway, some even as far away as Vicksburg, Mississippi, while others would never be found.

PART I

Andersonville, Georgia
Captivi in Inferno

PHILLIP ANTHONY PERRY

1

"Captured"

> "Fear none of those things, which thou shalt suffer:
> behold, it shall come to pass,
> that the devil shall cast some of you into prison,
> that ye may be tried, and ye shall have tribulation ten days:
> be thou faithful unto the death,
> and I will give thee the crown of life.
> Do not fear what you are about to suffer."
> —Revelation 2:10 GNV

"Fourscore and seven years ago our fathers brought forth, on this continent, a new nation, conceived in liberty, and dedicated to the proposition that all men are created equal. Now we are engaged in a great civil war, testing whether that nation . . . can long endure." —Abraham Lincoln's Gettysburg Address, November 19, 1863

November 1863—Brandy Station, Orange County, Virginia

How he wound up here was a complex question. It would be a long time before Robert Sneden could answer that one. His story was one of duality, spanning two countries, two sides, and two points of view. Two points on a compass and two colors. Robert's life would be divided in two—one before the war and one after. The thought passed through his mind to make a run for it. But he knew he couldn't outrun a bullet.

The Previous Day

Robert Sneden's satchel was now full of sketches. Upon leaving the regiment two days ago, nothing existed but blank pages, pencils, and the drafting tools provided by the federal army. He busied himself collecting topographical and geographical information to make maps for federal strategic purposes.

The small group of soldiers accompanying him had stealthily covered many miles of terrain, and it had been no picnic. Uncharted and unforgiving, the assigned journey was necessary. It wasn't just an order—General George Meade insisted he needed those damned maps.

Bleeding and brushing through the thickets of briers and locust thorns didn't help the group's mood. Every step reminded them of the blisters earned on every toe, on the balls of their feet, and on their heels.

Out here in the open, they stood exposed to the enemy. Rebels could hide anywhere, so on they quietly marched, wincing and grumbling with each painful step. At least the autumn foliage lay mostly on the ground, improving long-range sight. Confederate snipers would be more visible. Robert provided more of a target than the others since he was mounted.

He sat atop a mare with his left leg bent at the knee and propped across the saddle, his drawing board on top, drawing tools in a modified blanket with a pocket. His current sketch already had most of the pertinent information. He'd finish the final detailed drawings in the comfort of the camp. With the mission completed, the unit headed back.

That evening, as the V Corps under General George Meade moved out, a small group comprised of Robert Sneden, the clerks, the cooks, and a squad of about ten infantrymen stayed behind to clear up loose ends. The cooking mess left from a ten-day ration preparation needed to be cleaned and readied to move out. Papers, maps, and instruments for mapmaking had to be packed away also. Robert and his small group got the order to tidy up and catch up the next day to the huge, two-hundred-wagon train of troops just departing. Unfortunately, not a drop of whiskey remained among them to ring in the Thanksgiving holiday.

As the sun set, he watched as the miles-long caravan left them. The departure of most of his company concerned Robert, and his comrades must have sensed it. He was told he was being nervous and paranoid—and he should get some sleep. They would break camp and rejoin the regiment first thing in the morning. He couldn't doze and didn't understand how they could. Someone should probably stand watch.

Later, he walked outside in the darkness of the foggy night to take a look. Visibility was less than twenty feet, but despite a limited view, he saw a horseman wander out of the edge of the woods and then disappear back into the thicket. Then another. Appearing and disappearing like a vapor. Rushing to his group, Robert tried to alert the others of something out there. They groggily waved him off and told him again to get some sleep. He grabbed a blanket and sat near the fire. *Was he suffering psychosis? Maybe.*

In the peace and quiet, nestled by the fire, Robert eventually nodded off about four o'clock in the morning. His slumber wouldn't last.

He awakened to a whisper in his ear and a Colt revolver held against his head. Click, click. The distinctive sound made when the hammer ratchets into firing position.

"Be silent, or I'll blow a hole through you," the voice said.

Frozen by the chilling voice in the dark, he could barely swallow the lump in his throat. *What the hell?*

"Get into your clothes right smart. Mosby wants you."

Now, wide-eyed and suddenly sick to his stomach, Robert complied with the instructions. He looked around him and saw that his fellow soldiers shared his hopeless predicament.

On November 27, Confederate Rangers, under the leadership of the "Gray Ghost," John Singleton Mosby, all wearing blue overcoats to disguise their Confederate gray, captured Robert and twenty-two other Union soldiers in the pre-dawn fog.

Robert Sneden served as a prisoner of war for the next thirteen months. From November 1863 until February 1864, he was held at an old tobacco warehouse in Richmond, next to Libby Prison, where he contracted and suffered from typhoid fever. On February 22, 1864, after a prison escape, Robert and a trainload of POWs were shipped to a new camp under construction near Americus, Georgia.

They were loaded onto crowded cattle cars, forty or fifty prisoners per car, with little ventilation, and transported by rail to what would be their new home. Armed rebels—four or five in each car—guarded them. The cars still had animal feces on the floor where the POWs lay. The prisoners got very little sustenance in the way of food or water during the arduous six-day journey to the notorious Andersonville Prison.

When the train arrived at the depot in Andersonville, the prisoners, stiff and sore from the ride, were herded out of the cattle cars. By the time the POWs arrived on the last day of February, the stockade walls were nearly completed and had received the first influx of prisoners only four days prior.

The prisoners were marched into the stockade and down to the prison headquarters for a thorough search. They could retain sums of money less than one hundred dollars. The POWs had little cash, however, as they took precautions to conceal any valuables. After being searched, the men formed lines and counted off into detachments comprising ninety men each. These detachments were then subdivided into messes of men—thirty each, to simplify the distribution of rations and taking roll. Union POW officers were placed in charge of regimental mess management.

At about the same time, among the steady arrival of Union soldiers, Private John McElroy joined Robert Sneden as a POW at the Andersonville stockade.

For now, the commandant of the prison was General John Henry Winder. Opinions about the commandant among the prisoners were strong and unified. They despised him—and the feeling was mutual. Winder's callousness toward the prisoners matched their passion for his destruction. Winder would later point to the 3,081 newly dug POW graves—one month's worth—and boast that he was "doing more for the Confederacy than twenty regiments."

General John Henry Winder

John Henry Winder's features seemed to illustrate the evil within. He had scraggly, white locks of hair that fell beneath his slouch hat, nearly to his shoulders. A drunkard and a scoundrel, he had sunken, gray, bloodshot eyes set in a haggard face of contempt. The cowardly bully and impatient tyrant, with a mouth drawn into an ever-present puss, seemed angry and bitter over his inferiority as a human being. A decorated oppressor in a uniform, Winder took pleasure in inflicting pain and suffering. His cruelty was legendary.

Whether it was divine intervention or karma, no one knows, but John Henry Winder would not live to see the conclusion of this war.

2

"In Bonds"

"Remember them that are in bonds,
as though ye were bound with them:
and them that are in affliction,
as if ye were also afflicted in the body."
—Hebrews 13:3 GNV

It was amazing how quickly humanity, when deprived and suffering, could crumble into anarchy. Scant vegetation grew inside the prison walls, trampled by the human herd. Outside the stockade, trees stood on the surrounding hillsides but provided little comfort or protection. Inside the walls, men—their sooty faces blackened by smoky, pine-sap campfires—huddled in small groups, warming themselves and cooking their meager rations, consisting of a pint of course-ground cornmeal, usually with the cob ground into it.

A makeshift market had gradually developed on the prison's Main Street, the muddy path through the center of the stockade. All manner of bartering and trading went on all hours of the day among prisoners and Confederate guards. Many of the prisoners had already traded most of their valuables, including their clothes, for extra rations, leaving them weak, hungry, naked, and vulnerable to the elements. It was a macabre scene—the walking dead and dying circling like ants on a massive scale with nowhere to go.

Robert Sneden busied himself sketching camp images on secreted paper, while John McElroy sat and scribbled his testimony in his journal.

Seventeen-year-old John McElroy had been first sent to Richmond, then to Andersonville, arriving at the same time as Robert. John, a printer and journalist was sort of a kindred spirit to Robert, an illustrator and mapmaker. John kept a personal journal, a habit he maintained throughout his military service. In one journal entry, he quoted Andersonville commandant General John Henry Winder allegedly boasting, "I am killing off more Yankees than twenty regiments in Lee's army." The sick irony of that statement was that it was true. The prison system operated by the Confederate government would claim three times the casualties as the army had on the battlefield.

In a journal entry dated July 27, 1864, McElroy claimed General Winder issued order No. 13 that stated, if Union troops came within seven miles of Andersonville, the guards were to "open upon the stockade with grapeshot (using the numerous cannons that were trained on the prisoners) without reference to the situation beyond the lines of defense." In other words, they were to commit widespread murder of the POWs inside the prison walls.

After Robert Sneden entered the gates of Andersonville, he soon became acquainted with the harsh realities of being a POW in a rebel camp. Upon arrival, he first laid eyes on General Winder, the man who would come to represent evil to the prisoners.

Robert had somehow managed to keep his distance from an evil force within their own ranks. But he would soon learn about a prison scourge—a group of prisoners called the Raiders. Robert would witness savage brutality, beatings, and murder. It was survival of the fittest inside this dystopian prison society.

During the first half of the Civil War, Confederate officials relied on existing structures in the Confederate capital of Richmond to house prisoners of war. More than twenty locations around the city held sixteen thousand POWs in 1863. Prisoners of war made up twenty percent of the population of Richmond, held in camps like Belle Isle, Libby Prison, Castle Thunder, or one of the many repurposed tobacco or cotton warehouses around the city.

The growing POW population in the Confederate capital alarmed military leadership. Confederate General Robert E. Lee stated in an October 28, 1863, memo:

"I would respectfully suggest that the city of Richmond is not a suitable place for the accommodation and safe keeping of these prisoners. I think the presence of a large number there is, for many reasons, very injurious. It increases largely the number of supplies to be transported to the city, and thus employs transportation which might be used for the benefit of the citizens. This has a tendency to increase high prices and cause distress among the poorer classes."

The city of Richmond was pushed to the brink as the citizens could no longer support themselves, the nearby encamped armies, *and* the exploding POW population. Confederate Secretary of War James Seddon instructed Captain William Sidney Winder on November 24, 1863, to travel to rural southwest Georgia to secure a location to construct a new prison.

Local property owners in Albany, Georgia, discouraged Winder's attempts to establish a prison there, fearing the negative impact of high concentrations of Union POWs on the community. Winder then traveled to Americus, Georgia, where he learned of a small village on the Southwestern Railroad line originally named Anderson.

The selected site was chosen for several reasons. First, the property owners of a large, wooded lot—Benjamin Dykes and William Turner—were willing to lease the site to the Confederate government. Second, the rail depot in Anderson allowed for the transportation of military personnel, supplies, and prisoners, with trains running daily. Third, a stream, described as a "large supply of beautiful clear water" was available for use as drinking water. Additionally, there were farms nearby for food, lumber mills for building supplies, and the site was isolated from the front lines to reduce escapes or potential liberation attempts.

The site would be officially named for the county in which it was located—Camp Sumter. Due to the confusion of mail delivery to another town called Anderson, the village was renamed Andersonville. Soon thereafter, the prison would also be unofficially called Andersonville.

It was a family affair concerning the site selection, construction, and command of the new prison. General John Henry Winder's son, Captain William Sidney Winder had selected the site, and William's cousin and the general's nephew, Quartermaster Richard Winder, supervised its construction. General John Henry Winder, commander of all the Richmond prisons, would initially run it. He assumed command of the facility on June 3, 1864.

Under the Impression Act of 1863, Confederate citizens were required to tithe ten percent of their property to the Confederate war effort, which included their slaves. This statute was imposed to impress as many as nine hundred slaves from plantations in the region into providing labor to construct the prison stockade. For weeks on end, slaves labored, chopping down pine trees, digging five-foot-deep trenches, and setting the twenty-five-foot square-hewn logs vertically in those trenches to construct a high perimeter wall surrounding the stockade. Removal of the pine trees left a barren landscape inside and outside the prison. There were only two or three trees left standing inside the stockade walls to provide natural shade for the prisoners.

Before the perimeter walls could be completed, the first prisoners were brought to Andersonville on February 24, 1864. Construction continued and during the next few months, approximately four hundred more POWs arrived each day until, by the end of June, twenty-six thousand men were confined in a prison area originally intended to hold ten thousand. Slaves continued the stockade wall construction, while Confederate soldiers from the 26th Alabama and the 55th Georgia Regiments stood guard over them and the POWs.

The Andersonville facility became necessary after the prisoner-exchange system between the North and South collapsed in 1863 over disagreements about the handling of Negro soldiers. The federal government declared that White and Black POWs would be exchanged man-for-man, regardless of race. The Confederacy insisted that the Negroes were property, therefore not recognized as soldiers, or even human beings.

Enclosing some sixteen acres of land, the prison was supposed to include wooden barracks, but the inflated price of lumber due to the war and the inability to get supplies had prevented their construction. A steady flow of prisoners continued to arrive daily on the incoming rail cars. The Union soldiers imprisoned there lived under open skies, protected only by makeshift shanties called "shebangs", constructed from scraps of wood and blankets. Without these shebangs, the prisoners had no way to get out of the elements. There were so few of the shelters that the men were forced to sleep in stacked-spoon fashion—or to have only their heads under the scant cover, as spokes in a wheel, leaving their legs and torsos exposed to the rain, scorching sun, or snow.

Flowing through the prison yard was a stream called Stockade Branch, the camp's only water supply. The stream, however, quickly became a cesspool of disease and human waste. The creek banks eroded to create a swamp, which occupied a significant portion of the compound.

Makeshift shelters built by Andersonville's inmates called "shebangs".

Two entrances—the North Gate and the South Gate—were on the west side of the rectangular stockade. Eight earthen forts located around the exterior of the prison were equipped with artillery to quell disturbances within the compound and to defend against feared Union cavalry attacks.

Andersonville was built to hold ten thousand, but within six months, more than three times that number were incarcerated there. Rations were inadequate, and at times, half or more of the population was reported ill. Some guards brutalized the inmates, and violence broke out between factions of the prisoners.

General Winder sought to alleviate the overcrowding by enlarging the stockade to twenty-six acres, but his efforts were frustrated by the arrival of even more prisoners so that by August of 1864, the prison's population reached its peak of thirty-three thousand Union soldiers. That made Andersonville Prison the fifth most populous city in all of Georgia.

Repeated requests by General Winder for building supplies from local mills were denied, as were requests for food, medical supplies, and tents. Confederate officials, specifically Georgia Governor Joseph E. Brown, refused to release supplies to the prison, preferring to keep them on hand for Confederate troops.

After only eight weeks into his command of Andersonville, Winder was promoted to command of all Confederate prisons in Georgia and Alabama. Winder appointed his former assistant, Captain Henry Wirz, as his replacement.

The Andersonville stockade sloped down on both sides creating a valley around Stockade Branch, which was a yard or two wide and a foot deep. Since no arrangement had been made for sewage disposal, this singular creek provided drinking, cooking, and bathing water, while also serving as the latrine. The daily waste of two nearby Confederate camps and the grease and garbage from the cookhouse were thrown into the creek. Soon, the slow-flowing stream became a mass of thick, polluted ooze.

Thousands more prisoners came and milled about its banks. Some of the very sick were unable to extricate themselves from the mire. Others who could not reach the sinks, or latrines, had to relieve themselves in the mud.

Many of the prisoners had rags for clothes and no shoes. Some of them were completely naked. At the edges of the stream, maggots were squirming and dying, forming a crusty border between the red Georgia clay and the fetid water. One prisoner reported that "all the filth from the prison ran into the creek and we had to strain the water through our teeth to keep the maggots out."

As a measure to keep the prisoners away from the stockade walls, the newly appointed commandant, Captain Henry Wirz, ordered that an interior boundary fence inside the main stockade wall be installed. The "deadline", as it was called, was a light fence erected twenty feet inside the twenty-foot-high walls.

The rebel guards situated in towers atop the wall, nicknamed pigeon roosts, were spaced every thirty feet and overlooked the yard. The guards were instructed to shoot any prisoner touching, crossing, or even approaching the deadline—without warning. Some of the more desperate prisoners would deliberately violate these rules to end their suffering.

Robert Sneden's drawing depicting Andersonville's "deadline".

All new arrivals to Andersonville quickly learned of Captain Wirz's strict disciplinary regime. He would greet them at the gate, cursing at them in his heavy Swiss accent while brandishing his pistol, personally threatening to shoot any man who broke prison rules or attempted to escape. He offered prisoners a twelve-hour head start, promising that they would be hunted down by his men and the dogs—and that they would suffer the consequences. Those consequences usually involved being mauled by the dogs, being locked in the stocks, and having food rations withheld.

Most of the guard forces were comprised of old men, wounded soldiers, and young boys—all ineligible to serve in the active Confederate army. Captain Wirz was responsible for everything that happened inside the stockade, including issuing rations, keeping rolls, maintaining discipline and order, and securing the stockade. He often used intimidation and brutality to maintain order.

Keeping an accurate headcount was difficult, given the rate at which the prisoners were arriving and dying. Disease, dysentery, scurvy, chronic diarrhea, amputations, exposure, and malnutrition most often were the cause of death. The habitually disobedient prisoners were placed in stocks where some expired due to their frail conditions. Other prisoners were cuffed to a heavy iron ball to drag around the stockade.

Just outside the prison walls, a six-acre cemetery near the railroad tracks was where dead prisoners were buried. When the ration cart was not in use doling out meager rations to the captives, that same cart made daily runs through the camp to pick up the corpses. No one bothered to clean it in between.

In a May 25, 1864, report sent to his uncle, General John Henry Winder, Captain Richard Winder stated the dire need for relief at Andersonville prison:

"If the number of prisoners is very much increased and this camp made, as I suppose it will be, the grand receptacle for prisoners captured throughout

the Confederacy, then I would by all means recommend that another area be enclosed with a stockade similar to the present one and that the grounds selected be on a stream about one-quarter of a mile south of the present camp. Immediate arrangements should be made in which the prisoners may be sheltered from the rains and protected from the heat of the sun. Buildings should be commenced as soon as practicable for the winter, and in the meantime, tents should be furnished for their use during the summer. Without this they will die off by the hundreds and will be a dead loss to us in the way of exchange."

Captain Winder's suggestions were ignored.

In Andersonville, 6,721 prisoners died during the summer of 1864. August 23rd was the day with the highest mortality rate; a total of 127 men died that day—about one every eleven minutes.

A stickler for facts and figures, Robert Sneden did the math—twenty-six acres for thirty-two thousand men. By Robert's calculations, each prisoner was allotted a space inside the walls about twelve square feet, or equal to an area about the size of a burial coffin.

More than half of the prison population was sick. Among the sick was Robert Sneden.

By the end of the war, 45,613 Union prisoners would pass through the Andersonville gates, of which almost thirteen thousand died. Most of the deaths occurred from August to December of 1864, when prisoners died at a rate of approximately one hundred men per day.

3

"In the pit"

*"And they shall be gathered together
as the prisoners in the pit:
and they shall be shut up in the prison,
and after many days shall they be visited."*
—Isaiah 24:22 GNV

"God help you, I cannot."—Henry Wirz

To a newcomer, the stench was unbearable. Many gagged and vomited upon entering the stockade, emptying their stomachs once inside the North Gate. The ground was littered with dead and dying men and human waste. The hopeless vacant stare of the prisoners was a sickening sight. Captain Wirz had been there long enough to become inured to the smell and tragic conditions. He strode about like a game rooster looking for a fight.

Still, he tried to minimize his exposure to the general population for a couple of reasons. Wirz feared a personal attack; he was always accompanied by armed guards when he mingled with the prisoners. He also feared contagious diseases carried by the men.

Today, like most days, Captain Wirz planned to greet a new batch of POWs. His mare had been saddled and awaited the commandant of Andersonville.

Wirz wore a well-appointed gray uniform that was relatively clean, considering the stockade conditions. The uniform was decorated with gold piping and stitching to indicate his superior rank. Strapped on his left hip was a nickel-plated, pearl-handled revolver, the very same pistol he had threatened practically every POW with as they entered the gate. Knee-high jackboots and a gray wool Kepi hat completed his uniform dress. His right arm was cradled in a black sling made of coarse cotton fabric. A cozy military relationship with General Winder and the loss of the use of his right arm to a Minié ball during the Battle of Seven Pines three years earlier had consequently resulted in his promotion.

Captain Henry Wirz

Exiting the command headquarters cabin, Henry Wirz and his officers strode to the dusty corral where the mounts were saddled and ready. Once mounted, the unit began the short quarter-mile ride down the hill to the North Gate to perform the familiar inductee ritual, which included promises and threats, encouragement and terror. Today was already hot and muggy in South Georgia and about to get hotter still.

Heinrich Hartmann "Henry" Wirz was born on November 25, 1823, in Zurich, Switzerland, to Hans Caspar Wirz and Sophie Barbara Philipp. Wirz received elementary and secondary education there, and he aspired to become a physician, but his family did not possess funds to pay for his medical education. Instead, he became a merchant, working in Zurich and Turin.

Wirz married Emilie Oschwald in 1845 and had two children. In April 1847, he received a four-year prison term for his inability to return money that he had borrowed. The court commuted his sentence to a twelve-year forcible emigration, and since his wife refused to emigrate with him, she eventually obtained a divorce in 1853.

In 1848, Wirz first went to Russia and the next year to the United States, where he found employment as a translator in a factory and then at a water-cure establishment in Massachusetts. Five years later, he moved to Hopkinsville, Kentucky, and worked as a doctor's assistant. He tried to establish his own homeopathic medicine practice in Cadiz, Kentucky and worked at water-cure establishments in Cadiz and Louisville.

The year after his divorce, Wirz married a Methodist widow named Elizabeth Wolfe. They moved to Louisiana, where he worked for a successful plantation owner named Levin Marshall as his plantation overseer and physician. Marshall owned many cotton and sugar plantations in Mississippi, Louisiana, and Arkansas. He owned five plantations in Mississippi and Louisiana which spanned 14,000 acres, and another 10,000 acres in Arkansas. By the 1850s, Marshall produced over 4,000 bales of cotton every year. By 1860, he owned a total of 817 African slaves.

Upon the outbreak of the Civil War in 1861, thirty-seven-year-old Wirz enlisted as a private in Company A (Madison Infantry), 4th

Battalion of Louisiana Infantry of the Confederate army in Madison Parish.

After recovering from wounds received during the Battle of Seven Pines, he returned to his unit on June 12, 1862, and was promoted to captain "for bravery on the field of battle." Because of his injury, Wirz was assigned to the staff of General John Henry Winder, who oversaw Confederate prisoner-of-war camps, as his adjutant.

Confederate President Jefferson Davis made Captain Wirz a Special Minister and sent him to Europe carrying secret dispatches to Confederate Commissioners James Mason in England and John Slidell in France. Wirz returned from Europe in January 1864 and reported back to Richmond, where he resumed working for General Winder in the prison department. In April 1864, Wirz arrived at Camp Sumter (Andersonville) and remained there for over a year, holding the post of commandant of the stockade.

Captain Wirz came riding through the muck on his gray mare, his right arm cradled across the horn of his saddle and a stub of a cigar clenched in his teeth. The arm flopped when he galloped, so he walked the mare steadily and slowly.

"Death rides a pale horse," murmured one of the prisoners to another.

Most of the prisoners looked upon Wirz as if they were seeing the seed of the devil himself; however, some understood that he had been assigned an impossible task—with little assistance or resources from the Confederate government.

In this remote location with meager supplies and support, Wirz was expected to provide everything for the health and sustenance for the multitude of prisoners and the rebel soldiers assigned there. Even if the decision had been made to release the POWs, their condition and the remoteness of the camp would have assured their death.

Prisoners and guards alike suffered from the lack of food, clothing, blankets, shelter, and medicines. The medicines intercepted through the blockade were confiscated as contraband and delivered to the North. Food rations were supposedly furnished to the prisoners and Confederate guards in the same quantity and quality, guards and POWs suffering alike. The destruction of the railroads, nearby supplies, mills, factories, and farm implements by Union troops prevented much needed supplies from reaching the stockade. The men would often go a fortnight without being able to acquire quinine for treatment of fever and ague or opium for dysentery and diarrhea.

Late in 1864, Henry Wirz solemnly told groups of new POWs arriving at the stockade:

"God help you, I cannot. What can I do? I cannot make provisions. My own men have not enough to eat. They are now on short rations. . . . I would as soon send these unfortunate men into hell as into that damned bull pen. It sickens me."

For many, Andersonville was the final and fatal bivouac.

Captain Wirz fancied himself a great leader and orator, giving speeches to the POWs about how "the powers that be" on both sides of this war were currently negotiating prisoner exchanges, and they would be free any day and soon. The prisoners who had been there the longest knew the truth, which was they had heard this speech many times before. The newer arrivals were naturally elated by his encouraging spiel. Captain Wirz may have expressed in words sympathy for the prisoners and their conditions, but the warmth of that sympathy was seldom felt by the men held there. New prisoners eventually learned how Wirz toyed with the emotional frailties of desperate men.

After repeated correspondence by Confederate Commissioner of Exchange, Colonel Robert Ould, with Union Assistant Agent of Exchange, John E. Mulford, the prisoner exchange was not resumed. In the view of the Confederate authorities, "through the alleged obstinance of the Federal Government," an agreement on the exchange of prisoners of war could not be affected.

In August 1864, Colonel Ould recommended immediate action to relieve the thousands of sick POWs incarcerated at Andersonville. The obvious lack of progress in this regard moved Ould to offer Mulford the delivery of all the sick and wounded Union POWs in confinement without insisting upon the delivery of an equal number of Confederate POWs in return, reminding Mulford of the current terrible mortality rate and urged swift action to send transportation to the mouth of the Savannah River. The offer included all sick and wounded men at Andersonville, as well as other Confederate prisons.

Additionally, if those numbers did not fill the transports to make it economically feasible, the remaining seats would be filled with healthy men. The "stone under the wheel" of progress toward prisoner exchange was that Confederate authorities continued to refuse to recognize duly mustered Negro Union POWs as men instead of property—property that in their opinion was to be returned to anyone with a claim as their master.

Federal authorities likewise stalled the prisoner exchange for their own reasons. In their view, the exchanged Confederate POWs were better cared for and better fed than the exchanged Union POWs. Upon release, the Confederate soldiers would dutifully return to their regiments for active duty, while the malnourished and sick Union soldiers were in no condition to fight or serve active duty. This stalemate would continue until springtime of the following year.

4

"Drenched in blood"

"Thou art mine hammer, and weapons of war:
for with thee will I break the nations,
and with thee will I destroy kingdoms,
—Jeremiah 51:20 GNV

"This country will be drenched in blood…
War is a terrible thing."
—William Tecumseh Sherman

President Abraham Lincoln faced re-election in November of 1864. With the long and costly war, he had lost considerable support from his Republican base, and his challenger, George Brinton McClellan, Lincoln's former general-in-chief of the Union Army, favored a negotiated peace with the Confederacy. McClellan's position regarding the war and his plan for ending it was gaining momentum with the electorate.

In contrast, Lincoln strongly supported the Thirteenth Amendment, which would end slavery in the United States forever. Democrats opposing Lincoln exploited racial fears during the campaign, cautioning that freedmen would run off with their White women and take good-paying jobs away from the White man.

The war was now in its fourth year—with more than a half million dead, a million more wounded, and no end in sight. Northern support was wavering, and Lincoln needed a military victory, and he needed it now. The upcoming presidential election was a pivotal one for the United States. If Lincoln lost, it would likely be the end of the Union itself and the end of the dream of freedom for four million slaves. Some believed that only a miracle could save Lincoln from a crushing defeat. It was in this setting, in an atmosphere of desperation when in April of 1864, William Tecumseh Sherman invaded Georgia.

It could be argued that Sherman's actions would determine if there was to even be a United States beyond 1864. General Sherman had 110,000 men under his command versus 70,000 Confederates. The strategy for the Confederates was to eventually wear down Union forces until public outcry forced either a stalemate or the Union threw in the towel altogether.

Sherman understood that the Southern city of Atlanta was a critical chess piece of the war, and he intended to take it. Everything moving east or west in the Confederacy had to go through Atlanta, a strategic railroad hub and manufacturing center. The city was second only to Richmond in strategic value. Many of the Confederate supplies seized by Union forces bore the marking "Made in Atlanta." Sherman decided therefore, to take Atlanta, and take away a critical manufacturing supply from the Confederates.

The destruction of Atlanta began well in advance of Sherman's march there. Confederate troops, using slave labor, dismantled houses, fences, and farms a year prior and built a twelve-mile ring of fortifications around the city with the salvaged materials. Only Washington, D.C., and Richmond were more defended with fortifications.

General William Tecumseh Sherman

Part of the success of Atlanta as a major city was due to the Western & Atlantic Railroad, linking Atlanta to Chattanooga. This line of tracks fed Sherman's supply line and led him directly to Atlanta. Sherman's challenge was to feed and supply 110,000 men and 50,000 mules and horses in enemy territory. With intelligence gathered, Sherman knew where the supplies were, how much his troops needed, and how to acquire them. He proclaimed, "I didn't start this war, but by God, I will end it," and vowed to "make Georgia howl."

Forty-four-year-old William Tecumseh "Cump" Sherman was originally from Ohio. His father died when William was just nine years old, leaving the family deeply in debt. In desperation, his mother Mary was forced to turn Cump over to the neighboring Ewing family to raise. Mary Sherman had no choice. She had to give her boy up, as she had given up most of her other children to

sympathetic relatives and friends. These tragic circumstances were extremely unfortunate for the Shermans of Lancaster, Ohio.

The Sherman family legacy included founders of towns, lawyers, judges, and representatives in the legislature—with a lineage traced back to the Revolutionary War.

Burdened with anxiety over his father's crushing debt, Cump entered adolescence with a quiet determination to restore the natural order of success and respect to the Sherman family name. When he was sixteen, his foster father, Senator Thomas Ewing, got him an appointment to West Point. He entered the service upon graduation, and his first assignment was to Georgia, where he memorized the landscape—an advantage that would serve him well twenty years later against Confederate General Joe Johnston.

Long before the Civil War began, the talk of war circulated, soon becoming the main topic of conversation. On the subject, Sherman wrote to a Southern friend:

"You people of the South don't know what you are doing. This country will be drenched in blood, and God only knows how it will end. You people speak so lightly of war; you don't know what you are talking about. War is a terrible thing."

Cump Sherman continued to serve in the military, regularly corresponding with his foster sister, Ellen Ewing. While serving in the South, Sherman saw for the first time the Mississippi River and the cities that dotted its banks. Carefully he made notes of the landscape and everything he saw of the cities of Vicksburg and Memphis. Cump took every opportunity to explore the region—investigating Kennesaw Mountain and western Georgia, making a topographical sketch of the terrain.

He then spent a month stationed at the federal arsenal in Augusta. He became familiar with the area as he rode horseback across the landscape. Cump later stated that this experience "was of infinite use to me and consequently to the government" during the Civil War. It would be over this same ground that Sherman would march to Atlanta and to the sea.

When Cump returned to Moultrie, Georgia, in late spring 1844, he found himself at a major turning point in his personal life. During a furlough, he decided to renounce his confirmed bachelorhood and marry his foster sister and faithful correspondent, Ellen Ewing. Despite whatever differences or baggage this union bore, Ellen was the one woman he had a steady affection for, and her unwavering devotion to him was the stabilizing certainty he needed. Sherman wrote Thomas Ewing asking for his daughter's hand and his blessing. Despite some momentary apprehension at the thought of his daughter and foster son marrying, Thomas Ewing consented.

After they married, Ellen expressed her desire for Cump to become a Catholic and resign from his military career for a civilian one. Reluctantly, Sherman conceded and tried his hand at banking as a manager of a San Francisco branch in 1853 until it closed in 1857. Sherman was relocated to a New York branch that also closed due to a banking crisis in 1858. He then became a lawyer in Leavenworth, Kansas, without much success. In 1859 Sherman became the first superintendent of Louisiana State Seminary and Military School (which later became Louisiana State University). The military atmosphere of the school was an agreeable one to Sherman.

In January 1861, as more Southern states seceded from the Union, Sherman was required to accept receipt of arms surrendered to the state militia by the US Arsenal at Baton Rouge. Instead of complying, he resigned his position as superintendent and returned to the North, declaring to the governor of Louisiana, "On no earthly account will I do any act or think any thought hostile . . . to the . . . United States."

When war broke out in 1861, Sherman re-enlisted in the Army, against Ellen's wishes. Seeing firsthand how unprepared the federal Army was for an imminent conflict with the seceding Southern states, Sherman lobbied for more troops, more training, and more supplies. Most of his requests went not only ignored but regarded as folly.

Within a year, Sherman was labeled in anti-Union newspapers as suffering a nervous breakdown while stationed in Kentucky. Newspaper stories alleged Sherman saw images of hundreds of thousands of Confederate soldiers coming at him . . . attacking him. In fact, some yellow journalists called him insane or mad.

Sherman's exasperation at the lack of preparation and order concerning the readiness of Union troops (and the civilian politicians ignoring the problems) had increased his frustration to an all-time high. In Sherman's view, if something wasn't done without haste to address the situation, only absolute Union failure could be the result. Sherman was ready to quit the military. However, after six weeks of rest at home in Ohio with the help and support of his wife and good friend Ulysses S. Grant, Sherman recovered from his emotional distress. Grant recognized Sherman's talents and abilities and wanted him back in the Army.

Complicating things, the newspapers began reporting troop movements and strategy. The press appeared to Sherman as more of a threat than the opposing army. In Sherman's view, attacks from newspapers represented a great danger to the Union cause.

After a disastrous outcome at Chickasaw Bayou, the *New York Herald* published a scathing article blaming Sherman for the failure, even though General John McClernand was the responsible officer. The author of the article, Thomas W. Knox, went on to suggest that Sherman was insane.

Sherman responded by charging Knox with treason, being a spy, providing information to the enemy, and violating General Orders No. 8 (exclusion of all non-military personnel, especially reporters, from the expedition transports) and War Department General Order No. 67 (forbidding the printing of any information from any army area without the consent of the commanding officer). Knox became the first reporter in the United States to be court-martialed. He was found guilty of the third charge, disobeying orders. Thomas Knox escaped the noose. Had he been found guilty of the other two charges, he would have been hanged for treason.

Thomas W. Knox

5

"New tenant"

"Be not deceived:
evil speakings corrupt good manners."
—1 Corinthians 15:33 GNV

"...one of the best young men I ever knew..."
—Louis Weichmann

He never wanted to pursue a career in the priesthood. That was his mother's idea. His father was a Lutheran—his mother a devout Catholic.

When Louis Weichmann graduated from high school in February 1859, he pondered his vocational options. He preferred a profession as a druggist in an apothecary, but his mother insisted Louis should enter a Catholic institution as a student for the ministry. With little enthusiasm and at the coaxing of his mother, he began a correspondence with Father E. Q. S. Waldron, a former pastor of the Catholic parish in Philadelphia, who had been transferred around 1856 to the Archdiocese of Baltimore.

Born in Baltimore on September 29, 1842, Louis Weichmann's family moved to Washington City (D.C.) the following year. His father was a tailor and a Democrat, who would vote for Stephen A. Douglas in the 1860 presidential election against Abraham Lincoln. The elder Weichmann later changed his views politically, becoming a Republican and voting for Lincoln in 1864.

Young Weichmann and Father Waldron exchanged several letters until February of 1859, when Weichmann was directed to present himself to the preparatory college of St. Charles Borromeo in Howard County, Maryland, twenty miles outside Baltimore. The college exclusively devoted itself to the training of young men for the Catholic priesthood.

Louis Weichmann

The studies at St. Charles were quite severe, and discipline was rigid. The school permitted no interaction with the outside world, except for letters to family and friends. New students to the ministry trickled in periodically, and among the new arrivals in September of Louis Weichmann's first year was a young man named John Harrison Surratt, Jr. Weichmann and Surratt became fast friends.

Weichmann's first impression was that John Surratt stood tall and erect and had a boyish appearance with a prominent forehead and receding eyes. His nose was thin and sharp. Weichmann thought he

5

"New tenant"

"Be not deceived:
evil speakings corrupt good manners."
—1 Corinthians 15:33 GNV

"...one of the best young men I ever knew..."
—Louis Weichmann

He never wanted to pursue a career in the priesthood. That was his mother's idea. His father was a Lutheran—his mother a devout Catholic.

When Louis Weichmann graduated from high school in February 1859, he pondered his vocational options. He preferred a profession as a druggist in an apothecary, but his mother insisted Louis should enter a Catholic institution as a student for the ministry. With little enthusiasm and at the coaxing of his mother, he began a correspondence with Father E. Q. S. Waldron, a former pastor of the Catholic parish in Philadelphia, who had been transferred around 1856 to the Archdiocese of Baltimore.

Born in Baltimore on September 29, 1842, Louis Weichmann's family moved to Washington City (D.C.) the following year. His father was a tailor and a Democrat, who would vote for Stephen A. Douglas in the 1860 presidential election against Abraham Lincoln. The elder Weichmann later changed his views politically, becoming a Republican and voting for Lincoln in 1864.

Young Weichmann and Father Waldron exchanged several letters until February of 1859, when Weichmann was directed to present himself to the preparatory college of St. Charles Borromeo in Howard County, Maryland, twenty miles outside Baltimore. The college exclusively devoted itself to the training of young men for the Catholic priesthood.

Louis Weichmann

The studies at St. Charles were quite severe, and discipline was rigid. The school permitted no interaction with the outside world, except for letters to family and friends. New students to the ministry trickled in periodically, and among the new arrivals in September of Louis Weichmann's first year was a young man named John Harrison Surratt, Jr. Weichmann and Surratt became fast friends.

Weichmann's first impression was that John Surratt stood tall and erect and had a boyish appearance with a prominent forehead and receding eyes. His nose was thin and sharp. Weichmann thought he resembled a young Jefferson Davis, recalling he was sharply dressed in a necktie, provoking taunts from the older students. Weichmann described Surratt as "a very orderly student and one of the best young men I ever knew and could not have been excelled by anyone. His reputation for conduct and deportment was most excellent."

The rigorous study regimen at St. Charles, coupled with limited contact with people outside the school, led to feelings of isolation and despair for many of the young men, including Weichmann and Surratt. Despite hearing the boom of distant guns and seeing an occasional soldier gallop by during student walks into the country, very little news of the war or political goings-on reached the boys at St. Charles.

John Harrison Surratt, Jr.

By the spring of 1862, neither John Surratt nor Louis Weichmann felt that the ministry was their true calling in life. John left St. Charles in July of 1862. Louis left later that same month—vowing to never return.

Weichmann's reasons for leaving differed from Surratt's. Weichmann felt he had not been treated fairly and promoted as rapidly as the other students; others had already been selected for entry into St. Mary's theological seminary in Baltimore. He thought he was equally entitled to enter seminary training, made an application, and was refused, prompting his abrupt departure. It was suspected that John Surratt left St. Charles because his father had just died and his presence was needed at home.

Father Waldron encouraged Weichmann not to give up a vocation to which he was called and told him "to rest off a while and renew his studies." Father Waldron then made Weichmann an offer to become an assistant teacher at St. Matthews in Pikeville, Maryland, until arrangements could be made for entry into theological seminary. Weichmann saw an advertisement by Reverend Charles I. White, D.D. (Doctor of Divinity) in the *Catholic Mirror* of Baltimore for an available teacher's position. He applied and was hired, beginning in January 1863. He was installed as the principal of St. Matthew's Institute for Boys in Washington with a salary of $38 per month plus lodging—thus making his home in the center of war operations for the Union Army.

Among his earliest callers while at St. Matthew's was his old schoolmate, John Surratt.

Surratt's appearance had changed considerably from the boyish youth Weichmann had first met to that of a more worldly young man, bronzed from the sun. Surratt was regularly bringing fruits and vegetables from the family's country home in Surrattsville to Washington, D.C. to sell at the market.

During a spring visit shortly before Easter, Surratt invited Weichmann to accompany him on his return to the Surratt home to celebrate Easter. The Surratt home was in Prince George's County, Maryland, twelve miles from D.C. on the road leading to Bryantown and the Potomac River. The road ran an almost straight line from Washington to the lower Potomac through two Maryland counties—Prince George's and Charles.

On that line lay Surrattsville, and farther down near Bryantown was Dr. Samuel Mudd's farm, thirty miles from the capital—and farther still was the home of Colonel Samuel Cox. There were no two counties in the United States where there existed, during the war, more disloyalty to the Union.

The road was slightly guarded and used by many as a conduit for espionage. The route was frequented by thousands—those running blockades, spies, and agent go-betweens, and those aspiring to escape the north to join the Confederate army. Unbeknownst to Weichmann, one of the agents running intelligence back and forth in support of the Southern Cause was his old college friend, John Surratt. This same road would also be the escape route taken by John Wilkes Booth following the assassination of President Lincoln.

It is astounding that the federal government did not find out the nature of this road and put a stop to these shady activities. Apparently, the only true friends of the Union in the area at that time were people of color.

The Surrattsville Tavern & Inn

The Surratt home was a large, frame structure with a parlor, barroom, country post office, and dining room on the main floor. Beneath that was a large cellar and above, numerous bedrooms. The property included a farm where vegetables were grown, as well as a fruit orchard. The surplus produce harvested from the farm was what John Surratt sold in the market in D.C. At the time, six or more Negroes who had previously been Mrs. Surratt's slaves were residing on the country property.

In addition to the Surrattsville farmhouse, Mrs. Surratt also owned a valuable house at 541 H Street in Washington, D.C.

When they arrived, Surratt introduced Weichmann to the family, consisting of Mrs. Surratt, her eldest son Isaac, and daughter Anna. John was the youngest of the siblings and the obvious apple of Mrs. Surratt's eye. Their father, John Sr. had died in July 1862. Isaac Surratt was a civil engineer by profession, soon to join the Confederate army. After he mustered in, Isaac would not return to the family until after the tragic events of April 1865.

Miss Anna Surratt—about twenty-years old, tall, fair in complexion, and well-proportioned—received a good education at Saint Mary's Female Institution in Bryantown, Maryland, becoming a young woman of much culture, as well as an accomplished pianist.

Mary Surratt

Mrs. Surratt—Mary, about forty, fair, with dark brown hair parted down the middle, and eyes described as "steel gray . . . quick and penetrating,"—possessed the rare faculty that made a stranger feel at home immediately. Almost as quickly, one realized she was a woman devoted, body and soul, to the Southern Cause.

Her maiden name was Jenkins, and she had been the belle of her hometown, Uniontown, Maryland. Mary's brother Zadoc Jenkins resided with their mother near Surrattsville. It was during this initial visit to the Surratt home that Weichmann discovered that though the family was agreeable and pleasant, they were all bitter secessionists.

The Surratt country home had by then become a regular stopping place for numerous secessionists and Confederate sympathizers. In fact, the Confederacy had no more active friends in any border state than Mary Surratt and her youngest child John. The character of the Surratt home as Confederate-friendly was known throughout the county. It had become a resort, a regular secessionist headquarters, for the blockade runners, spies, and agent parties who passed this way to cross the Potomac.

Mary and John were known to have hostile feelings toward the Union as evidenced by the testimony of a former mail carrier and Union soldier named John Tibbett. He had known the Surratt family for more than ten years. Tibbett would later testify that he heard Mary Surratt say in his and her son John's presence that "she would give anyone $1,000 if they would kill Mr. Lincoln," and "the damned Northern Army and the leader thereof ought to be sent to hell."

The morning after Louis Weichmann's arrival at the Surratt home, he was aroused by the sound of music outside his bedroom window. He quickly dressed and encountered John Surratt meeting a section of the Marine Band of Washington, who had arrived to serenade some newly elected officials. Enjoying the performance with them was a frowzy-headed youth of sallow complexion and coal-black hair named David Herold.

On the Monday morning after Easter, John Surratt accompanied Weichmann on his return to Washington. Upon reaching the city, Surratt stopped the buggy in front of a drug store near the Navy Yard. David Herold worked in this apothecary as a prescription clerk. Being only a casual acquaintance, Weichmann merely acknowledged recognition and exchanged pleasantries.

Returning to his post at the school, Weichmann resumed his teaching duties until he vacationed in Philadelphia during the summer of 1863. He renewed his efforts to enter the seminary but was rebuffed again.

In January 1864, the wheel of fortune made a sudden and unexpected turn in Weichmann's favor. He learned from an acquaintance of a vacancy for a clerk in the Commissary General of Prisoners, a bureau of the War Department. The job was awarded to Weichmann and was an agreeable one. Instead of the $38 per month that he was currently earning, his salary would more than double to $80 per month.

Louis Weichmann and John Surratt remained friends and visited periodically. On a return visit to Surrattsville, Weichmann attended Sunday service at a small Catholic church in nearby Piscataway. As fate would have it, he again ran into David Herold.

It was also during this visit that John Surratt informed Weichmann that his mother intended to lease the country home in Surrattsville and move to the residence in Washington, D.C. The city residence would become a boardinghouse, and Weichmann was invited to make his home there with the Surratt family. He cheerfully accepted.

6

"The drummer boy"

*"And ye shall hear of wars, and rumors of wars:
see that ye be not troubled:
for all these things must come to pass, but the end is not yet."*
—Matthew 24:6 GNV

"Boys, train up right…we may need you someday."
—Abraham Lincoln

Originally, the area of Illinois that would become Bloomington was at the edge of a large grove occupied by the Kickapoo people—before the first Euro-American settlers arrived in the early 1820s. Springing from the settlement of Keg Grove (later called Blooming Grove), Bloomington was named the county seat on Christmas Day, 1830, when McLean County was created.

James Allin, one of the new county's promoters, offered to donate sixty acres of his land for the new town, and Bloomington was laid out. Its lots were sold at a well-attended auction on the 4th of July in 1831.

There were few roads then, but rich soils brought new farmers who began commerce by conducting their business. People came from all over to trade and do business at the town's center. One of those was a young man named Abraham Lincoln, who started his career as an attorney in Illinois.

Eppenetus Washington McIntosh, nicknamed "Epp," was born in October of 1843 in Terre Haute, Indiana. He and his family moved to the Bloomington area in 1852, when he was nine years old. Epp's father, Joseph McIntosh, was a shoemaker by trade. The move provided an opportunity for Joseph to practice his trade and grow his business in a thriving town. The census taken two years prior tallied the population of Bloomington as 1,594 patriotic souls.

Joseph's first wife, Nancy Beach McIntosh, died in 1837 in Terre Haute. The first marriage had produced a son, John Wesley McIntosh, Epp's half-brother and ten years his senior.

With his colorful, outgoing personality, young Epp made friends easily. People seemed to instantly like him. He naturally gravitated toward boys his own age with similar interests. Play often involved exploring the outdoors—wading in the creek, fishing, or catching crawdads and turtles barehanded. Sometimes, the boys played "army." Epp and his pals would be the "good army" against an unending supply of imaginary combatants.

Today's adventure for Epp and his friends was playing a noisy game of pretend soldier in the street in front of Mr. Lincoln's law office. Epp later recalled, "A dozen or so of us urchins were playing soldier in my father's yard, which was across the street from Lincoln's office. I was the drummer boy, using a tin pan and a couple of sticks."

He thought his dad was a tall man until he saw Mr. Lincoln. The lawyer looked over the fence and told Epp and his friends, "Boys, train up right—we may need you someday."

Christmas came soon, and with it a gift from Abraham Lincoln—a little toy drum. Upon that drum, Epp learned to play.

During his time in Bloomington, Lincoln appeared to have indulged in only one work luxury—an office boy. Lincoln was known for his affection for children. With the little drum, Epp thrummed himself into Lincoln's further notice until one day, he offered Epp the job of whitewashing his fence. With the job well done and as Lincoln stood admiring Epp's work, he asked if Epp cared to be his office boy. Epp eagerly accepted the position and served as Lincoln's office boy for the next two years.

Young Illinois attorney Abraham Lincoln

Epp eventually became a Union drummer in the Civil War. Seven years had passed, and Epp's former boss called the nation to arms. President Lincoln made the request for 75,000 men to enlist to quell the rebellion. Epp answered the call to duty—to serve his beloved country and show honor to the great flag.

A well-grown youth of seventeen and a good drummer, Epp was eager to take a stand in front of the old Illinois Courthouse. There on the steps, he beat the roll that called for volunteers. It was neither the little tin pan he had used that day when he and his fellow urchins played soldier in front of the law office nor the toy drum Lincoln had given him for Christmas, but a new one—one that could be heard all over town. Doing his duty, he beat the roll on that spring day in May 1861.

Epp's unit, the 14th Illinois Infantry was one of the regiments raised under the "Ten Regiment Bill," which anticipated the requirements of the general government by organizing, equipping and drilling a regiment in each congressional district in the state for thirty days, unless sooner required for services by the United States.

The companies met at Camp Duncan, in Jacksonville, Illinois, on the eleventh day of May 1861, and were mustered into state service. On the twenty-fifth of the same month, the regiment was mustered into the United States service for three years. The field officers were elected by ballot—officers and soldiers all voting. To Epp, this was all part of a great adventure. He was going places and seeing things he had only heard and read about. He wanted to "see the elephant."

The regiment was always busy—drilling, training, marching, and learning. One of the primary lessons for Epp was learning all the different drum signals, a military language unto itself.

The regiment proceeded to Memphis, and from there on to Bolivar, Tennessee. On October 4, 1862, the 4th Division under Union Major General Stephen A. Hurlbut was ordered to proceed to Corinth to relieve the beleaguered garrison of that place. But before the regiment reached Corinth, Union General William Rosecrans had already severely punished the enemy, and Epp's regiment met the retreating rebels at the village of Metamora, Tennessee, on the Hatchie River.

Epp's regiment took an active part in the Battle of Shiloh and the Siege of Corinth. In the aftermath of the huge losses on both sides at Shiloh, Union Major General Henry Halleck decided a more deliberate and cautious approach would yield better results with fewer casualties. In the victory that followed eight hours of hard fighting, Epp's 14th Illinois Infantry sustained the reputation it had earned at Shiloh. It was during the Siege of Corinth that Epp McIntosh was cited as picking up the colors and bravely charging the rebel lines, waving the banner.

Upon the expiration of his original enlistment in the Union Army, Epp returned to Illinois in 1863 and re-enlisted as a regular US Army private. He was retained in the combined 14th and 15th Infantry, Illinois Battalion, as a "veteran private." Epp's new company, Company A, was assigned to guard rail stations that were key to providing General William Tecumseh Sherman's Army with supplies during the march through Georgia.

Confederate General John Bell Hood's Army of Tennessee entered Cobb County, Georgia, and prepared to strike the lifeline of the Union invaders, the Western & Atlantic Railroad. It was thought that if the gray coats could cut the railroad, Sherman, lacking supplies, would be compelled to abandon Atlanta.

The Illinois Battalion was detailed to guard railroad communications at and near Acworth, Georgia, a most important and dangerous duty, as it was the only route by which General Sherman could re-supply his immense Army with sustenance, ammunition, and supplies.

General Hood indicated in an October 4, 1864, dispatch to Lieutenant General A. P. Stewart that if the Confederates could "fill up the deep cut at Allatoona Pass, north of Acworth, its destruction would be a great advantage to the rebel army." The problem was, the

Union Army was strongly entrenched there and could be expected to fiercely resist any attempt to block the railroad.

In the month of October 1864, when Confederate General Hood made his demonstration against Sherman's rear guard, a large number of the battalion were killed, and the majority of the balance was taken prisoner and sent to the infamous Andersonville Prison.

Among those captured and taken as a prisoner of war that day was an Illinois drummer named Epp McIntosh.

Inside the stockade, prisoners were up all night over little fires in a desperate attempt to stave off the October chill. All the ovens in the Andersonville cookhouse were going full blast cooking pancakes and cornbread to sell in the morning, though wood was scarce. Nearly all the tree stumps had been dug up and the roots used for fuel. This was laborious work, as the roots of the tree stumps went ten or twelve feet into the ground. The swamp was filling up fast with filth. Still, the men delved into it to get at the roots, which were dried in the sun and sold.

Tent poles, fuel, and other things were sold to the new prisoners who paid high prices for them. Practically every day, there were new arrivals, and they stood out like sore thumbs.

As if on cue, the Raiders, a nasty band of rogue soldiers—thieves and murderers—incarcerated at the prison, crowded the gate looking for victims and allies. Like vultures on a carcass, the Raiders swooped down on the unsuspecting naive new arrivals.

Most of the Raiders were former inmates of a Confederate prison in Richmond—Belle Isle. Numbering close to two hundred, the Raiders always traveled around the camp in packs, assuring a physical advantage whenever an opportunity presented itself. They were given a wide berth when passing through the camp, and anyone unwise enough to find themselves in the band's midst or venture into their campsite quickly learned his mistake.

The new prisoners initially kept to themselves, not knowing whom to trust. Nearly all the new prisoners had blankets; some had rubber blankets, which were not to be bought for less than fifty dollars each. Rubber blankets were used for building shanties.

The rubber blankets were prized in Andersonville, and if the new arrivals weren't cautious and quick, the Raiders would take them all. Their weapons of choice were wooden clubs, blackened and hardened in pine sap fires, and these predators seldom roamed the camp without them.

7

"The Angel of Andersonville"

"I was naked, and ye clothed me:
I was sick, and ye visited me:
I was in prison, and ye came unto me."
—Matthew 25:36 GNV

"When I give for Christ's sake,
I give the best."
—Father Peter Whelan

During May of 1864, Reverend William Hamilton, pastor of Assumption Church in Macon and the man responsible for missions in southwest Georgia, visited the small town of Americus. He accidentally came upon Andersonville Prison and learned how many Catholics were imprisoned there. After a brief time, he departed and returned a week later to stay for three days.

What Father Hamilton saw at Andersonville led him to write a report to the bishop about the conditions of the stockade and prison hospital. He suggested a priest be provided immediately. Bishop Verot sent Father Peter Whelan to Andersonville.

Father Whelan had distinguished himself as a chaplain to both Confederate and Union troops during the conflict that pitted brother against brother. Initially ministering to the Confederate troops, including the Montgomery Guards, an Irish company established in Savannah for the 1st Georgia Volunteer Regiment, he remained with them during the Union siege of Fort Pulaski. He volunteered to remain with them during their imprisonment in New York in 1862. He was released in a prisoner exchange. A year later he received his assignment to minister to the Union POWs held at Camp Sumter, where he eventually became known as the "Angel of Andersonville."

Father Peter Whelan arrived at Andersonville on June 16, 1864. On his approach, he paid little attention to the committee of vultures circling above the camp. Drawn by the irresistible stench of decay, those scavengers of carrion were always present. Father Whelan, instinctively looking up, gazed beyond the swirling black and said a silent prayer for strength and comfort for what he must do.

Irish-born Catholic priest, Father Peter Whelan stood over six feet with round, swinging shoulders, long arms, a short body, long legs, and feet of more than ordinary size. His drab coarse hair stuck up all over. If he possessed a comb or brush, his appearance gave no indication of it.

His coat was not of the latest or approved fashion. The sleeves exposed several inches of the lower part of his arms above the wrists and large, rough hands. His pants extended only a little below the knees, exhibiting a considerable portion of his stockings and unpolished, ash-colored dusty shoes.

It was not as if Father Whelan wasn't aware of his appearance. He was. To him, it was of little significance. His focused dedication was to the flock he shepherded. His flock was the men inside the stockade walls of Andersonville—both guards and prisoners alike.

One day Father Whelan met a brother priest, to whom nature was no more cosmetically kind to than himself. "Well," said Father Whelan, "your mother and mine must have been women of great virtue . . . because they did not drown us when they first saw us. None but mothers of great . . . patience would have raised such ugly specimens of humanity."

On another day, Father Whelan was presented with a new suit by the officers, as his own had become so threadbare. The next day he was seen wearing his same old garb. When asked where his new suit was, he explained that he had given it to a soldier who had been captured wearing nothing but his underclothes. He was asked why he hadn't given his old suit to the soldier. Whelan replied, "When I give for Christ's sake, I give the best."

That statement was to be the rule he followed his entire life.

A week after Father Whelan's arrival at Andersonville, Private Thomas P. "Boston" Corbett was captured by Colonel John Mosby's Confederate Cavalry at Culpepper, Virginia. Boston Corbett and other Union POWs were brought to the Andersonville stockade.

While other priests and even the bishop would come for brief periods to Andersonville, Father Whelan alone remained for nearly four months during the hottest season of the year and the period of the highest mortality, the summer of 1864. Bishop Verot wrote:

> "The prisoners were penned up in an improvised enclosure made of tree trunks sunk vertically in the ground. . . . [They] were under a tropical sun. Some unfortunates tried to help by hanging rags on the end of a stick. Most . . . were without clothes and a good number were entirely naked. It was necessary to receive the confession of the sick . . . in the middle of the crowd; but the imminence of death left no place for respect. Without advancing more than twenty steps I confessed and administered nine sick men and I only stopped at the most urgent cases. The continuous sight of death finally dulled all human feelings. What was most painful was the horrible stench which spewed from this huge agglomeration in so small a space."

Father Whelan ministered to the inmates and guards of Andersonville, regardless of their religious affiliation, political alliance, or color, with compassion and decency that was comforting and inspiring to the men. Whelan's duties were performed in such heat that he had to cover his head continuously with an umbrella. As the elderly priest moved about the stockade, men followed the umbrella and collected around him to ask questions concerning news from the outside of the stockade—especially war reports and the possibility of a prisoner exchange.

Into this daily nightmare Peter Whelan came to perform a ministry unlike any he had done before or would ever encounter again. He worked days, returned to his bunk in a little twelve-by-eight-foot hut about a mile from the prison, spent restless nights, rose each day at dawn, took a scant breakfast, and said his prayers. He then walked the hot, dusty path back to the Andersonville stockade, where he stayed from 9 a.m. until nearly sundown—then it was back to the hut for night prayers and some food.

Father Whelan was joined by Father Henry Clavreul in August. Clavreul became violently ill and later wrote:

"Whelan decided that I should leave, so I took the trains back to Savannah whilst the . . . old priest retraced his steps to the stockade."

As the number of prisoners grew steadily to about 33,000, Whelan requested more help. First, Reverend John Kirby and then Reverend Anselm Usannez joined Whelan, but both became violently ill, revolted by the conditions in the stockade. They couldn't stand it. Both left after serving two weeks.

In late August, as Sherman was about to enter Atlanta, Union POWs were transferred to Savannah and Charleston. Confederate authorities feared that Sherman would attack the prison and release the prisoners, so the authorities sent the POWs to other prisons to prevent their rescue and alleviate the overcrowding. With these developments, Whelan decided he could leave.

But before he left Andersonville Prison, the priest contacted Henry Horne, a devout Catholic and successful restaurant owner in Macon. Whelan borrowed $16,000 in Confederate money. With this, he went to the town of Americus, Georgia, purchased ten thousand pounds of wheat flour, had it baked into bread, and distributed it at the prison and makeshift hospital at Andersonville. The prisoners referred to it as "Whelan's bread." This much-needed gift was enough to provide the men with rations for several months. Whelan would depart in October 1864 after many of the prisoners had been removed to other locations.

Although the priest did not leave a record of his initial shock upon his first entry into Andersonville, Father Hamilton who initially visited Andersonville with Father Whelan described his impressions of subsequent visits vividly:

"I found the stockade extremely filthy; the men all huddled together and covered with vermin [lice]. . . . I found [the hospital] almost as crowded as the

stockade. The men were dying there very rapidly from scurvy . . . diarrhea and dysentery. . . . They were not only covered with the ordinary vermin but also maggots. . . . They had nothing under them at all except the ground."

Most nights, Father Whelan fell asleep exhausted and "full of sorrow for what he had seen all day."

8

"Mad as a hatter"

"For there are some eunuchs,
which were so born of their mother's belly:
and there be some eunuchs,
which be gelded by men:
and there be some eunuchs,
which have gelded themselves for the kingdom of heaven.
He that is able to receive this, let him receive it."
—Matthew 19:12 GNV

At first, they were just small tremors. The kind that created a muscle spasm or made an eyelid twitch. Then they became more frequent and greater in severity. He ignored them as best as he could, not knowing what was causing his malady. He consulted the holy scriptures for answers and found several passages that gave him comfort. *It could be sin trying to exit the body*, he thought—*or was it attempting to enter?* He didn't know. Another thing he didn't know was that these symptoms were a manifestation of chemical changes in his brain. These doctors didn't know everything—of that he was confident.

As soon as he saw an opportunity, Boston Corbett vowed to leave this hospital bed and return to his unit. These medical people didn't understand how important it was for him to get back to where he was needed. He'd sworn an oath to defend and protect the United States, and by God, he intended to keep it.

Late fall 1864, the leaves were down, and a frost covered the cold ground surrounding Annapolis Hospital. The doctors told him he was suffering from exposure, scurvy, and malnutrition. After food and rest, he felt much better, but unfortunately, the tremors nagged and persisted.

Born in London, England, January 1832, Thomas P. Corbett eventually found his way to Troy, New York, as a young man, where he worked in a hat-making shop. As a hatter, Corbett was regularly exposed to the fumes of mercury nitrate, a chemical used in the treatment of fur to produce the felt used on hats. Excessive exposure to the compound could lead to hallucinations, psychosis, and twitching—known as the "hatter's shakes," thus popularizing the phrase "mad as a hatter."

Historians have theorized that the mental issues Corbett exhibited before and after the Civil War may have been caused by this chemical exposure.

After working as a hatter in Troy, Corbett moved to New York City. He married, but his wife and child died during childbirth. Following their deaths, he moved to Boston. He became despondent over his losses and began drinking heavily. Unable to hold a job, he eventually became homeless. After a night of heavy drinking, he was confronted by a street preacher, whose message persuaded him to join the Methodist Episcopal Church. Corbett immediately stopped drinking and became devoutly religious. After being baptized, he changed his name to "Boston," the name of the city where he was converted and reborn.

Thomas P. "Boston" Corbett

In 1857, he began working at a hat manufacturer's shop on Washington Street in downtown Boston. He was reported to be a proficient hatter but was known to evangelize, frequently stopping work to pray and sing for co-workers who used profanity in his presence. He also began working as a street preacher, sermonizing and distributing religious literature in North Square. Corbett quickly earned a reputation around Boston for being a "local eccentric" and a religious fanatic.

Once, as Corbett walked home from a church meeting, two prostitutes approached and propositioned him. The encounter deeply disturbed him. Returning to his room at a boardinghouse, he opened his Bible and read from chapters five and nineteen in the Gospel Book of Matthew:

"Wherefore if thy right eye cause thee to offend, pluck it out and cast it from thee ... and there be some eunuchs, which have gelded themselves for the kingdom of heaven."

Corbett contemplated his spiritual devotion, and in order to avoid future sexual temptation and remain holy, he castrated himself with a pair of scissors. He then ate a meal and went to a prayer meeting before seeking medical treatment for the self-mutilation.

Three years later, in April of 1861, Corbett enlisted as a private in Company I, 12th Regiment, New York Militia. That same month, the regiment—comprised of ten companies and commanded by Colonel Daniel Adams Butterfield—left the state en route to Washington, D.C.

Corbett's eccentric behavior quickly got him into trouble. He always carried a Bible with him. He read passages aloud from it regularly, held unauthorized prayer meetings, and argued with his superior officers. He also condemned officers and superiors for what he perceived as blasphemy and violations of God's word.

Colonel Daniel Butterfield

In one instance, he verbally reprimanded his commanding officer, Colonel Daniel Butterfield (the man credited with writing "Taps"), for using profanity and taking the Lord's name in vain.

Colonel Butterfield had earned the nickname "Little Napoleon" because of his bad temper and meddlesome assertiveness. Butterfield found no humor in Corbett's defiant criticism and failure to observe strict military decorum. As a disciplinary measure, Butterfield sent Corbett to the guardhouse for several days, but Corbett refused to apologize for his insubordination. As a matter of fact, he enjoyed the imposed solitude with his Bible. Butterfield was not amused.

Due to his continued disruptive behavior and refusal to take orders, Corbett was court-martialed and sentenced to be shot. His sentence was eventually reduced, and he was discharged from service in August 1863.

Undeterred, Corbett stubbornly re-enlisted later that month as a private in Company L, 16th New York Cavalry Regiment.

On June 24, 1864, Corbett was captured by Confederate Colonel John S. Mosby's men in Culpepper, Virginia, and held captive at Andersonville Prison for five months. He was released in an exchange in November 1864, admitted to the Army hospital in Annapolis, Maryland, and treated for exposure, scurvy, and malnutrition.

Corbett returned to his company, and five months later, his regiment, the 16th New York Cavalry, was assigned to be part of the largest nationwide manhunt in U. S. history—the search for the assassins of President Abraham Lincoln.

9

"The Reckoning"

> *"And Reuben answered them, saying,*
> *Warned I not you, saying,*
> *Sin not against the child,*
> *and ye would not hear?*
> *and lo, his blood is now required."*
> —Genesis 42:22 GNV

Starvation, exposure, and disease weren't the only evils the prisoners at Andersonville had to face. On top of these perils and the unmitigated cruelty of the rebel guards was a group of even more sinister POWs that preyed upon the rest of the prisoners. These jackals were some of the meanest, most cruel villains ever encountered. The Andersonville Raiders terrorized their fellow prisoners, stealing their possessions and even committing murder.

They were Army deserters, bounty jumpers, cut-throats, and thieves, banding together to become the bane of practically every miserable inmate in Andersonville. These thugs robbed other prisoners of anything of value that could be traded for money or more rations. With the proceeds of their heartless deeds, they became stronger, while their hapless victims became weaker.

Within each group of new arrivals to the prison came like-minded criminals—additional members to the gang—increasing their numbers to around two hundred. Whenever the gates opened to receive "fresh fish," or new inmates, a number of the vicious hoodlums were positioned to spot them and note their possessions.

They tracked the targeted victims day and night, and under the cover of darkness, the Raiders attacked and robbed them. If the victim resisted, he would be unmercifully beaten, or his throat cut. It was useless to complain to the rebel guards. There was no protection to thwart this bloodthirsty gang.

The Raiders were an organized force to be reckoned with. They had five or six leaders, with groups under their leadership who plundered and victimized the weaker prisoners. The Raider groups numbered anywhere from five to twenty-plus men each and were armed with pine logs, brass knuckles, knives, and pine roots. Pine roots were dried and baked in a slow fire to produce sharp points—an effective and deadly weapon.

As a result of their preying on the weaker prisoners, they were generally healthier and better fed. Among the prison population, the Raiders were feared and thought an invincible force. Immediately following an attack by the Raiders, the attacker would quickly retreat to the swamp on a far corner of the prison with the ill-gotten loot. No one dare chase the villain into the swamp area, because twenty Raiders armed with clubs awaited there for a brutal response.

At last, driven by desperation, a handful of men decided that enough was enough.

Tiring of the constant intimidation, the robbing, and the beatings at the hands of the Raiders, a new prisoner "police force" was formed to stop the reign of terror at Andersonville.

This new group, the Regulators, was headed by Sergeant Leroy L. Key from Bloomington, 16th Illinois Infantry.

Sergeant Key, a man of strong will and great nerve, committed himself to stopping the Raiders' cruelties, whatever the costs. More than one hundred men comprised Key's Regulators—all sworn to the same goal. The members were the most fit and healthiest soldiers in the camp not aligned with the Raiders.

Sergeant Leroy L. Key

Fourteen of Sergeant Key's regiment, including his own brother, had died inside the stockade walls of Andersonville, some at the hands of the Raiders. Key felt he owed his efforts to honor these men.

The Regulators organized and divided into companies, each commanded by a sergeant. Each man armed himself with a pine log club lashed about the wrist and stationed strategically around the camp every night, but never occupied the same place repeatedly.

The Regulators continued to increase in number and courage as days passed. Raider attacks tapered off due to the Regulator sentries' presence but did not stop.

Captain Henry Wirz, commandant at Andersonville, announced that he was not involved in inner-prisoner conflicts and as long as the prisoners stayed inside the walls of the stockade and did not encroach the deadline, his responsibilities were satisfied. Wirz was not particularly interested in refereeing melees in the camp, therefore, by default, sanctioning inner-prisoner hostilities.

Tensions soon mounted in Andersonville to a fever pitch. Captain Wirz was aware of the pending standoff between the Raiders and the Regulators. His primary fear was an attempted breakout amidst the hostilities.

Finally, on July 3, 1864, there was excitement in the camp among the prisoners. Right or wrong, it felt good that the prisoners had hope of any kind. It was obvious to the prisoners and the guards alike that something big was going to happen.

There was a reckoning brewing.

10

"Running the gauntlet"

"But he that doeth wrong,
shall receive for the wrong that he hath done:
and there is no respect of persons."
—Colossians 3:25 GNV

"... and may Got haf mercy on you and on dem."
—Captain Henry Wirz

Robert Sneden and John McElroy watched as the rival forces began to assemble on opposite ends of the stockade. After they quickly wolfed down their breakfast rations, they walked the muddy thoroughfare of Main Street to position themselves in a safe area to watch. As usual, vultures circled slowly overhead, drawn by the putrid stench wafting from the camp. Neither Robert nor John was recruited to join the Regulators. They fully supported the

Regulators—mind and soul. But physically, they weren't healthy enough to effectively engage in the conflict.

On the north side of the prison camp, the Regulators began forming a skirmish line at about 11 a.m. Sergeant Key assembled his men, now numbering about two hundred fifty, along Main Street.

The Raiders formed up along the south side of the camp. Every eye in camp would witness the battle.

Once organized, the Regulators in purposeful stride, began the slow deliberate advance with a skirmish line ten paces apart and advancing readily toward the Raiders.

The nearer the Regulators got to the Raiders, the louder their war cries became. The two forces viciously collided, screaming and crushing shebangs in their paths, bloodying one another with their primitive weapons.

Key's Regulators did a flanking maneuver and attacked the Raiders—front and side. After about ten minutes of brutal fighting, the Raiders retreated to the swamp. But the Regulators had anticipated this and established a force there to cut off their retreat.

Both sides were bloodied, but the Regulators had clearly won. A cheer went up from the prisoners celebrating the victory. Captain Wirz allowed his guards to lend Sergeant Key several lengths of rope to tie and restrain the captured Raiders. The battle was done for the day, but the war wasn't over quite yet.

The next morning, Sergeant Key's Regulators marched through the camp, armed and ready. Their mission today was to capture or fight the remaining Raiders. They seized the main tent of the most prominent Raiders and found the stolen treasures.

Blankets, clothes, watches with chains, knives, shoes, and every other kind of plundered booty were recovered. Even four or five decomposing bodies of victims were found buried under their makeshift tent. Some of the Raiders resisted but were pummeled into total submission or unconsciousness.

The Regulators scanned the camp for unaccounted Raiders to make their arrests. As the day progressed, more Raiders were captured, bound with rope, and turned over to the rebel guards for confinement in an enclosure at the north gate. The Raiders were conquered as a group. Their fate now awaited the decision of the rebel captors.

When asked by Captain Wirz what they thought should be done with the Raiders, one of the Regulators suggested a trial. After nervous laughter in disbelief at the recommendation, the agreement was made and word from the rebel hierarchy was that a trial was indeed in order to determine the Raiders' fates.

Juries would be selected from among the newest arrivals to minimize prejudicial bias. Attorneys, both prosecution and defense, were selected from among the prisoners, as well. The judge had been selected in short order, but his name was not revealed until the beginning of the trial. The appointed judge, Private Peter McCullough, was known among his fellow prisoners as "Big Pete" of the 8th Missouri Infantry, Company G. The trial was conducted as professionally and as honestly as the circumstances allowed. Evidence, witnesses, and proof of their crimes were in abundance.

The court-martial panel consisted of thirteen sergeants, also selected from the latest arrivals. The trial was conducted and concluded by July 8, 1864. Six Raiders were found guilty of first-degree murder. These six were the chiefs of the Raider gangs: Charles Curtis, William "Mosby" Collins, Patrick Delaney, W. R. Rickson, John Sarsfield, and a sailor named Andy Munn. They were all sentenced to hang within the walls of the stockade between sunrise and sunset on July 11.

The day before the execution, guards selected prisoners to go outside the stockade walls under the watchful eyes of sentries to "gather firewood"—wood to build the gallows. The same day, Father Peter Whelan visited the condemned men in the stocks.

The next morning, as the gallows were readied, Whelan tried in vain to obtain a stay of execution. Except for the scheduled execution, it was a typical July day in Georgia—sunny, hot, and sticky.

Among the remaining 125 Raiders arrested, 86 were sentenced to "run the gauntlet" inside the stockade, 20 were sentenced to be "bucked and gagged," 15 were sentenced to be attached to a ball and chain for 30 days, and about a dozen were to receive 20 lashes, then sent to the stockade to "run the gauntlet."

"Running the gauntlet" involved all the prisoners lining both sides of Main Street, armed with clubs and sticks, and one by one, the convicted prisoners, thrust through a gate at one end of the prison, had to run the entire length of the stockade. The prisoners beat the runners mercilessly and with reckless abandon until the convicted prisoners either reached the other side of the prison, were unconscious, or were dead. Three Raiders that ran the gauntlet died within the first hour.

As the time for the execution of the six convicted murderers approached, excitement inside and outside the camp grew. Farmers and other nearby residents came and found spots on a shady hill overlooking Andersonville Prison. At 2 p.m., well over 30,000 prisoners, a large group of civilian spectators outside the stockade,

Confederate guards, and the convicted men themselves were set for an execution.

The locals who had gathered on a hill overlooking the inside of the stockade had brought picnic baskets and blankets, awaiting the morbid spectacle. At a quarter past two the south gate opened, and in rode Captain Henry Wirz on his gray mare. Walking behind him was a group of rebel guards and Father Peter Whelan.

Following them through the gate came the six convicted men between a row of double guards. Their hands were bound with rope behind their backs, as were their elbows. Sergeant Key and his men formed a square around the gallows with six of them acting as executioners.

As soon as the doomed Raiders came inside the square, two barrels were fixed under the drop plank, one barrel stacked atop the other with the pull rope stretched on the ground. Three strong men stood ready to snatch the barrels from underneath when the time came.

Meanwhile, Father Whelan read from the scriptures nonstop.

Captain Wirz dismounted, strode to the front of the gallows, and addressed the convicted men. Speaking with his thick European accent, Wirz said loudly enough for most within earshot to hear:

"Prisoners . . . I return to you dese men so goot as I got dem. You have tried dem and found dem guilty. I haf had noting to do wit it. I vash my hans of everyting connected wit it. Do wit dem as you like, and may Got haf mercy on you and on dem. Garts! About face! Forwarts. March!"

And with his short speech concluded, the rebel guards marched out, muskets at shoulder-arms, with Wirz following on his mare. The convicted stood there, dazed for the moment. They thought maybe it was all a bluff, to get their attention. They perhaps thought that there would be a last-minute reprieve.

But no. There would be no clemency granted today.

11

"Time's up!"

*"O serpents, the generation of vipers,
how should ye escape the damnation of hell!"*
—Matthew 23:33 GNV

"Time's up!"
—Sergeant Leroy Key

Throughout June and July of 1864, it rained for twenty-one consecutive days. During a heavy storm, none of the prisoners could keep from getting soaked, and those poor fellows who were without any shelter were much worse off than those who had only a blanket for a roof. Main Street was a muddy trough trampled by Andersonville's massive population.

The gallows, quickly constructed the previous day, demonstrated the stark materials available. It consisted of two heavy vertical timbers spaced about twenty feet apart—angle-braced at the ground and at the top for strength and rigidity, rising to its full height—more than twenty feet at the heavy crossbeam across the top. Six rope nooses had been evenly spaced and secured to the crossbeam. The drop beneath the beam was supported in the center by two wooden barrels, stacked one upon the other. A wooden cleat affixed on the vertical timbers was installed to support the drop on the outer ends. At the appropriate moment, the barrels would be snatched by ropes, causing the drop to fall in the center. The fall was deemed adequate—between seven and eight feet.

Among the prisoners, there was a great deal of yelling and excitement. Outside the stockade, the civilian spectators could hear little more than the roar of the inmates. Inside, however, was a different story. One of the condemned Raiders screamed, "My God, men! You don't really mean to hang us up there?"

"That's about the size of it. You and the rest of the damned gang have to now swing," coldly replied Sergeant Key.

Then all the condemned Raiders commenced shouting, swearing, and begging. One of them, Patrick Delaney finally screamed, "All stop now; let the priest talk for us!"

Father Peter Whelan stopped reading and closed his Bible. He turned to face the crowd and began earnestly pleading for mercy for the condemned men. At first, the priest's words were difficult to hear over the crowd. Upon understanding his words, the crowd shouted, "No, hang them!"

The clamor of rebukes rose in volume until Father Whelan could no longer be heard. He raised his hands, one clutching the Bible, trying to calm the masses, to no avail. The roar of the victimized witnesses continued to increase in volume.

Then one of the condemned men, William "Mosby" Collins, screamed, "By God, I say die this way first!"

And with that, Collins managed to wriggle out of his restraints and break free. He ran over people in his path as he made his way toward the swamp. Bulling and ramming his shoulders into people in his way, Collins frantically plowed into the weakened prisoners, collapsing shebangs and tents in his wake.

Collins made it as far as the bog before a group of Regulators chased him down and returned to the square with him in custody again, panting, swearing, and pleading. All were covered in the muck from the swamp. Collins was allowed to rest for a moment after the exertion. He commenced crying and pleading for mercy, begging for his life.

Patrick Delaney admonished Collins, telling him to "stand up like a man and die game."

The six condemned men were forced up the ladder and placed in position under the beam, directly under the nooses. Sergeant Key took out his pocket watch, looked at the face, and announced, "Two more minutes to talk!"

Delaney said goodbye. He continued, "If oive hurted any of yez, I hope yez forgive me. Shpake up now!"

But no one among the witnesses seemed to be in a forgiving mood. The crowd inside Andersonville grew quiet. After the pause, Sergeant Key glanced at his watch again and declared, "Time's up!"

Atlanta, Georgia

General William Tecumseh Sherman realized that he couldn't stay in Atlanta—at the end of a long supply line that the Confederates could destroy. He decided to go on the offensive, abandoning his supply line.

One hundred miles north of Andersonville, Sherman presented a new plan that involved leaving Atlanta and crushing the enemy once and for all. To accomplish this, Sherman divided his forces, sending half his troops north to deal with General Robert E. Lee in Virginia and the other half to Savannah to re-supply the army by sea.

Sherman determined to leave behind him a wasteland, destroying anything and everything the Confederates could possibly use to continue to make war. His scorched earth philosophy would leave a fifty-mile-wide swath of destruction in his wake. Sherman also understood the psychological impact his trail of terror would generate on the enemy.

After he took Atlanta, Sherman and his men knocked down factories, mills, buildings, and gasworks with battering rams. Fearing uncontrollable fires, he ordered that no fires be set until the last moment. He instructed his men to leave the churches and private homes unscathed, but to destroy all the railroad tracks leading out of Atlanta, save one. The one leading north.

Armed with recent census maps, Sherman knew where the critical supplies were located. With this information, he was able to develop a 250-mile route to Savannah, not totally living off the land, but close to it. Sherman had gathered intelligence about where the grain, fodder, cattle, hogs, and farms were—and he planned accordingly the route for the march to the sea.

Atlanta burned. Against Sherman's orders, a huge section of the city's homes was torched. Before leaving the city, troops enjoyed dinner in some of Atlanta's finer mansions. Afterward, they piled all the remaining contents into large parlors and set them ablaze. One of

Sherman's subordinate officers offered a $500 reward for information on who started the fires. Even though the reward was nearly triple a private's annual pay, no one among the soldiers snitched.

Sergeant Key raised his right hand as the signal that it was time to start the execution. The sound from the crowd swelled. The hangmen on the platform pulled cornmeal sacks over the heads of the condemned men and secured the nooses around their necks, as the other executioners clasped the rope at the barrels.

Father Whelan continued to read the service for the dying as the roar of the crowd increased to full throat. Civilian spectators on the hillside paused their picnics to watch.

Key dropped his hand. The Regulators on the barrel rope snatched it, causing the plank to drop. Five of the men fell the full lengths of their ropes, near about seven feet, squirming and kicking. Collins, being a heavy man, broke his rope—falling in a heap onto the ground below the gallows, unconscious. After the meal sack was removed from his face and water dashed on his head, Collins regained consciousness and asked, "Where am I? Am I in eternity?"

Sergeant Key's brother had allegedly been one of Collins's murder victims. Naturally, Key responded accordingly with vengeance in his voice.

"We'll soon show you where you are, damned you!", as the plank was being reset atop the barrels.

While the other five dangled and squirmed, Collins was ordered to "get up on that plank," which he did, crying and pleading for mercy all the while. His noose was again readied with a new rope. The barrel was reset, and Collins stood atop the drop. As soon as he was in position and noosed, the drop barrel was kicked out from under him, the executioner not bothering with the barrel rope. Collins fell the length of the rope again, struggling and kicking. All six convicted murderers were swinging now. They were left dangling on the beam for the next twenty minutes in the hot July sun before being checked for dead.

Only one of the six died of a broken neck. The rest died from slow strangulation.

After the execution, Robert Sneden, John McElroy, and Boston Corbett returned to their shebangs to assess what damages, if any, had occurred during the commotion.

12

"Skeletons in rags"

> *"He that oppresseth the poor, reproveth him that made him:*
> *but he honoreth him, that hath mercy on the poor."*
> —Proverbs 14:31 GNV

> "He possessed... a voice that was rich
> and musical in its tones.
> In dress, he was faultless." —Louis Weichmann

The ration cart creaked into the square, and prisoners loaded the executed Raiders' bodies, one on top of the other like cordwood, and took the cart outside the stockade. They transported the corpses to the far side of the cemetery—away from the other prisoners interred there to avoid polluting the sanctity of the cemetery. They dug a shallow mass grave seven feet square and three feet deep.

First, they stripped the bodies naked of all articles of clothing, then placed them shoulder to shoulder in the freshly dug earth. No coffin, no box, no barrier of any sort. They shoveled red Georgia clay directly over the corpses. But then, none of the graves in the prison cemetery contained burial coffins. They could not spare the materials required to build them.

Fortunately for the families, numbered wooden stakes and duplicate records of the dead had been made to help identify the victims of Andersonville. Much later, the burial plots would be carefully marked with painted wooden tablets, with the assistance of a nurse named Clara Barton—including the graves of the executed Raiders.

Andersonville mass burial

Robert Sneden's life encounters prior to capture and imprisonment had not prepared him for life inside. But Robert became hardened during his Andersonville experience. His physical and mental toughness were honed by default. Robert was not a victim of circumstance but instead became a *victor* of circumstances.

Dark rain clouds provided a backdrop for the ever-present vultures swirling above the camp. The putrid stench of decay summoned their attendance. Prayers and moaning continued day and night—ignored by the guards, who were indifferent to the prisoners' suffering. It had all become part of the gloomy landscape.

The reign of terror from the Raiders was over, but the horrors of Andersonville remained. After the executions, Robert returned to his shebang to assess its condition. It rained hard all day and most of the night. He was drenched, and so was his shebang.

The dugout pit where he lived beneath the blanket roof soon filled with water. He and his comrades scrambled to pull the weaker ones out of the pit to prevent them from drowning. Everything was soaked. No fires could be lit to combat the chilling rain. Muddy water infested with maggots and vermin flowed into their pit. Robert was forced to move from his campsite and find another one to escape the vermin swimming there.

Dead and dying men lay all around, delirious in their miserable state. They died all hours of the night and day, the living men lying with the corpses, as they were too weak to crawl away from them. Some of the prisoners held prayer meetings for the dying and sang hymns. The liveliest preaching came from Private Boston Corbett.

When the rains eventually paused and the skies cleared, dozens crawled on their hands and knees to the gates to receive whatever herbs or root medicines were available. Capable ones carried or dragged the weaker ones on old, ragged blankets. The ones too far gone for the medicines to have any effect upon stayed in the blazing sun to await what the others deemed a sweet and merciful death. Doctors, fearful and reluctant to enter the camp, didn't want to catch a disease from the prisoners and kept their distance.

It was still hot and muggy in mid-September as Robert Sneden watched a column of prisoners march into the gate of the Andersonville stockade. He thought, *they are no more than skeletons in rags.* Prisoners were routinely delivered daily, but he recognized these men. They were the same prisoners selected as parolees that had left a week earlier for prisoner exchange.

After inquiries, Robert learned that they had been taken to a small village near Atlanta under a banner of truce for exchange with General William T. Sherman. Sherman selected only the men from his own command and sent the remaining 740 POWs back to captivity in Andersonville.

This revelation dashed all hope of exchange among the men who were clearly puzzled by Sherman's abandonment. At first, the prisoners were outraged and could not fathom why Sherman would do such a thing to fellow Union soldiers. As the conflict dragged on, it became a war of attrition. The Union had far greater resources and kept Confederate soldiers out of the war and off the battlefield by denying prisoner exchange.

The death rate at the stockade remained high and climbed even higher, averaging between sixty to eighty fatalities daily. Sherman's actions would kill hundreds more.

Two days later, Robert Sneden was informed by his captors that he was among a group of prisoners selected for exchange. He had heard these rumors before and didn't trust them to be genuine. Besides, he had just witnessed the return of 740 prisoners from a failed parolee exchange. Also, capitalizing upon his artistic talents, Robert had issued counterfeit passes inside the prison to sell for rations, and he suspected that one or more of the other prisoners may have ratted him out in exchange for more food.

War news coming through the grapevine said that General Grant had pinned Lee's army down in Richmond and Union victory was imminent. Closer to the prison, word was that a Union push through Tennessee into Georgia offered the best hope of relief for Andersonville's prisoners. Though encouraged by the news of the Union Army's success, Robert was still leery of the offer of a prisoner exchange. He was instructed to report to the Officer of the Gate for important papers awaiting him.

Taking extra precautions, Robert concealed all his drawings, maps, and journal writings in all parts of his ragged clothing and pasted some between the pages of his Bible using pine sap glue. He used false linings in his cap, fake linings in his shirt, and double insoles in his shoes to hide his treasured papers. Satisfied with his covert preparations, he reported to the gate to find that his suspicions were unjustified. He was told to pack his belongings and make himself ready for transport for exchange.

Guards marched him to the station, where he boarded a train car, resolved that even if the train didn't take him to freedom, at least it would take him away from Andersonville. The cattle car took Robert and a small group of prisoners due east to Savannah. Robert was elated when informed by the guards that their orders were to send small groups of sailors among them to Charleston for exchange. He took this opportunity to write letters home, sending them, along with his journal, with the paroled soldiers to deliver to loved ones.

A month later, Robert and his comrades were loaded onto rail cars again—this time, hog cars. This train took them back in the direction from which they had come to a newly built stockade, Millen Prison at Camp Lawton, Georgia. Coincidentally, Boston Corbett was exchanged at about the same time as Robert Sneden.

While Robert and Boston were lucky enough to leave Andersonville, others had the misfortune of arriving there. On October 4, 1864, Epp McIntosh's luck ran out during maneuvers preceding the Battle of Allatoona, when infantry and artillery units formed into positions for battle. Confederate cavalry under Nathan Bedford Forrest captured Epp, along with more than a hundred other Illinois soldiers at Acworth Station.

As prisoners of war, they were marched across Georgia in cold, drizzling rain for five days with little food, little water, and only two or three stops to rest. They were delivered to the Andersonville stockade on October 9, 1864. The Andersonville records spelled Epp's name with one "p," listing him on their rolls as Epenetus W. McIntosh.

Epp remained at Andersonville Prison, praying for an opportunity at prisoner exchange. It would be a while yet to come. Epp's health took a rapid downward spiral, much like everyone else's unfortunate enough to pass through the gates of the Andersonville stockade.

The Surratt Boardinghouse – Washington, D.C.

Besides his clothes and personal effects, Louis Weichmann didn't have a lot of things to move. On November 1, 1864, Weichmann became a boarder at Mrs. Surratt's boardinghouse in Washington, D.C., agreeing to pay her the sum of $35 per month rent. For that amount, he shared a bedroom with John Surratt on the second floor which was furnished with a bed, a chifforobe, a desk, and a chair.

On the day he moved in, Mrs. Surratt wasn't there—but John Surratt Jr. and his sister Anna were. Mary Surratt did not come until the first of December; she was closing her deal with the rental of the country home in Surrattsville to a former policeman named John M. Lloyd for $500 per year. Weichmann incidentally witnessed the lease agreement and thereby became acquainted with Mr. Lloyd.

Shortly after Weichmann became a boarder in the Surratt home, a friend of Anna's named Honora Fitzpatrick came and boarded, sharing a bedroom with Anna. A little later, John T. Holohan, his wife Eliza, and their two children moved in, and later still, a nine-year-old girl named Apollonia Dean came to reside there to attend school. Thus, the house was filled and profitable from the beginning.

On November 25, John Wilkes and two other Booths played New York City in a presentation of *Julius Caesar*: Junius as Cassius, Edwin as Brutus, and John Wilkes as Marc Antony.

To a standing-room-only, sold-out crowd, the three received and merited the applause of their historic performance. Engagements at Ford's Theatre in Washington paid John Wilkes Booth as much as $700 per week—the equivalent of more than $13,000 per week in 2023 dollars.

In major cities, crowds of adoring fans would wait after his performances to catch a glimpse of the dapper John Wilkes Booth as he would exit the theater.

L-R John Wilkes, Edwin, and Junius Brutus, Jr. November 25, 1864

13

"Is that scarecrow really a provost?"

> "Be not forgetful to entertain strangers:
> for thereby some have received
> Angels into their houses unawares."
> —Hebrews 13:2 GNV

A winter chill had set in at Millen Prison. Robert Sneden, along with a few hundred fellow prisoners, had traveled 160 miserable miles in cattle cars to get there. Still, it had to be better than from where he had come. He exited the cattle car stiff and sore from the arduous journey, squinting and shielding his eyes in the sudden light. He used his hand to visor the sun while he got his bearings. Robert inhaled deeply, expecting what should have been fresh air. The smell of wet campfire and animal excrement wafted into his nostrils as he was ushered toward the gate in the south wall. He scanned the camp for distinguishing features.

Pine bark still clung to the tall poles that made up the recently erected perimeter walls. The newly constructed camp, the largest prison in the world at 42 acres, was intended to alleviate overcrowding at Andersonville. It wouldn't last, however.

Millen Prison at Camp Lawton

Camp Lawton, or Millen Prison as it was called, would have to be evacuated just six weeks after it opened due to Sherman's advance through Georgia. When Robert walked into Millen Prison, he was still wearing the same clothes that he had on when he first walked into Andersonville. Threadbare and ragged as they were, he was glad to still have them.

He stood close to a fire, trying to avoid freezing to death without scorching his trousers. There was very little wood to be had inside the walls, so masses of men clustered around what few fires they had. The smoke from the pine sap blackened their skin. Sooty, blackened faces and hands made it difficult to discern Caucasian from Negro. Since they had no soap issued to them to wash it off, sand was used instead. It wasn't very effective and left their skin raw.

At roll call on November 11, 1864, the sergeant announced that a man was needed to go outside the stockade to assist the surgeon as a clerk. Robert requested the job—knowing that in exchange for his services, there would be extra rations. He was accepted as a candidate for the duty. First, he had to be screened by Confederate officers to see if he met the requirements.

A guard escorted Robert outside the gates, while one of the sentries stationed in the "pigeon roost" trained his musket on him. To avoid being shot, Robert placed himself behind the escort, even though the escort all the while was telling the sentry that this prisoner had permission to exit the stockade. The sentry apparently thought, *It could be just another Yankee trick!* and aimed at Robert—following his movements with the barrel of a musket. With the rising sun at his back, Robert was marched several hundred yards to a cluster of log shanties located on the hill overlooking the prison.

He entered an L-shaped pine-log shack situated between the cookhouse and the quartermaster's office. It turned out to be General John Henry Winder's headquarters. Mud was caked on the wooden floor, thick and heavy near the door from boot traffic. The officers' boots were likewise crusted with either muddy earth, horseshit, or both. The cabin was noticeably larger than the surrounding buildings. There was space enough for a desk, a table, a cabinet, and a small group of officers. Most of the officers were standing, as there were only four chairs. The upholstered chair behind the desk was occupied by General Winder.

A brick fireplace was located on the west wall directly across from the large window facing the stockade to the northeast. The remaining furniture was arranged near the hearth. A low fire of embers burned in the fireplace. Unlit coal oil lamps sat atop the crude mantle. Winder sat at his desk filled with papers and was surrounded by eight subordinate officers. He appeared disheveled and intoxicated as Robert inhaled the unmistakable stench of whiskey and noted the general's bloodshot watery eyes.

The warmth inside the shack made the smell of collective body odor and horseshit stronger. The clothes the officers wore were dirty and of poor homespun quality. Robert stood patiently a few feet back from Winder's desk. After a few minutes, the general noticed his presence, and the screening began. Winder asked how long he had been a prisoner and whether or not he could write Latin invoices for medicines. The question aroused Robert's suspicions—remembering the fake passes he had forged back at Andersonville. *Did one of his comrades betray him? Was this a ruse to entrap him?* His eyes scanned the officers' faces for any indication of such a conspiracy. He paused before he answered the question.

"Well?" Winder bellowed. "Can you?"

Robert stalled by answering the first question first. "I've been a prisoner since November of '63."

"Alright then, what about them Latin invoices? Ya gotta be able to do that if you want the damn job helpin' the doc."

Robert made up his mind that answering the question was a chance he would have to take. *Besides, how much worse could it get?* "Yes, I can do that."

Winder shuffled some papers on his desk and slid one out. After briefly scanning it, he handed it to one of his subordinates. The officer stepped forward, handed it to Robert, and stepped back to his position next to Winder's desk. Robert began to read. In the document, Robert was offered a written parole, stating that he would pledge his oath as a military man that he would not attempt to escape from the Confederate States of America, and that if he did try to escape, he would be shot without a trial.

After reading the parole document, Robert defiantly said to Winder, "It's my business to run away, and your business to try to catch me." He also calmly stated, "I don't recognize any such Confederate States of America—in fact, the meanest nation on earth had not recognized them or their bogus Confederacy." At this, Winder sprang up behind his desk, scattering papers and swearing at Robert, slobbering and threatening him with execution for his disrespectful outburst.

Winder had his provost marshal read some sort of document to Robert of the consequences of his actions, but the provost had much difficulty making out the words and spelled some that he was not familiar with. Obviously lacking in education and possessing a limited ability to read, the provost bumbled his way through the document as Robert tried to listen above the din.

The provost marshal was an older man of about sixty years with unkempt dirty, gray hair, and dressed in a sad, yet comical way. He wore dirty, homespun clothes with a red sash across his breast that was too short for his torso and ill-fitted. The seat of his pants was scorched brown from backing up to a fire and standing there too long. His shoes were made of rough-cut cowhide and were clownishly several sizes too big. He wore a slouch hat cocked on his head that did little to complement his ensemble. The front of his shirt was stained with tobacco juice, evidenced by the same stains on his chin.

The provost continued to haltingly read the document but could not be heard well above the talking and yelling by the others in the room. The provost tongue-rolled the wad of chewing tobacco and continued reading louder, peppering the air with brown spittle. Before the provost could finish reading the document, Robert couldn't help himself and laughed at the spectacle.

"What the hell you laughin' at?" boomed Winder.

Robert pointed and asked, "Is that scarecrow really a provost?"

This question caused some of the officers to horselaugh and make sport of the provost, which enraged Winder even further. The general had lost control of the proceedings and let loose with a blistering tirade that again included threats of execution. Winder instructed the guards to take the prisoner away.

The guards escorted Robert out of Winder's headquarters. As he exited, one of the better-dressed officers stepped to Robert and caught his hand, passing along a secret Masonic sign of some sort. He wasn't sure of the meaning, but took it as a sign of a confidence shared. He wore a dress coat much like the ones Union officers wore.

The guards led Robert into the yard and shackled him to a fallen tree with leg irons. A cold rain fell that night. There was no shelter for Robert, but he did have a fire. The young guards assigned to take turns watching him were amiable enough, but Robert would not sleep a wink that night. The guards openly talked about Winder's drunken tirade and what a tyrant he was. Robert wondered throughout his hours awake if he would not be shot that very night and buried in a shallow grave before daylight.

At about 9 p.m., the officer who had given Robert the handshake signal appeared and sat alongside Robert on the fallen tree. He asked Robert whether or not he was a Yankee.

Robert volleyed with his own question. "What do you call a Yankee?"

The officer replied, "You know, people from places like Massachusetts, Vermont, or Connecticut."

Robert replied, "I don't belong to either."

The officer introduced himself as Dr. Isaiah H. White, Confederate Chief Surgeon. It turned out that they shared an acquaintance in New York. The conversation led to the possibility of an assistant position being offered. Dr. White added that General Winder's threat of execution had not been sanctioned with paperwork and that he would try to reason with the general after he sobered up.

The next morning Robert was led into headquarters again, but General Winder was not present. Among those in attendance were the provost marshal, Dr. White, and a few other officers. Robert was given an amended oath agreement that simply stated he was indeed a POW at a Confederate camp and that on his word of honor as a soldier, he would not attempt to escape, lest he be shot trying.

In return for signing the agreement, Robert became Dr. White's assistant. He was also given a five-pointed tin star with a couple of holes in it. The star was meant to be sewn onto a hat or article of clothing to identify paroled prisoners who had different access privileges from the other prisoners.

Dr. White led him to a tent near the hospital ward. His new shelter would be an office tent with a plank floor. Inside the tent were desks, a medicine cabinet, and stools. A cot was in the corner for Robert's use. The doctor's quarters were in the larger hospital tent. These accommodations were by far the finest Robert had been afforded since becoming a prisoner.

That afternoon, he accompanied Dr. White on his rounds. They visited the rebel soldiers' hospital filled with the sick and injured. During the rounds, Robert came across boxes full of clothes donated to Union POWs from the U.S. Sanitary Commission. The rebels had apparently kept the supplies for themselves. When he inquired about the boxes, the doctor told him to take what he needed.

Robert grabbed the clothes, dashed to his tent, and immediately set about exchanging his wardrobe. He quickly stripped and was completely layered from drawers to an outercoat in minutes. Then he began the task of removing all his drawings and writings that had been secreted away in the tattered rags on the floor. With this task completed, he burned his old clothes.

Four days later, three prisoners froze to death in the Millen stockade. The camp buzzed with activity as Winder received the order that the prisoners were to be moved as soon as possible. To where was not yet known. Robert read in a newspaper left behind by Dr. White, dated November 14, that the rebels were calling for all men, regardless of age. What this meant to Robert was: The Confederate war machine was running out of human resources. The exchange policy preventing paroles was cruel and heartless—equally reviled by the Union POWs and Confederate leadership. But the results stated in the newspaper were proof of its effectiveness. By 4 p.m., the entire camp was packed and ready to move out.

Camp Millen was empty except for light artillery stationed on the camp's perimeter. Sherman's forces would later burn it to the ground when they happened upon the empty stockade. Robert marched with Dr. White and his group to the railroad depot where they were loaded onto trains. The train arrived at Savannah at 6 a.m. the next morning. During the stop in Savannah, more boxes of goods donated by the U.S. Sanitary Commission for the Union POWs were found.

When Robert woke the next morning, rebel officers were lying all around in drunken slumber with the door standing wide open. The chain of command among the rebel guards was beginning to evaporate. There was little discipline from the officers all the way down to the enlisted privates. Leaving no one responsible, the rebels plummeted into chaotic disarray. It was apparent that the Confederacy was imploding, and Sherman's advance through the South served as a catalyst.

Robert had distributed some of the uniforms found in the boxes to many of the rebel guards accompanying him. So now to a stranger Robert looked like one of them. Since he had been eating better during his parole with Dr. White, he had regained some healthy weight and could pass for one of the rebel soldiers. To an untrained eye, he traveled among the enemy incognito.

By this time, Union artillery and musket fire could be heard nearby, and Robert was confident that freedom, real freedom, was near. Dr. White had left Assistant Quartermaster Captain C. F. Stubbs behind to pack up supplies, while the doctor went ahead to Florence, South Carolina.

Captain Stubbs was a cripple. Robert had also come to know him as a drunk. Yet he was an easygoing sort, and Robert got along well with him. They became traveling partners, and with his appearance and Stubbs's passes in hand, he could move among the Confederates freely.

Robert and Stubbs traveled on to Florence, arriving at 2 a.m., December 4. They presented themselves at General Winder's headquarters at breakfast. When informed that Stubbs didn't have the supplies with him, Winder had him arrested. During those days of Stubbs's arrest, Robert had little supervision from the guards.

By the time Stubbs was released four days later, Robert had discussed with Dr. White the possibility of being put on the cartels for exchange. He added that he would like to go home—to enjoy turkey for Christmas dinner with loved ones.

14

"Found alive"

> *"And when he cometh home,*
> *he calleth together his friends and neighbors,*
> *saying unto them, Rejoice with me:*
> *for I have found my sheep which was lost."*
> —Luke 15:6 GNV

"Found alive" —Robert Sneden

December 8, 1864, General William T. Sherman marched his armies toward Savannah and a base of supplies. But the Left Wing lagged behind the Right Wing, and the last thing Sherman wanted was isolated columns that might invite a Confederate sortie from Savannah. So "Close up!" was the order of the day.

To continue its line of march, the 14th Corps had to cross a deep swamp cut by several streams. Overnight, pontoniers of the 58th

Indiana Infantry began repairing the bridge span over the creek, which had been burned by retreating Confederates. On either side of the crossing points, soldiers and freed slaves labored to lay corduroy roads or log roads. Trees had to be cut, and limbs had to be trimmed and lashed together to form the corduroy roads, and these preparations took time. With that time spent, the corps fell further behind schedule.

Once they got past the swamps and the corduroy roads, the troops pressed on, but the terrain and Confederate annoyances prevented the 14th Corps from covering much ground. The lead regiments were only four miles past the bridges by nightfall. At least the weather was cooperating. The wagons rolled reasonably well on the frozen ground.

Florence County—Northeastern South Carolina

After contemplating Robert's request to go home, Dr. White wrote out orders to Lieutenant Colonel John Iverson to achieve the parole request. With orders in hand, Robert trudged on alone, walking the railroad tracks for two and a half miles until he reached the prison camp outside Florence, South Carolina. When he arrived, there were no shelters. Robert slept a miserable night on the frozen ground when he and the others weren't moving and stirring around to keep from freezing to death.

They woke the next morning to 17 more dead prisoners, expired from hypothermia—freezing to death on the raw ground. After a meager breakfast, they reported to the railroad station, boarding cattle cars that took them all to Charleston—a distance of over 135 miles. After the five-hour train ride, they marched to the pier to board a side-wheel steamship.

On December 11, 1864, Robert Sneden was officially exchanged at Charleston. He and a large group of fellow POWs walked across two gangplanks one by one, and were counted as they boarded the large vessel. The POWs were packed aboard like sheep. From his view from the deck, he made a sketch of Charleston Harbor.

Braving stormy seas, the steamboat *Varuna* began its 300-mile journey, steaming toward Cape Hatteras. As it pitched in the waves, most prisoners stayed between the decks lying down, as they had no "sea legs." Robert, more familiar with sea travel than his mates, fared better than his comrades in avoiding sea sickness.

The seas got even rougher as the *Varuna* neared the coast at Cape Hatteras. Huge swells tossed the ship, pounding her hull against the waves. A thin line of white smoke that emanated from the forward part of the boat near the winch soon turned into a thick black puff of smoke. Robert then realized the boat was on fire.

The ship's bell sounded the alarm, and seamen came running. Paroled prisoners below deck began screaming and running, with both gangways jammed with men trying to get topside. Men battled the blaze for a half hour, extinguished the flames, and restored order. The crew checked the boilers and engines, finding them in acceptable condition to continue their journey.

The prisoners, after their long and demoralizing captivity, acted like wild animals. The sudden taste of freedom caused them to behave unpredictably. The guards were nowhere in sight—most likely playing cards below deck—and not really concerned about the welfare of the parolees. When Robert went below deck, he found that six or seven prisoners had been trampled to death or suffocated in the confusion of the fire. It was then that he discovered the fire's origin.

One of the prisoners had gone below deck to look for something to eat. He had apparently taken a lit candle with him, and in the darkness, accidentally set the forage on fire. After this incident, the guards took a keener interest in watching the POWs to stifle any reckless behavior.

Before reaching the Chesapeake Bay, several more prisoners died. By the time the *Varuna* reached the wharf at Annapolis, Maryland, dozens of men lay dead on the deck, secured in boxes hastily made by the ship's carpenter.

It rained all the following day. The paddle wheel arrived at Annapolis in the gloom at 4 p.m., where Boston Corbett was already a patient recovering at the Annapolis Hospital.

Robert finally arrived at the port in Washington, D.C., three days before Christmas Eve. He explored "Camp Parole" after breakfast the next morning. The grounds there was level but muddy from the more than two thousand former POWs assigned there, tromping through the muck to get to the cookhouse and quarters.

Outside the camp, a large stockade housed 12,000 men—a mix of Union army deserters, bounty jumpers, Raiders, murderers, and "Galvanized Yanks" (Union POWs who had agreed to work for the Confederacy).

Robert reported to his old Union headquarters to check on his pay, as he had not drawn any Army salary since his capture and imprisonment. Searching the records for his last payment revealed that he had been marked in the ledger in pencil as being "missing or dead." He took out a pencil of his own and amended the ledger to reflect that Robert Knox Sneden was "found alive."

The day before Christmas Eve that year at 6 p.m., Louis Weichmann and John Surratt stood on the sidewalk in front of the boardinghouse enjoying the Christmas festivities and decided to take a stroll along

Pennsylvania Avenue. Weichmann wanted to purchase Christmas gifts for his sisters. They went down 7th Street together, viewing store window displays. They were directly opposite Odd Fellows Hall when someone called out,

"Surratt! Surratt!"

"John, someone is calling you," Weichmann said.

Dr. Samuel Mudd

John turned to recognize an old friend from Charles County, Maryland—Dr. Samuel A. Mudd, standing with another man.

"Why, Doctor, how do you do?" John said, grasping him by the hand.

"I am so glad to see you. Let me make you acquainted with my friend, Mr. Weichmann."

"And you, gentlemen, let me present to you my friend, Mr. Boone," responded Dr. Mudd.

Boone. Such was the name that Weichmann heard. It was not abundantly clear if he misheard the name upon introduction, or if it was a deliberate alias given.

Louis Weichmann later gave his first impression:

Mr. Boone was "a young man of medium figure, apparently about twenty-eight years old. A heavy black mustache rendered the pallor of his face very noticeable. He possessed an abundance of curly black hair and a voice that was rich and musical in its tones. His bearing was that of a man of the world and a gentleman. In dress, he was faultless."

After the introductions, Weichmann shook hands with Dr. Mudd and Mr. Boone. Mr. Boone invited all to forgo shopping and join him to enjoy the hospitality of his room at the National Hotel.

Booth's Washington, D. C. residence – The National Hotel

When they arrived at room number 84, the host invited everyone to be seated. Boone pulled a call bell and requested milk punches and cigars for four. After they sipped the milk punches and engaged in some desultory conversation, Dr. Mudd arose and stepped out into the entry, calling Mr. Boone to join him. After about five minutes, both Mudd and Boone returned to the door and called out Surratt. The three stayed in the entry, leaving Weichmann alone in the room.

When the three men returned, Dr. Mudd apologized for the rudeness of leaving Louis alone, stating: "I hope you will excuse us for the privacy of this conversation—the fact is Mr. Boone has some business with me. Between you and me, he desires to purchase my farm, but he does not wish to give me enough for it."

Boone made similar apologies to that effect. The three seated themselves some distance of eight feet away and had low conversations inaudible to Weichmann. After about twenty minutes, Dr. Mudd invited everyone to the Pennsylvania House on C Street where he was staying. The party adjourned there to Dr. Mudd's room. After a while, the party was winding down, and Mr. Boone was the first to leave, bidding all a good night at about 10:30.

On the return home that night, John Surratt remarked that the brilliant and accomplished young gentleman they had just met was none other than John Wilkes Booth, the famous actor.

Louis Weichmann would discover much later that in reality, Booth had no intention whatsoever of buying Dr. Mudd's or any other land. He simply wanted to familiarize himself with the roads and the people he felt he could trust in the area surrounding Washington, D.C.

PART II

Conspiracy and Surrender

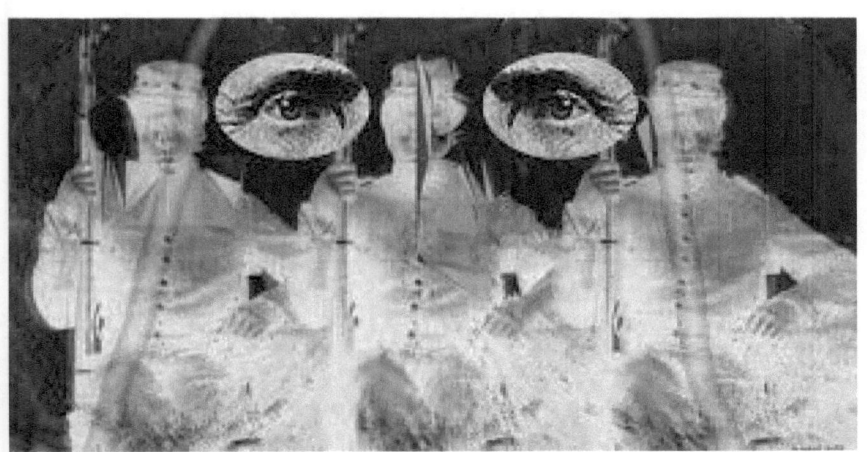

15

"Inauguration Day"

*"Eye for eye, tooth for tooth, hand for hand, foot for foot,
Burning for burning, wound for wound, stripe for stripe."*
—Exodus 21:24-25 GNV

*"...until every drop of blood drawn with the lash
shall be paid by another drawn with the sword."*
—Abraham Lincoln

March 3, 1865

Abraham Lincoln was weary, and haggard in appearance, with dark circles around his eyes and noticeable bags underneath. Lines in his face were deeper and more obvious against the deathlike pallor of his complexion. The duties of his office—and the war—had robbed him of sleep. Still, he was joyous in his demeanor.

The Thirty-Eighth Congress was in session and would work throughout the night, as the president debated and cajoled members of the House to get what he passionately believed in, what he felt the country desperately needed. Lincoln signed a bill creating the Bureau of Refugees, Freedmen, and Abandoned Lands. Known as the Freedmen's Bureau, this federal agency oversaw the difficult transition of Blacks from slavery to freedom.

Secretary of War Edwin Stanton interrupted Lincoln to request a conference. They exited the House Chamber to have a private chat. The conference concerned a letter sent from General Robert E. Lee to General Ulysses S. Grant, proposing a meeting to end the hostilities of the Civil War.

Lincoln instructed Secretary Stanton to notify General Grant that the conference could be granted, but only on the basis of General Lee's surrender. Lincoln issued directives on surrender discussions, giving General Grant wide-ranging powers on military matters, but reserving political matters for himself.

At last, Stanton and Lincoln could see the end of the four-year bloody fratricidal war. As they exchanged congratulations, Lincoln, from his greater height, dropped his long arm upon Stanton's shoulders, and the two embraced over the potential closure of the long and tragic struggle.

March 4, 1865

Vice-President Hannibal Hamlin, the first Republican to hold the office and the most influential politician from the state of Maine, escorted his successor, Vice-President-Elect Andrew Johnson, to the Senate Chamber to be sworn in.

Democrat Johnson of Tennessee was named to replace Hamlin as Lincoln's running mate in the 1864 election. Lincoln was seeking to broaden his base of support and was also looking ahead to Southern Reconstruction. Johnson had proven himself adept as military governor of occupied Tennessee.

After Johnson was sworn in, Lincoln led the audience out of the chamber and onto the East Front inaugural platform for his swearing-in ceremony, where he raised his right hand, placed his left hand on the Bible, and took the oath of office for the second time. Following the ceremony, Lincoln delivered his second inaugural address.

He suggested that the death and destruction wrought by the war was divine retribution to the United States for possessing slavery, saying that God may will that the war continue—

> *"...until every drop of blood drawn with the lash shall be paid by another drawn with the sword ... With malice toward none, with charity for all, with firmness in the right as God gives us to see the right, let us strive on to finish the work we are in, to bind up the nation's wounds, to care for him who shall have borne the battle and for his widow and his orphan, to do all which may achieve and cherish a just and lasting peace among ourselves and with all nations."*

While Lincoln delivered his inaugural address on Capitol Hill, a place where most were collectively devoted to saving the Union without war, insurgent agents were present, seeking to destroy it without war—seeking to dissolve the Union. In attendance among the crowd was the popular, young, and handsome actor John Wilkes Booth.

With a ticket of admission to the event procured by his fiancé Lucy Hale, Booth was in the grandstand seething. He stood near and just behind the president with the purpose and intent to stab the Commander-in-Chief, should the opportunity present itself.

Lincoln's 2nd inaugural address. *Note Booth in balcony above the president.

With the words "with malice toward none, with charity for all" ringing in the air, Booth fancied a plan to murder the president. In the confusion of the crowd, he firmly clutched the knife, the instrument with which he intended to stab Lincoln to death. After Lincoln passed through the door to the platform where the ceremonies were to be held, Booth forcibly broke through the line of Capitol policemen shielding the president. One of the policemen, Lieutenant J. W. Westfall seized Booth, and after a struggle, forced him back into the crowd. Remarkably, Booth was not detained or arrested for his murderous attempt against the president.

Following the inaugural address, Booth wrote in his diary: "What an excellent chance I had, if I wished, to kill the president on Inauguration Day!"

Upon his return to Surratt's boardinghouse, Booth assembled his loose-knit band of Southern sympathizers, including David Herold, George Atzerodt, Lewis Powell (also known as Lewis Payne or Paine), and John Surratt Jr. The fuming and disgruntled Booth held court over his pro-Confederate, anti-Union loyalists, a splinter faction of a larger group called the Know-Nothings.

The Know-Nothing movement was a nativist political party that operated nationally in the mid-1850s. Nativism is a policy that favors native inhabitants as opposed to immigrants. Know-Nothings was a secret society, with hand signs and passwords. Members had a pure-blooded pedigree of Protestant Anglo-Saxon stock. The party rose to prominence in 1853 and included more than one hundred elected congressmen, eight governors, a controlling share of half a dozen state legislatures, and thousands of local politicians. Members supported nationalism, deportation of foreign beggars and criminals, elimination of all Catholics from public office, and mandatory Bible reading in schools. Their aim was to restore their vision of what America should look like, with Protestantism, temperance, self-reliance, and American nationality and work ethic enshrined as the nation's highest values.

Abraham Lincoln had expressed his own disgust with the Know-Nothing political party movement ten years earlier. In a private letter to close friend Joshua Speed written on August 24, 1855, Lincoln asked: "How can anyone who abhors the oppression of Negroes, be in favor of degrading classes of white people? Our progress in degeneracy appears to me to be pretty rapid. As a nation, we began by declaring that 'all men are created equal.' We now practically read it 'all men are created equal, except Negroes.' When the Know-Nothings get control, it will read 'all men are created equal, except Negroes, and foreigners, and Catholics.' When it comes to this, I should prefer emigrating to some country where they make no pretense of loving liberty—to Russia, for instance, where despotism can be taken pure, and without the base alloy of hypocrisy."

16

"Starstruck"

> *"Dearly beloved, believe not every spirit,*
> *but try the spirits whether they are of God:*
> *for many false Prophets are gone out into the world."*
> —1 John 4:1 GNV

March 1865—Downtown Baltimore

The breeze shifted, causing the man to draw his coat up tight to fend off the cold winter chill. He was only four blocks north of Inner Harbor, and the air coming across the bay was cold. He flipped his collar up and shrank further down into his coat. Lewis Powell stared at the Baltimore sidewalk as he shuffled east along Fayette Street, pausing at the corner of Calvert and Fayette with no place to go. Not only that, but wherever he might be destined, he had no money to get there.

He trudged on with his fists jammed into his empty coat pockets, stomach burning with hunger. He was close to desperation. Cold and starving was no way to be in Baltimore at the tail end of winter.

Strange. He thought he heard his name carried in the wind. It almost sounded musical to his ears. Lewis Powell lifted his eyes and turned his head toward the sound.

John Wilkes Booth's destiny was inescapably one of ego and vanity. His parents, noted British Shakespearean actors Junius Brutus Booth, Sr. and his mistress Mary Ann Holmes, were accomplished thespians. John's older brothers Junius, Jr. and Edwin were also successful stage actors by the time John joined the stage in his teens.

John Wilkes Booth made his stage debut in 1855 at age 17, in the supporting role of the Earl of Richmond in *Richard III* at Baltimore's Charles Street Theatre. The audience jeered at him when he missed some of his lines. Being hissed off the stage was a stinging rebuke he felt for the rest of his life. This occurrence in a northern city fueled his disdain for the Union. Conversely, his successes in the South forever endeared him with equal measure on stages like the ones in Richmond.

With practice, Booth honed his craft to become somewhat of a heartthrob stage actor in his prime. By the end of the Civil War, he was earning the equivalent of more than $700,000 annually. (Ford's Theatre paid Booth $700 per week or $36,400 annually. When adjusted to 2022 dollars, the amount equaled $708,105.)

Despite his good fortune, fame, and success as an actor, he was an angry young man. He could not keep his political views to himself, and his disdain toward President Lincoln would not be silenced. He loathed the president and wanted everyone to know it.

By 1860, a disgruntled Booth was arguing so passionately with his older, pro-Union brother Edwin about Lincoln and the war that Edwin finally told him he was no longer welcome at his New York home.

Booth didn't mind expressing his feelings about Lincoln to anyone who would listen—with an unrelenting vitriolic condemnation. He railed against Lincoln in conversations with his sister Asia, saying: "That man's appearance, his pedigree, his coarse low jokes and anecdotes, his vulgar similes, and his policy are a disgrace to the seat he holds. He is made the tool of the North, to crush out slavery."

John Wilkes Booth

In the spring of 1861 just after the opening salvos of war, Booth played in Richmond—acting with more than his usual zest and reaping a rich measure of approval and applause. In the audience that night was a young Florida soldier named Lewis Thornton Powell. It was the first play Powell had ever seen, and he was spellbound by the magical influence wielded by the actor. Powell was chiefly attracted by the voice and persona that defined John Wilkes Booth.

Booth possessed large, lustrous eyes, a graceful form, delicate mold, and a rich voice that lingered in the ears. Powell was starstruck. Booth was everything that Powell was not. Powell was tall and awkward, rough and frank, generous and practically illiterate. Booth on the other hand was polished and sophisticated, subtle with a brilliant fancy, and abundantly well-read. After the performance, Powell sought and gained an introduction to the actor. Never were two men so different and on a collision course of destiny, yet so well calculated—one to rule, the other to be ruled.

Lewis Powell was the eighth child of twelve, the youngest son of a Baptist minister. The family had moved to Live Oak Station on the railroad between Jacksonville and Tallahassee, Florida, just before the outbreak of the war in 1859. Lewis's oldest brother had been maimed and the Confederacy sent home a crippled veteran. His remaining brother was killed during the Battle of Stones River in Murfreesboro, Tennessee. During the battle at Gettysburg on July 3, 1863, Lewis Powell was wounded and taken prisoner.

During his confinement, Powell was detailed as a nurse at Pennsylvania College Hospital. From Gettysburg, he was sent to West Building Hospital in Baltimore, where he remained until October 1863. With no hope of prisoner exchange, he deserted his regiment and subsequently became a member of Company B, in General John S. Mosby's Cavalry, a notorious outfit known as Mosby's Rangers.

As a member of Mosby's Rangers, Powell gained a reputation for being "boldest of the bold and rashest of the reckless." He was a good horseman and knew the area well in the Shenandoah Valley and the Piedmont region of Virginia.

He knew the highways and byways—the shortcuts across fields and woods, enabling him to travel from Warrenton to Winchester, or from Fairfax Court House to Port Royal in

Lewis Thornton Powell

one-third the time normally required. Powell would often go off riding alone, penetrating enemy lines and returning with prisoners, horses, and plunder.

On one occasion, he was surrounded by federal troops in a cabin with a slim chance of escape. Powell cleverly disguised himself by blackening his face with lampblack and walked out of the house right past the enemy. One of the Union soldiers remarked, "That is a damned tall ni**er," and let him pass.

Determined to make his way north, Powell went to Noakville, on the Virginia-Midland Railroad, where he left his horse and donned a suit of civilian clothing. He proceeded to walk down the railroad tracks toward Alexandria, where he encountered federal pickets. Powell portrayed himself as a refugee who didn't understand or speak English very well and was conveyed to Alexandria.

Lewis Powell's role in the presidential assassination plot almost came to an end before it started, when on March 12, 1865, he beat a Black maid at the Margaret Branson boardinghouse in Baltimore on Eutaw Street. Powell had met Mrs. Margaret Branson during his time in the Gettysburg Hospital. Powell asked the Negro servant to clean up his room, and she refused, giving him what he considered impudent backtalk, stating that she would not do it. For this, Powell struck her, threw her on the floor, stomped her body, struck her about the head, and threatened to kill her. She promptly had him arrested and accused him of being a Confederate spy.

Espionage was a serious charge, one that drew attention from the authorities. At the time, Maryland was under martial law. The Union Army's Provost Marshal, James Barnet Fry, had supervision over such cases. As a former member of Mosby's Rangers, Powell was well acquainted with deception and used this skill to his advantage.

In his capacity as provost marshal, Fry was responsible for tracking deserters, enforcing military laws, and overseeing the Invalid Corps. Using the name "Lewis Paine," Powell swore he was from Fauquier County, Virginia, and knew nothing about the war. Declaring he was only 18 years old, he pretended to be stupid and not understand the English language.

Lacking evidence that proved he was a spy, the provost marshal released Powell on March 14. Powell took an oath of allegiance to the United States, and the provost marshal wrote on his allegiance form that "Lewis Paine of Fauquier County, Virginia," was to live north of Philadelphia, Pennsylvania, for the duration of the war.

The provost marshal had carelessly written the "stay north" order in pencil. Lewis Powell later erased it from his oath of allegiance and remained in Baltimore—homeless, hungry, and broke.

Lewis Powell had no means of support and was in a pitiable condition. He dragged himself along the downtown Baltimore street past the Barnum Hotel. A familiar musical voice hailed him from the hotel steps. Looking up, Powell saw the handsome face of John Wilkes Booth. Booth expressed astonishment at the obvious plight and frantic straits of Lewis Powell. They exchanged a few words, with Powell pleading: "Booth, I want bread—I am starving."

Ordinarily, Booth would have said to a friend in such despair to come and eat without haste, but Booth instantly saw an opportunity to further his scheme. He did not straightaway tell his friend to come and eat. Nor did he tell him to go away and die. Booth seized with eagerness the prospect of a willing accomplice, plying this young man's hunger to wind him about with tendrils of deceit. "I will give you as much money as you want, but first you must swear to stick to me. It is in the 'oil business.'"

Then and there, Lewis Powell swore an oath of fatal consequences—binding his very soul to John Wilkes Booth. Booth took Powell into the hotel where he feasted. The following morning, Booth gave him enough money to buy a change of clothes and expenses for a week.

Powell persisted in wanting to know more about Booth's oil business, but Booth was evasive in his answers, stringing him along for the moment. Booth knew well that he must get total control of this desperate creature for his own ends.

Accordingly, Booth proceeded to secure every thought and emotion of Lewis Powell—eloquently painting a picture for Powell of Southern injuries, devastated homes, ravished women, orphaned children, freed Negroes, and the graves of his Southern brethren on a thousand hillsides and so many battle sites.

When Booth was convinced that Powell was fully indoctrinated and completely under his spell, he disclosed his mysterious plan to abduct the president while he was traveling to the Soldiers' Home on the outskirts of D.C. to force the Union to resume prisoner exchanges. Lewis Powell became one of Booth's most physically powerful and trusted lieutenants in the conspiracy—soon finding his way to the "nest that hatched the egg"—Mrs. Mary Surratt's boardinghouse.

17

"Reconnaissance"

> *"Thou shalt keep thee far from a false matter,
> thou shalt not slay the innocent and the righteous:
> for I will not justify a wicked man."*
> —Exodus 23:7 GNV

At the Surratt boardinghouse, Mrs. Mary Surratt, her daughter Anna, Honora Fitzpatrick, and Louis Weichmann had finished dinner and were enjoying social time in the parlor when the doorbell rang. Weichmann rose, excused himself, and opened the door to find a tall, robust man with black hair and a ruddy countenance, wearing a dark, felt slouch hat and a seedy black overcoat. His hands were buried deep in his coat pockets. He stared at Weichmann and asked if Mr. Surratt lived there and if he was home. Weichmann replied that it was indeed Mr. Surratt's home, but he was not in. The man then inquired if Mrs. Surratt was at home and asked to see her, identifying himself as Mr. Wood.

Weichmann returned to the parlor, informing Mrs. Surratt that a gentleman named Wood was at the door. At her instruction, Weichmann brought the man into the parlor and introduced him as Mr. Wood. Wood approached Mrs. Surratt and said something to her in a low voice to which she remarked to Weichmann, "The gentleman would like to have some supper, and inasmuch as the dining room is disarranged, I will be very much obliged to you if you will take the meal to him in your own room."

Weichmann sat in his room and watched while Mr. Wood devoured his food. When Weichmann asked where he was from, Wood replied, "I am from Baltimore and a clerk in the china store of Mr. Parr." Upon finishing his meal, Wood stated that he would like to retire for the night and was given a bed in the attic. In the morning, Wood was gone.

Three days later, on March 15, 1865, John Wilkes Booth rented the presidential box at Ford's Theatre for the performance of the play *Jane Shore*. A ticket seller at Ford's Theater, Thomas J. Raybold, sold Booth 6 tickets for box number 10 (the presidential box), for $10 each. Booth provided tickets for himself, Lewis Powell, John Surratt Jr., and their female companions in order to familiarize themselves with the layout of the theater and how to access the box. For the night out, John Surratt asked to borrow Louis Weichmann's blue cloak.

The group attended the theater, as planned, in the company of two of Mrs. Surratt's female boarders, Honora Fitzpatrick and Apollonia Dean. Eleven-year-old Mary Holohan, preparing for her first communion, declined her invitation. The young ladies were thrilled at the attention given them but were unaware of the true motive for the outing—to carry out a covert reconnaissance mission.

While at the theater, Booth called Surratt and Powell into the entry for a private conversation. After the play, the men returned the girls to the boardinghouse, then had a late-night planning meeting at Gautier's Restaurant on Pennsylvania Avenue. It was the first time Booth revealed his alternate plan to kidnap Lincoln from Ford's Theatre instead of intercepting the president on his way to visit the Soldiers' Home.

On the afternoon of March 16, Louis Weichmann returned home from work at the War Department and rang the bell for Dan, the young Negro who did chores around the Surratt house. Louis requested some water for washing up and asked Dan where John Surratt was. Dan replied, "Massa Surratt rode away from the front of the house about two o'clock with six or seven on horseback."

Ford's Theatre Washington, D.C. 1865

"Who were they?"

"One was Massa Booth, another was Payne [Powell], then Port Tobacco [Atzerodt], and David Herold."

Dan claimed he didn't know the other two men, but upon description, Weichmann knew he was describing Samuel Arnold and Michael O'Laughlen.

A little later in the evening, Weichmann met Mary Surratt in the hallway weeping bitterly. Concerned at seeing her tears, he asked what was wrong. "Go down, Mr. Weichmann, and make the best of dinner that you can. John is gone away . . . John is gone away."

Honora Fitzpatrick

Mrs. Surratt did not come to the dinner table that night as she usually did. The only ones dining were Louis Weichmann, Honora Fitzpatrick, and Anna Surratt. During the meal, Anna became suddenly agitated and brought down the handle of her knife upon the tabletop with great force, the slam stopping the others mid-bite.

"Mr. Weichmann," she exclaimed, "do you know that if anything happened to my brother John through his acquaintance with Booth, I would kill him!"

Startled, Weichmann and Fitzpatrick eyed one another with raised brows and finished their meals in silence, while Anna smoldered. After dinner, Weichmann was in his room reading Dickens's *Pickwick* when John Surratt burst in, visibly anxious. Surratt was wearing his pantaloons in his boot tops and spurs on the heels. In his hand, he held a small four-barrel Sharp's Pepperbox Derringer.

"What's the matter?" asked Weichmann.

Unconsciously, Surratt waved the pistol around, leveled it at Louis, and exclaimed, "Weichmann, my prospects are gone! My hopes are blasted! I want something to do. Can you get me a clerkship?"

"You are foolish; why don't you settle down and be a sensible man?"

Weichmann continued trying to calm Surratt down, and about ten minutes later, Lewis Powell entered the room, excited, his face flushed. Powell said nothing but paced about the room like a caged animal, at one point adjusting his clothing and revealing a large revolver on his hip. Shortly afterward, Booth entered the room wearing dark clothes with a riding whip in his hand. Booth walked a few circles around the room before noticing Weichmann.

"Hallo, you here? I did not see you."

Booth then signaled Powell and Surratt, and the three went upstairs to the little room in the attic where Powell had slept. They stayed there for about half an hour and left the house.

Booth was always a welcome guest in the Surratt house, visiting frequently and at all hours of the day. No sooner than Booth crossed the threshold, he created a fluster among the females of the house. Handsome, famous, and fascinating, Booth fancied himself a charmer. Though he cared little for Anna Surratt or Honora Fitzpatrick, he was content to pay them salutations with a theatrical flourish, to which they would swoon.

Booth took pride and pains to let it be known he was paying special attention to the daughter of New Hampshire Republican Senator, John P. Hale. He often told how he sent "Bessie" Hale beautiful flowers, neglecting to talk about the mistress he kept in one of D.C.'s gilded houses of pleasure. This mistress—a petite, sensual, red-headed prostitute named Ella Turner—upon learning of Booth's philandering deeds, unsuccessfully attempted suicide with poison.

While a clerk at the War Department, Louis Weichmann befriended fellow clerk, Captain Daniel H. Gleason, a former soldier and member of the Veteran Reserve Corps, who had been wounded during the war. Weichmann confided in him the comings and goings at the Surratt boardinghouse, especially the frequent visits by John Wilkes Booth. At the time, he considered his casual acquaintance with Booth a fine thing. What Weichmann first told Gleason was, in his view, harmless gossip. But as time wore on, Weichmann began to suspect the character of Booth and his dubious circle of friends.

Chats with Captain Gleason at the War Department continued, taking a more suspicious tone regarding Booth and his associates. Gleason told Weichmann to keep an eye on them and report anything serious to him, and if he felt it was warranted, they would report it to Secretary of War Stanton. If need be, Gleason suggested they could go to General G. H. Rucker of the Quartermaster's Department to secure horses to pursue them should they flee.

Later, upon entering his room, Weichmann found John Surratt sitting before the fire, staring blankly into the flames, looking as if he had lost his last friend in the world. Concerned for his friend, he asked, "What's the matter, John? Why are you so dejected?"

"I can't tell you; you are a Yankee."

Once again, Lewis Powell appeared at the front door of the Surratt house. When Weichmann answered the doorbell, the guest identified himself as Mr. Payne and requested John Surratt. He was told that John was not home and was escorted into the parlor where Mrs. Surratt and the ladies of the house were gathered. Weichmann announced the guest as Mr. Payne.

One of the ladies remembered him from his previous appearance and addressed him as Mr. Wood. It dawned on Weichmann that indeed the man had given different identities on the two visits. Now, Payne/Wood/Powell wore a new gray suit with a black tie. On this occasion, he presented himself as a Baptist preacher. One of the ladies, Mrs. Holohan, remarked, "Queer preacher; I don't think he will convert many souls."

The following day, John Surratt returned home in the late afternoon and lay on the bed in their room while Weichmann was writing at the table. Payne/Wood/Powell entered and asked, "Is this Mr. Surratt?"

"Yes, sir, it is."

"I would like to talk privately with Mr. Surratt."

Weichmann thought it was odd that Payne/Wood/Powell was obviously acquainted with John Surratt yet pretended to have never met him. Powell was deliberately attempting to deceive Weichmann—for what ends he did not know. Perplexed, Weichmann stood and left the room.

The next day while searching for John Surratt, Weichmann ascended the steps to the back attic and upon entering, he beheld Surratt and Powell seated on a bed surrounded by a menagerie of items including eight pairs of spurs, two Bowie knives, and two revolvers. Initially, they attempted to shield the articles from view until they realized who had surprised them.

Concerned, Weichmann immediately went downstairs and reported his discovery to his landlady. "Mrs. Surratt, I do not like this."

Mary told him to think nothing of it, informing him that John's habit of riding into the country required these things for his personal protection.

Booth had taken on the financial responsibilities of virtually everyone involved in the conspiracy. John Surratt now claimed ownership of horses boarded at Howard's Stables on G Street, though Brook Stabler, an employee of Howard's, admitted that Booth paid for their keep. Likewise, the arms carried by John Surratt, Lewis

Powell, and the other conspirators—all were paid for by Booth. Additionally, Booth paid room and board for these same men, as none had the means or occupation to earn the money for their expenses.

On the morning of March 17, Booth learned that President Lincoln had been invited to attend a matinee theatrical performance at the Soldiers' Home. The Soldiers' Home was in a rural part of D.C., about one mile from the city limits, and Lincoln usually visited the facility without an escort.

Booth's group of conspirators met in front of the Surratt boardinghouse at 2 p.m. to receive instructions from Booth. He sent David Herold out to the Surrattsville Tavern with equipment and informed the others that they should wait at a local saloon while he rode out to the Soldiers' Home to scout the area. When Booth arrived at the Soldiers' Home, he discovered that Lincoln had decided to address a group of Indiana soldiers at a downtown hotel instead. Lewis Powell and the other conspirators never left the tavern to perform any deeds on Booth's behalf that day.

Later, Booth held a meeting at the Lichau House on Pennsylvania Avenue. In attendance were Samuel Arnold, Michael O'Laughlen, George Atzerodt, John Surratt, David Herold, and Lewis Powell. During the discussion, Booth became angry with Arnold. Arnold remarked that if the thing [the kidnapping of Lincoln] was not done that week, he would withdraw from the plot.

"You ought to be shot!" roared Booth.

"Two can play at that game!" Arnold yelled back.

Booth brought his fist down hard on the table.

"Well, gentlemen, if the worst comes to the worst, I shall know what to do!" thundered Booth.

"If I understand you to intimate anything more than the capture of Mr. Lincoln, I for one will bid you goodbye," replied Arnold.

Booth seethed.

In the evening, John Surratt returned home alone. When Weichmann asked what had become of his companions, he replied that Booth had gone to New York and Powell had gone to Baltimore. This was probably true of Powell, but not likely so of Booth. Booth did not leave D.C. for New York until March 21, returning on March 25.

By this time, both Arnold and O'Laughlen had withdrawn from the conspiracy to abduct the president. No record whatsoever of them returning to Washington, D.C., exists. On April 1, Arnold accepted a job 180 miles away in a store working as a sutler.

He would be there at the store in Fort Monroe when he was arrested following the assassination. Authorities would point out that Arnold's and O'Laughlen's mistake was thinking that withdrawing from the conspiracy plot was enough. It wasn't. They should have informed authorities of Booth's scheme.

18

"One of the largest and best steamers ever constructed..."

*"Pride goeth before destruction,
and an high mind before the fall."*
—Proverbs 16:18 GNV

March 21, 1865

He arrived where he thought the shot could be heard. Davy sat still and quietly in the buggy.... listening. Nothing but a gentle breeze stirred and the squeak of leather. Steam rose from the sweaty horse flesh, smelling like dusty hay. The sun was peeking through the woods on the east side of the road. The calendar would indicate that today was the day after the March equinox, late winter and still raw.

He unholstered his revolver and rested his wrist in his lap. Stillness. A few birds chirped while squirrels rustled among the leaves. Facing the direction they should approach, Davy Herold fired his pistol into the air, signaling to John Surratt and George Atzerodt of his whereabouts on the road to Surrattsville. His horse reacted to the shot skittishly, and he tightened his reins. The animal resisted, its ears twitched and rotated backward toward Herold as the whites of the horse's eyes enlarged in terror. The mare pranced in a circle backing up. It wasn't long until he heard clops from approaching horses. The three men—Herold, Surratt, and Atzerodt—greeted one another on the road and galloped away together toward Surrattsville.

They arrived at Lloyd's Tavern with a cache of two carbines, ammunition, twenty feet of rope, and a monkey wrench. John Surratt asked Lloyd to take care of and conceal the items. Lloyd, a former police officer, was visibly uncomfortable with the request but realized that he had an unspoken obligation to his landlord's son. Lloyd told him he did not wish to store such things and there was no good place to conceal them anyway.

Upon hearing Lloyd's reluctance, Surratt took Lloyd to an unfinished chamber above the storeroom in the back part of the building and showed him where to stow the items—underneath the floor joists of the second floor. Surratt informed Lloyd that he just wanted to keep the supplies there for a few days and would call for them soon.

The scheme was supposed to go like this: In the event of the successful capture of the president, the rope was to be stretched between two trees across the road on which they were to make their escape—to break the pursuit of any cavalry that might follow. The purpose of the monkey wrench was to remove the wheels from the carriage that would transport Lincoln to the ferry. The wheel-less body of the carriage was to be set onto the boat and ferried south across the Potomac River.

March 24, 1865

Along the waterway, the long winter gave way to fresh buds popping out along the branches. Despite sunny skies, it was still chilly, with a high temperature of 44 degrees, but on the river, it felt even colder. The red-cheeked crew of the *Sultana* was dressed for the raw weather. The swollen Mississippi River was bone-chilling cold.

The *Sultana* was licensed to operate on the Lower Mississippi between her home port of St. Louis and New Orleans. The license listed Captain James Cass Mason as a three-eighths majority owner of the vessel. The other majority owners were Sam DeBow, W. J. Lewis, and Mr. William A. Thornberg. The boat was valued at $80,000, and she was insured for a large amount.

By the end of the war, one month later, Captain Mason—to offset his financial problems—had sold most of his interest in the *Sultana* to his first clerk, William J. Gambrel.

The paddle-wheel boat was chugging south at a favorable clip, taking advantage of the Mississippi's southward current. The bill of lading for today's load was for the shipment of 31,000 lbs. of dry hemp—for the fare of 50¢ per 100 lbs.—from St. Louis to New Orleans, for a total of $155. The document, signed by first clerk and part-owner William J. Gambrel, listed James Cass Mason as the captain of the *Sultana*.

James Cass Mason

Mason was born in Virginia in 1831 and moved to St. Louis as a child. A lanky man in his mid-thirties who kept his face clean-shaven, Mason typically wore a black, frock dress uniform coat and khakis, whether he was on duty or off. He wore his sandy brown hair cropped short, military style. His icy blue eyes gave him the appearance of intensity. Captain Mason was a capable navigator, who took his responsibilities seriously and firmly believed that his rank as captain demanded respect from other crew members and passengers alike.

Mason had married well, wed to Rowena M. Dozier, a member of a prominent family in St. Louis. Rowena Dozier's father, James Dozier, owned a steamboat that he had named after his daughter. Coincidentally, Mason's name first surfaced publicly when he was the captain of that steamer, the *Rowena*. The vessel was confiscated by the federal government in February of 1863, for smuggling Confederate contraband during the Civil War. James Dozier lost a boat, and Mason lost his job. Mason and James Dozier broke off relations after the incident. Mason was never publicly connected with the Confederates again and was henceforth considered by many secessionists as a turncoat.

He next became captain of the *Belle Memphis*. As a riverboat pilot, he earned a reputation as a careful operator, though many in the business viewed him as a speed demon. Mason occasionally raced other Mississippi riverboat operators from port to port for bragging rights. The winning vessel of the race earned the right to proudly display a trophy signaling victory—a large rack of elk antlers affixed between the twin smokestacks.

The *Sultana*, built in Cincinnati in early 1863 for Captain Preston Lodwick, was reported to be "one of the largest and best steamers ever constructed." The wooden steamship was built by the John Litherbury Shipyard on Front Street in Cincinnati and was originally intended to be used for the Lower Mississippi cotton trade.

With a legal carrying capacity of 376 people, the *Sultana*, which had a crew of eighty to eighty-five, was legally permitted to take on about 290 passengers. Lodwick owned the *Sultana* until March 1864 when he sold her to three investors, one of whom was James Cass Mason, the steamer's captain and master.

She was state of the art at the time, including the most modern safety equipment: safety gauges that fused open when the internal boiler pressure reached 150 pounds psi (per square inch), three fire-fighting pumps, a metallic lifeboat, a wooden yawl, 300 feet of fire hose, 30 buckets, five fire-fighting axes, and 76 life belts.

The *Sultana* measured an impressive 260 feet in length and 42 feet in width at her side paddle wheels. Each paddle wheel measured 34 feet in diameter with fenders rising above the third deck. Emblazoned across the fender housings in tall, capital, red letters in western script was her christened name, *SULTANA*.

Four decks proud, her gleaming white paint made her look like a giant, layered wedding cake. The bottom deck housed the kitchen, crew's quarters, two steam engines, four interconnected coal-fired tubular boilers, and the cargo hold. Her two side-mounted paddle wheels carried 11-foot-long plank buckets and were powered by pistons 25 inches in diameter with an eight-foot stroke. The propulsion mechanism was driven by the four tubular, or fire-tube, steam boilers. Introduced in 1848, they could generate twice as much steam per fuel load as conventional flue boilers. Each fire-tube boiler was 18 feet long and 46 inches in diameter and contained 24 five-inch flues, tubes that ran from the firebox to the chimney.

The economic advantages of the tubular boilers, however, came with a safety trade-off. The water levels in a tubular system had to be carefully maintained at all times. The flues clogged easily, and the mineral buildup on the tubes and boiler sides was especially heavy when the river water used in the system carried lots of sediment.

It was difficult to scrape off. Even the slightest dip in water level could cause hot spots leading to metal fatigue, thereby significantly increasing the risk of an explosion.

In the bow of the *Sultana*, a wide central staircase led to the next level—the passengers' promenade deck, which exhibited carved balusters, arched spandrels, and ornate finials. Behind the staircase sat a wooden crate about the size of a coffin, containing the ship's mascot—a small alligator named Buford.

Running through the promenade deck was a saloon leading to a dining area in the stern. The dining room featured ornate woodwork, glass chandeliers, and luxurious carpets. Dinners were served on white linen tablecloths and fine china and crystal. The *Sultana* boasted a bar for men and a Ladies' Lounge—rare on riverboats. Staterooms flanking the saloon were small—eight square feet, but smartly appointed, and reserved for passengers paying extra for the privilege. They contained bunk beds, a wooden Windsor chair, a wash basin, a white porcelain chamber pot, and a brass cuspidor.

Above the promenade deck lay the hurricane deck, so called because it was exposed to the elements with no roof overhead. On top of that sat the smaller Texas deck, which held the cube-shaped pilothouse. The pilothouse was encased in glass windows on the sides and back—leaving the front open for optimal views. Two fluted smokestacks, jet black, 35 feet tall and held in place by a web of cables, bracketed the pilothouse and Texas deck. Behind the smokestacks lay a long, narrow structure, the officer's quarters, small and sparsely furnished, but adequate. Fastened to the crossbeam bracket between the *Sultana's* towering smokestacks was a trophy indicating Mason's paddlewheel had won a big river race—a huge rack of elk antlers.

In the pilothouse, the ship's wheel stood 10 feet high. Also housed in the pilothouse were the ship's navigational chart table, a rope to ring the ship's brass bell, and a cord for the ear-piercing steam whistle. At the stern behind the pilothouse rested a small two-masted yawl, lowered by winch to check water depth ahead. Weighing 1,719 tons, the steamer drew less than seven feet of water.

For two years, the *Sultana* ran a regular route between St. Louis and New Orleans. Regular trips up and down the Mississippi took a toll on her and her boilers.

Steamships were sometimes commissioned by the War Department to carry troops and supplies. By the war's end, boat operators were recruited for transport duty since Sherman's March to the Sea had crippled the country's Southern transportation infrastructure—the railroads.

In their attempt to disable rail transportation, both Union and Confederate forces employed sabotage. Whenever Sherman's troops encountered a railroad in Confederate territory, they removed the tracks. But whenever Confederates came upon a disassembled track, they would simply put it back together so rail transport could resume. Consequently, Union troops eventually adopted a more permanent method of destruction. "Sherman neckties," they were called. Troops removed the rails, heated them by piling the crossties into a bonfire until they were cherry red, then wrapped them around trees to prevent their re-installation.

As a result, the transportation of any federal goods or personnel going north or south would have to travel the Mississippi River on government-contracted steamships. Among the many boats that ran those routes, cash-strapped Captain James Cass Mason's *Sultana* eagerly lined up for its share of the shipping bonanza.

19

City Point

*"They that be slain with the sword,
are better than they that are killed with hunger…"*
—Lamentations 4:9 GNV

"Good-bye gentlemen, God bless you all!"
—Abraham Lincoln

Captain Henry Wirz knew it was inevitable and there was not a lot he could do about it. He had repeatedly requested food and medicine from the Confederate Quartermaster. Scouts had been dispatched to search the area surrounding Andersonville, scavenging what they could. His own men were on half rations now, like the POWs. The corral had fewer horses and mules. Driven by hunger, the men were forced to "grease their chins" with horseflesh—eating their livestock. A few weeks at best were all Wirz could imagine the food to hold out. And that was if everything in stowage wasn't rotten and ruined already. The war was coming to an end. He could feel it.

The late winter rains continued nonstop. The POWs camped near Stockade Branch stood in muddy water nearly crotch-deep. The steady rains had flooded the penitentiary's sole water supply. The creek was so polluted with the solid waste of men and beasts that more than half of the inmates had dysentery, but at least the flooding flushed the diseased waste from the surrounding swamp.

Captain Wirz had not received word about when there would be forthcoming supplies. Andersonville Prison was in a very bad way. Telegraph lines had been in tatters since December, and rail transport was hit or miss. News traveled slowly in southwestern Georgia. An overwhelmed Henry Wirz could only watch helplessly as a steady stream of new prisoners poured daily into the stockade. He only wished there were supplies on those same train cars bringing the POWs.

March 27-29, 1865

Spanish Fort, Alabama, on the Gulf Coast, was heavily fortified as an eastern defense of the city of Mobile. Up until this point, Mobile had remained in Confederate hands.

Union forces embarked on a land campaign in early 1865 to take Mobile from the east. The fall of Spanish Fort allowed Union forces to concentrate on Fort Blakeley six miles to the north and hence destroy the last organized resistance east of the Mississippi River. The fall of Spanish Fort and Fort Blakeley permitted Union troops to enter Mobile unopposed.

As part of the Anaconda Plan—a strategy to end the war—Union forces choked off any attempts by rebel forces to re-supply or move troops on the waterways by a blockade of Southern ports. Control of the Mississippi River was now in Union hands.

Sherman, Grant, Lincoln, & Porter at City Point, Virginia

President Lincoln met with Union Generals Ulysses S. Grant, William T. Sherman, and Admiral David Dixon Porter at City Point, Virginia, to plot what was hopefully the last stages of the Civil War. Lincoln went to Virginia just as Grant prepared to attack Confederate General Robert E. Lee's lines around Petersburg and Richmond, an assault that promised to end the siege that had dragged on for ten months. Meanwhile, Sherman's force was steamrolling northward through the Carolinas.

The three architects of Union victory—Lincoln, Grant, and Sherman—convened for the first time as a group at Grant's City Point headquarters. Prior to meeting with his generals, the president reviewed troops and visited with wounded soldiers. When he sat down with Grant and Sherman, Lincoln expressed concern that General Robert E. Lee might escape Petersburg and flee to North Carolina, where he could join forces with General Joseph Johnston to forge a new Confederate army that could continue the war for months.

Nearing the end of the war brought about fears of desperate acts by the rebels. One of the bigger concerns was that if cornered, Lee's Confederate forces would resort to retreating into the woods and continue fighting as guerrillas, prolonging the war indefinitely.

Grant and Sherman assured the president that the end was in sight. Lincoln emphasized to his generals that any surrender terms must preserve the Union and its war aims of emancipation and a pledge of equality for the freed slaves.

On March 29, President Lincoln walked to the railway station in City Point, where General Grant was leaving on a train headed to the front. Grant told Lincoln he hoped this would be the final offensive against Lee.

Lieutenant Colonel Horace Porter wrote of his observations of Lincoln that morning: "Lincoln looked more serious than at any other time since he had visited headquarters. The lines on his face seemed deeper, and the rings under his eyes seemed of a deeper hue." Sleep had continued to elude the president, and it showed in his facial features but did not diminish his resolve.

As the train pulled away from the platform, Grant and his party tipped their hats to honor the president. Returning the salute, his voice broken by an emotion he could ill conceal, Lincoln said, "Good-bye, gentlemen, God bless you all!"

Less than four weeks later, Grant and Sherman would secure the surrender of the Confederacy they had promised, and President Lincoln would be dead.

20

"Options"

> *"Furthermore when ye shall hear of wars, and rumors of wars,*
> *be ye not troubled, for such things must needs be:*
> *but the end shall not be yet."*
> —Mark 13:7 GNV

Friday, April 7, 1865—City Point, Virginia

President Lincoln forwarded to Secretary of War Stanton telegrams from Generals Andrew Humphreys, George Meade, and Horatio Wright. Lincoln telegraphed General Grant: "General Sheridan says, 'If the thing is pressed, I think Lee will surrender.' Let the thing be pressed."

General Robert E. Lee had two options in mind, and neither one was surrender. Lee's troops had once again crossed the Appomattox River, arriving in Farmville, Virginia, where a much-needed respite was allowed. The troops were bone-tired and hungry, after marching virtually nonstop for days. While troops prepared bacon and cornbread on campfires, Lee contemplated his options.

He could try to turn south toward Danville or head west for Lynchburg and the protection of the Blue Ridge Mountains. Lee chose to continue westward.

General Grant and his Union Army advanced to Farmville and arrived just after Lee's departure but continued hot on his heels. Grant wrote a communique directly to General Lee. Wishing to end the hostilities and needless loss of more lives on both sides, Grant ordered his inspector general and special envoy Brigadier General Seth Williams to deliver the letter to the Confederate picket lines that night.

Under a flag of truce, Brigadier General Williams and an orderly set out for the rebel lines in the darkness. Upon reaching the Confederate pickets around 8 p.m., they were met with gunfire, killing the orderly. An hour later, again displaying the flag of truce, Williams delivered the letter. It was another hour before Lee was handed the communique.

Headquarters, Armies of the United States
General R. E. Lee, Commanding C. S. A.

5 PM, April 7, 1865

The results of the last week must convince you of the hopelessness of further resistance on the part of the Army of Northern Virginia in this struggle. I feel that it is so, and regard it as my duty to shift from myself the responsibility of any further effusion of blood by asking of you the surrender of that portion of the Confederate States army known as the Army of Northern Virginia.

U.S. Grant, Lieutenant-General,
Commanding Armies of the United States

Lee absorbed the content of the letter in silence, afterward handing it to thirty-five-year-old General James Longstreet. Lee referred to Longstreet as "Old War Horse," one of the foremost Confederate generals of the Civil War and the principal subordinate to General Lee.

James Longstreet had been a poor student academically and a disciplinary problem at West Point, ranking 54th out of 56 cadets when he graduated in 1842. He was popular with his classmates however, and befriended a number of men who would become prominent figures during the Civil War, including William S. Rosecrans and Ulysses S. Grant, who was one of the West Point graduating class of 1843.

Longstreet was commissioned a brevet second lieutenant. He joined the 4th U.S. Infantry at Jefferson Barracks, Missouri. Longstreet spent his first two years of service at the post.

In 1843, he was joined by his friend, Lieutenant Ulysses Grant. In 1844, Longstreet met his future first wife Maria Louisa Garland, called Louise by her family. She was the daughter of Longstreet's commander, Lieutenant Colonel John Garland. At about the same time as Longstreet began courting Garland, Grant became acquainted with and courted Longstreet's fourth cousin, Julia Dent, and the couple eventually married. Reports suggest that Longstreet served as Grant's best man at his wedding, or at least may have been a groomsman.

A South Carolinian, born and bred, Longstreet was serving in the United States Army as a paymaster in Albuquerque when the first shots of the Civil War were fired on Fort Sumter. When he got the news, he joined his fellow Southerners who had decided to leave their posts as a result. Longstreet's memoirs reveal that this was a particularly "sad day" for him, that several Northern officers had tried to convince him to stay. While Longstreet was not enthusiastic about secession, he believed in state's rights and felt his obligation as an officer was first and foremost to his home state. Longstreet accepted a commission as a lieutenant colonel in the Confederate army on May 1, 1861. He submitted his resignation papers to the U.S. Army, and the resignation was accepted on June 1, 1861.

The newly commissioned officer arrived at the executive mansion of Confederate President Jefferson Davis in Richmond on June 22, 1861. Longstreet was informed that he had been appointed the rank of brigadier general and ordered to report to P.G.T. Beauregard in Manassas, Virginia.

General James Longstreet

Seven months later, in January 1862, a scarlet fever epidemic in Richmond claimed the lives of Longstreet's one-year-old daughter Mary Anne, his four-year-old son James, and eleven-year-old son Augustus, all within a week. The losses were devastating for Longstreet, and he became withdrawn, both personally and socially.

His headquarters had always been known for parties, drinking, and poker games. After he returned from the funerals, the previous headquarters for social life became, for a time, more somber. He rarely drank, and his religious devotion increased.

Longstreet quietly read Grant's letter, handing it back to Lee with the comment "not yet" and suggested a response was in order. Lee agreed, concluding that the letter must be answered. Lee personally composed a response, stating:

Genl

I have read your note of this date. Though not entertaining the opinion you express of the hopelessness of further resistance of the Army of Northern Virginia – I reciprocate your desire to avoid the useless effusion of blood, and therefore before considering your proposition, ask the terms you will offer on the condition of surrender.

R. E. Lee, Genl

21

"...and I would rather die a thousand deaths."

"The pride of a man shall bring him low: but the humble in spirit shall enjoy glory."
—Proverbs 29:23 GNV

Saturday, April 8, 1865

After leaving Farmville, Grant's troops caught up to Lee's Confederate Army of Northern Virginia. Though they outnumbered Lee's army nearly six to one, the disparity did not end there. Lee's troops were exhausted and malnourished after a nonstop six-day march west. Grant's men conversely were well-armed, adequately rested, and well-fed.

Lee's army had struggled west after the detachment covering their rear was overwhelmed at Sayler's Creek. Left in their wake was a sad testament to the Confederate army's struggles. Weary, starving rebel soldiers were deserting the Cause in alarming numbers. The once mighty rebel army was irreparably weakened and coming unraveled.

Abandoned rebel wagons, artillery pieces, and injured Confederate soldiers, horses and mules that could not go any farther littered the desperate trail of retreat. Grant's Union Army closely pursued General Lee's hungry and exhausted men, pushing them westward. Grant pressed on—shadowing rebel movement like a trident—on parallel and trailing routes.

Union General George Armstrong Custer's cavalry division was informed that a well-stocked supply train awaited Lee's army at Appomattox Station. Custer pressed forward and engaged in a battle characterized by the absence of a Union infantry. The engagement involved Custer's cavalry versus Confederate artillery plus an assortment of soldiers.

Confederate Brigadier General Reuben Lindsay Walker commanded, with support from some dismounted cavalrymen, artillerymen armed with muskets, and some stragglers. It was an ill-equipped, ragtag group.

Custer's cavalry rampaged through the trains, killing or capturing about fifteen-hundred Confederates. It not only dispersed the trains that Lee desperately needed for rations and supplies, but it served notice to Lee that Union cavalry now sat astride his route of withdrawal. Disorganized fighting continued until well after dusk.

As the sun set, Union campfires ringed Lee's troops, completely surrounding them. Just before dark, Lee received a second letter from Grant, stating that his great desire was peace. He offered Lee an opportunity to designate an officer to accept the terms of surrender—to allow Lee to avoid the personal humiliation himself. The ever-resilient Lee wouldn't hear of it.

Lee responded to Grant with the following letter:

Genl

I received at a late hour your note of today. In mine of yesterday I did not intend to propose the surrender of the Army of Northern Virginia, but to ask the terms of your proposition. To be frank, I do not think the emergency has arisen to call for the surrender of this army, but, as the restoration of peace should be the sole object of all, I desired to know whether your proposals would lead to that end. I cannot, therefore, meet you with a view to surrender ... but as far as your proposal may affect the Confederate States forces under my command, and tend to the restoration of peace, I should be pleased to meet you at 10 AM tomorrow on the old state road to Richmond, between the picket-lines of the two armies.

Very respy your obt. Servt

R. E. Lee, Genl

Sunday, April 9, 1865

4 a.m.

One of General Grant's aides entered his quarters to awaken him but found the room empty. A search of the camp found Grant already up and dressed, pacing in the darkness outside, complaining of a migraine headache that had tortured him for several days.

5 a.m.

General John Gordon, in command of the Second Corps of the Army of Northern Virginia and one of Lee's most courageous officers, was chosen to lead a charge that would hopefully tear a hole through Grant's Army that now surrounded them. Hopefully, this action would provide a possible escape route for Confederate troops.

8 a.m.

A message to Lee from Gordon said, "I have fought my corps to a frazzle and I fear I can do nothing."

Emerging from the tree line below them, a wall of blue coats—two Union infantries had formed a skirmish line two miles wide and advanced on their front, with another two infantries blocking their rear. Now, Lee couldn't go forward, backward, or sideways.

10 a.m.

General Lee, dressed in full general's dress uniform—complete with a red silk sash, jeweled and engraved sword, and a pair of fine thread gloves, mounted his horse, Traveller. "Aide-toi et Dien t'aidera" the engraving on Lee's ceremonial sword said in translation, "Help yourself and God will help you." The meaning was not lost on Lee. He told his men, "There is nothing left for me to do than go see General Grant, and I would rather die a thousand deaths. I have probably to be General Grant's prisoner today, and I thought I must make my best appearance."

General James Longstreet advised Lee of his belief that Grant would treat them fairly, but as Lee rode toward Appomattox Courthouse, Longstreet said, "General, if he does not give us good terms, come back and let us fight it out."

General Lee rode to the picket line with a great many things on his mind. After looking back over the past four years, Lee probably asked himself how he had wound up on this road. Above all, he felt a sense of tremendous sadness. Lee felt the tragedy of war and wanted to spare his loyal soldiers further useless bloodshed. General Lee was a man who would have taken every advantage afforded him, any military option that came his way, but now there were no more options left. General Lee arrived at the designated meeting site with a small somber group of aides and officers.

Lee presented himself to the Union commander under a banner of truce. But there was no General Grant. Grant had composed a letter asserting that the meeting "would lead to no good." With General Gordon's charge on Union lines that morning, Grant assumed that hostilities had resumed. But after some additional back-and-forth letters between Grant and Lee, the two generals ultimately agreed to meet face to face.

Grant, normally calm and composed during any crisis, was rather nervous about his scheduled meeting with General Lee. The ride to the meeting site required sixteen miles on horseback and afforded a lot of time to think.

General Lee, exhausted and depressed, had anxiously been awake until just before dawn. He was now taking a nap under a nearby apple tree. He still had not eaten a morsel of food since his last communique with Grant. Lee's aide, Charles Marshall, had been given the assignment to find a proper meeting site to finalize the terms of surrender of the Army of Northern Virginia.

22

April 9, 1865

*"He that hath knowledge, spareth his words,
and a man of understanding is of an excellent spirit."*
—Proverbs 17:27 GNV

"I suppose, ...that the object of our present meeting
is fully understood."—General Robert E. Lee

April 9, 1865 – Palm Sunday

The midday sun was directly overhead. It was shaping up to be a warm and sunny spring day in Virginia. Daffodils were beginning to bloom. Besides the birds chirping and an occasional dog barking, the only sound heard was the squeak of leather and the clopping of horses as their riders approached a small Virginia town. What little conversation exchanged among the riders was clipped and sobering.

Appomattox Court House had been the county seat of Appomattox County, Virginia, since 1845. The little town was comprised of some twenty simple structures: a town center including the once busy Clover Hill Tavern, a half dozen clapboard houses, several small stores, one handsome red-brick house, and the courthouse itself. Used as a way station for weary travelers on the Richmond to Lynchburg Stage Road, Appomattox had become known as a "bare and cheerless place," perhaps due to the ravages of a grueling four-year war.

Following a brief inspection, Lee's aide, Charles Marshall, rejected the first site considered as the location for the planned event. It was too dilapidated to honor the momentous occasion. Instead, the handsome red-brick home of Wilmer McLean was chosen. Newly built in 1848, McLean had retired there in 1861 after his former home, located at the site of the first Battle of Bull Run, took a mortar shell through the kitchen. Selecting the McLean house as the surrender site gave credence to Wilmer McLean's claim. He would later boast the Civil War practically started in his kitchen and ended in his parlor.

The McLean House- Appomattox Courthouse, Virginia

The McLean house was situated a fair distance from the road with the perimeter of the property defined by a split-rail fence. Pecan and locust trees stood tall on the property, and lilacs abutted the porch like fragrant bookends. A white picket fence surrounded the house.

The main structure was flanked on one side by a low smokehouse with slave quarters directly behind. A horse stable and barn occupied the property on the opposing end of the house. A brick sidewalk led from the picket fence to the base of the broad front steps.

At a glance, the red-brick house was a symmetrical two-story structure, with chimneys situated at both ends and a full-length porch across its entire face. The front porch was supported by large, square pillars and covered overhead by the second-floor veranda. Encased by a painted white handrail and decorative spindles, a broad set of stairs ascended to the front door, replete with a prism-cut transom. The second-story veranda was accessed through another door directly above the front entrance. Both doors were bracketed by large full-length windows.

Charles Marshall entered the house first, followed by one of Grant's aides. The house was splendidly appointed and well-kept, most likely the finest in town. The parlor at the front of the house was spacious and cozy. The room exuded a subtle elegance. A low fire burned in the hearth with an abundance of embers. The fireplace mantel was deep mahogany and accented by ceramic vases and decorative lamps. The polished hardwood floor was almost entirely covered with fine carpeting. The aroma of burned logs of hickory and oak lingered.

At one o'clock, General Lee entered the McLean house resplendent in his magnificent gray dress uniform and engraved sword. He sat down at a small wooden table in the parlor and silently waited. At 1:30, the sound of hoofbeats signaled General Grant's arrival.

Grant and his officers entered the home. General Grant was swordless and wore a muddy private's uniform shirt. His boots and pants were splattered with mud. The contrast between the two generals was remarkable.

Grant and Lee met face-to-face for the first time in 20 years—both sharing a desire to conclude the long-suffering war.

General Ulysses S. Grant

Lee stood as Grant crossed the room, and the two shook hands. They took their seats at different tables strategically placed eight feet apart. The officers and aides in attendance distributed themselves around the perimeter of the parlor. Among those Union officers in attendance was the president's eldest son, Captain Robert Lincoln.

Grant, in an attempt to ease the obvious tension in the room, spoke first: "I met you once before, General Lee, while we were serving in Mexico, when you came over from General [Winfield] Scott's headquarters to visit Garland's brigade, to which I then belonged. I have always remembered your appearance, and I think I should have recognized you anywhere."

Lee acknowledged, "Yes, I know I met you on that occasion, and I have often thought of it, and tried to recollect how you looked, but I have never been able to recall a single feature."

Lee cordially continued, "I suppose, General Grant, that the object of our present meeting is fully understood. I asked to see you to ascertain upon what terms you would receive the surrender of my army."

Grant replied, "The terms I propose are those stated substantially in my letter of yesterday, that is, the officers and men surrendered are to be paroled and disqualified from taking up arms again until properly exchanged, and all arms, ammunition, and supplies to be delivered up as captured property."

Lee nodded. "Those are about the conditions I expected would be proposed."

General Grant reassured Lee. "Yes, I think our correspondence indicated pretty clearly the action that would be taken at our meeting; and I hope it may lead to a general suspension of hostilities and the means of preventing any further loss of life."

General Lee quietly contemplated the gravity of the discussion. For Lee, the battle-seasoned soldier, this was uncharted territory. He was intimately familiar with every facet of war except one: surrender.

"I presume, General Grant, we have both carefully considered the proper steps to be taken, and I would suggest that you commit to writing the terms you have proposed, so that they may be formally acted upon," Lee said after solemn consideration. Grant responded, "Very well, I will write them out."

23

"We are all Americans."

> *"Again, verily I say unto you,
> that if two of you shall agree in earth upon anything,
> whatsoever they shall desire, it shall be given them
> of my Father which is in heaven."*
> —Matthew 18:19 GNV

Grant lit a pipe instead of his trademark cigar and asked for his order book to be brought and placed before him. An assistant brought the book. Grant wrote steadily and paused briefly to eye General Lee's sword. After completing the document, Grant conferred with his secretary, Lieutenant Colonel Ely Parker about clarifications and revisions. Satisfied with what he had written, Grant stood and walked the short distance to personally hand the book to General Lee. The order book passed from Grant's hand to Lee's.

General Lee pushed aside candlesticks and other items on the table and laid the order book down in front of him. Removing his eyeglasses and handkerchief from his breast pocket, he carefully wiped the lenses and adjusted them onto the bridge of his nose.

Lee began to read:

Appomattox C. H. Va.
Apr. 9th, 1865
Gen. R. E. Lee,
Commanding C.S. Army

General:
In accordance with the substance of my letter to you of the 8th instant, I propose to receive the surrender of the Army of Northern Virginia on the following terms to-wit: Rolls of all the officers and men to be made in duplicate—one copy to be given to an officer designated by me, the other to be retained by such officer or officers as you may designate; the officers to give their individual paroles to not take up arms against the Government of the United States until properly exchanged, and each company or regimental commander sign a like parole for the men of their commands. The arms, artillery, and public property to be parked and stacked, and turned over to the officers appointed by me to receive them. This will not embrace the side-arms of the officers, nor their private horses or baggage. This done, each officer and man will be allowed to return to their homes, not to be disturbed by the United States authority so long as they observe their paroles and the laws in force where they may reside.

Very respectfully,
U. S. Grant, Lt. Gn.

After he read the terms of surrender, Lee's expression brightened. Before him, the terms were more civil and as generous as Lee could have hoped or expected. The surrendering Confederate soldiers would not be imprisoned as traitors or suffer the embarrassment of being paraded through the streets and jeered at as conquered rebels.

Looking over at Grant, Lee cordially said, "This will have a very happy effect upon my army."

General Robert E. Lee

"Unless you have some suggestions to make in regard to the form in which I have stated the terms, I will have a copy of the letter made in ink, and sign it," Grant replied.

General Lee paused. "There is one thing I should like to mention. The cavalrymen and artillerists own their own horses in our army. Its organization in this respect differs from that of the United States. I should like to understand whether these men will be permitted to retain their horses."

This revelation pointed out just one of the significant differences between the well-supplied Union Army and the underfunded Confederate troops. Grant, not unsympathetic to Lee's request, responded in a gentle, yet firm way, as to who was dictating the terms to whom.

"You will find that the terms as written do not allow this. Only the officers are permitted to take their private property."

Referring back to the surrender agreement, Lee admitted, "No, I see the terms do not allow this, that is clear."

Grant acknowledged, "Well, the subject is quite new to me. Of course, I did not know that any private soldiers owned their animals, but I think we have fought the last battle of the war—I sincerely hope so." He added, "I will arrange it this way—I will not change the terms as now written, but I will instruct the officers I shall appoint to receive the paroles to let all the men who claim to own a horse or a mule take the animals home with them to their little farms."

"This will have the best possible effect upon the men," Lee responded. "It will be very gratifying and will do much toward conciliating our people."

Charles Marshall, preparing to write the copy of the document, borrowed some paper from Grant's aide, who then borrowed ink from Marshall.

The Confederate aide then wrote out Lee's reply:

General:
I have received your letter of this date containing the terms of surrender of the Army of Northern Virginia as proposed by you—As they are substantially the same as those expressed in your letter of the 8th instant, they are accepted—I will proceed to designate the proper officers to carry the stipulations into effect—

Very respectfully, your obedient servant
R. E. Lee, General

There was one more thing of importance on General Lee's mind Explaining that he had more than a thousand Union prisoners in addition to his own men with no rations, Lee admitted to Grant his dilemma concerning foodstuffs.

"Indeed, I have nothing for my own men," Lee confessed.

Without hesitating, Grant proposed sending rations for 25,000 men across the lines. "Would this be enough?" Grant asked.

Gratefully, Lee replied, "Plenty. An abundance, I assure you."

After the preliminary papers had been signed, introductions were made around the parlor between Grant's staff and Lee's. Grant's personal secretary, Ely Parker, a Seneca Indian, shook hands with Lee, while Lee stared at him for a moment and finally said, "I am glad to see one real American here."

To which Parker replied, "We are all Americans."

Colonel Ely S. Parker

24

"My heart is too full to say more."

> *"I am able to do all things through the help of Christ, which strengtheneth me."*
> —Philippians 4:13 GNV

> "I think we are near the end at last."
> —Abraham Lincoln

With ink copies of the surrender agreement completed and signed by both parties, Lee somberly shook Grant's hand, gave a courtly bow, and left the room. A cluster of anxious sightseers had gathered on the McLean front porch, and a multitude of sightseers filled the yard. With his face red and flushed, Lee exited the house and stepped out onto the porch. Lee slapped his gloves into his hand a few times, breaking the silence. Donning his hat and gloves, Lee paused to look out over the fields beyond the McLean yard. Solemn faces, black and white, stared back without a word.

Looking for his mount, Traveller, Lee called out, "Orderly! Orderly!"

Traveller was brought around to the front of the house. Lee grunted as he pulled himself astride the animal. Once comfortably saddled, he slowly exhaled. Grant stepped out onto the porch and watched the general gather himself and his bridle. As Lee sauntered away, he turned his head back to the porch, and both generals tipped their hats to one another. Union and Confederate soldiers alike saluted the departing general.

Addressed to Secretary of War Edwin Stanton and dated April 9, 1865, 4:30 p.m., General Grant sent a message simply stating: "General Lee surrendered the Army of Northern Virginia this afternoon on terms proposed by myself."

General Lee ended his day by speaking to a crowd of weeping soldiers who had gathered at his tent. With a voice strained with emotion, Lee addressed his troops:

> "After four years of arduous service marked by unsurpassed courage and fortitude, the Army of Northern Virginia has been compelled to yield to overwhelming numbers and resources. . . . Boys, I have done the best I could for you. My heart is too full to say more."

Lee was acutely aware of his power to set an example for the South and urged his former troops to swallow their anger and return home to re-build their lives.

News of General Lee's surrender at Appomattox reached John Wilkes Booth and his co-conspirators. To say Booth was disappointed would be an understatement. Now, his original plans of kidnapping were for naught. Months of planning and preparation, wasted. Yet, Booth had one last role to play. His theatrical swansong.

The steamboat River Queen—en route to Washington, D.C. from City Point, Va.

President Lincoln was in a cheerful mood. The war was essentially over now. As the *River Queen* gently steamed, Lincoln wrote in his journal:

> "It is my intention to make the transition from insurgents to citizens as smooth and seamless as possible. I hope that my concessions will reduce hostilities and prevent additional loss of life on both sides. I want to bring the Southern states back into the Union and prevent Congress from imposing punitive measures against our brethren. I must bear the horrors of war, too. Oh, this war! This awful, awful war.
>
> "He from whom all blessings flow, must not be forgotten. A call for a national thanksgiving is being prepared and will be duly promulgated. My fondest desire has come to pass; a messenger just arrived and informed me that General Lee has surrendered to General Grant and it is up to me to try and bring about reconstruction.
>
> "There is one part of me that just wants to continue to float along the river and allow the gentle rhythmic motion of the River Queen soothe my troubled soul and help me temporarily forget my troubles. Oh, how I wish I were back home in Springfield or traveling towards California enjoying the company of Mrs. Lincoln and the boys.
>
> "God almighty how am I to bring about the reconstruction of the insurgents when there is no one true political entity in which to negotiate with? No one

man has the authority to give up the rebellion for any other man. How will I keep those blood thirsty northern vultures in Congress from picking clean the bones of the Southern states and taking advantage of the poor men and women hurt the most by this bloody war?"

That whole day steaming up the Potomac, the conversation turned to literary readings. Mr. Lincoln read aloud to the passenger guests for several hours. Most of the passages he selected were from Shakespeare.

The president returned to Washington, still suffering from insomnia but otherwise in excellent health. The *River Queen* arrived at 6 p.m., bringing the president, Mrs. Lincoln, Tad Lincoln, and their entourage to the Washington docks.

The River Queen

The streets were alive with people. Jubilant post-war celebrations had broken out. General Robert E. Lee had at last surrendered. Bonfires were everywhere—one on practically every street corner. Grown men—young and old—were hugging, laughing, and crying in the streets. Women were equally excited with the prospect of the triumphant return of their boys—sons and husbands, brothers and beaus, after four years of brutal war.

The president visited Secretary of State William H. Seward, who was recuperating at home after being severely injured by a fall from a carriage the previous week. Seward's injuries were serious but not life threatening.

Secretary of State William Seward

Seward and his family had planned to go out for a pleasure ride in their carriage on April 5th, 1865. Second oldest son Frederick, 20-year-old daughter Fanny, and Secretary Seward had ridden a short distance to pick up Fanny's friend near the Seward home. When Henry, the driver, stopped and stepped down to open the carriage door, Frederick exited the coach to retrieve Fanny's friend. At that moment, the horses were spooked, and the carriage leapt forward. Frederick attempted to grab the reins but missed and fell, injuring himself. In a flash, the team bolted down Vermont Avenue at breakneck speed without anyone in control of the animals. In a panic, Secretary Seward made the decision to jump from the runaway carriage as it slowed for the turn onto H Street. He misjudged his jump in the turn and was thrown violently onto the pavement. Witnesses carried him home bleeding and unconscious. His face was swollen and bruised beyond recognition. A doctor was immediately called to attend to the secretary's injuries.

Seward was suffering from facial lacerations, numerous abrasions a fractured jaw broken in two places, and a right arm broken just below the shoulder. His neck and jaw were fastened in a brace made of metal and canvas and he was covered in bandages. His arm was set in a cast and sling.

Lincoln eased into the bed, lying next to Seward. He told Seward cautiously, "I think we are near the end at last." Unable to speak well with the broken jaw, Seward extended his good arm to Lincoln to congratulate him on the great news. The president squeezed Seward's hand and wished him a speedy recovery, then returned to the White House.

Crowds had gathered in front of White House, calling for the president, chanting, "Speech! Speech!"

Abraham Lincoln responded briefly, but pleasantly. He would prepare a suitable speech to be delivered later.

It would be his last.

25

"I'm done playing."

*"Wherefore my dear brethren, let every man be swift to hear,
slow to speak, and slow to wrath.
For the wrath of man doth not accomplish the righteousness of God."*
—James 1:19 – 20 GNV

Monday, April 10, 1865—Vicksburg, Mississippi

The Big Black River was the dividing line between the part of Mississippi, including Vicksburg, held by the Union Army and the part held by the Confederate army, which included the area closer to Jackson. With the surrender agreement signed the day before, most of the fighting had ended, but only after the POWs had reached the camp held by the Union Army were they truly free. There, after crossing the Big Black River, the paroled POWs were given clean clothes and food at Camp Fisk, a federal processing center for the former prisoners of war.

After the POWs were released, they had a hard time making their way west across the South to Vicksburg, There, they had been told, steamboats await to carry them to their homes in the North. Traveling north from Vicksburg on the Mississippi River, these steamboats could reach the Missouri, Ohio, and Tennessee Rivers and, from there, the towns of the American Midwest the soldiers called home.

But to get to the Mississippi River at Vicksburg, the soldiers had to travel by boat, by train, and even on foot. Because they were so weak from their war and prison experiences, some of them tragically died along the way. Making matters worse, some of the trains loaded with POWs derailed en route due to sabotaged railroad tracks, stranding the POWs.

While arrangements were being made to transport them north on the Mississippi River, the freed POWs stayed in the camps outside Vicksburg. Thousands of captive federal soldiers had been moved from the prison stockades of Andersonville and Cahaba to Camp Fisk, about four miles east of Vicksburg.

Four-Mile Bridge

An agreement was made between the Union Army and the remnants of the Confederate army that a neutral zone be recognized, honored, and patrolled by both Union and Confederate sentries in their respective designated areas. The equivalent Confederate camp nearby was called Camp Townsend. The neutral zone was approximately one mile on either side of the railroad tracks that ran between the two camps.

Approaching the camps by rail, views of Four-Mile Bridge and the nestling of tents at Camp Fisk and Camp Townsend were a welcome sight for the weary POWs. This vision—the reality of freedom at last—held the promise of a return to loved ones, and hot nourishing food and proper medical care. It brought whoops of joy and unbridled elation to those approaching the camps.

With the unofficial end to the Civil War pending, twenty-year-old former POW Epp McIntosh rode a train across Four-Mile Bridge into Camp Fisk after being exchanged at Vicksburg. During his short stay, he would finally receive medical treatment, good food, and decent clothing. As soon as arrangements could be made, McIntosh would ride a steamer up the Mississippi with his fellow Union POWs to their next stop, the military hospital at Camp Benton, located in St. Louis, for a recovery furlough. From Camp Benton, Epp McIntosh, Ohio Sergeant William Fies, and their comrades would continue until reaching their final destinations.

Washington, D.C.

Noah Brooks had breakfast at the White House with President Lincoln. Brooks, a journalist and editor who had worked for newspapers in Sacramento, San Francisco, Newark, and New York, authored a major biography of Abraham Lincoln based on personal observations, since he had become close personal friends with Lincoln.

A procession from the Navy Yard, led by the Marine Band and joined by the Lincoln Hospital Band and the Quartermaster's Band, grew to thousands, and marched to the executive mansion. The president made a brief speech at noon from a second-story window and requested the band play "Dixie," since Union forces had "fairly captured it."

Crowds serenaded the president throughout the day, and he responded by making short, impromptu speeches. The Cabinet met with the president. Lincoln had photos made by famed photographer, Alexander Gardner. These would be the last photographs taken of Lincoln alive.

Last photograph of Lincoln taken alive.

At 5 p.m., a large crowd with several brass bands assembled at the White House. A tired but joyous president responded to the serenade and promised to prepare a more eloquent speech for tomorrow.

About 6 p.m., a delegation of fifteen men entered the White House and met the president in the hall. A spokesman for the group made a speech and presented Lincoln with a picture of himself in a silver frame. Lincoln thanked the delegation and suddenly remembered something that needed his attention. He promptly stepped into his office and wrote a quick note to Secretary of War Edwin Stanton: "Tad wants some flags. Can he be accommodated?"

Stanton wrote a note to Secretary of the Navy Gideon Welles: "Let master Tad have a Navy sword."

John Wilkes Booth again visited Surratt House, where he encountered Louis Weichmann. Weichmann noted that Booth appeared to be in a foul mood. Making casual conversation, he asked Booth why he was not playing in the theater.

"I'm done playing. The only play I care to present is *Venice Preserved*," answered Booth.

At the time, Weichmann didn't know what he meant by that statement, as he had never seen nor read the play. Years later, however, Weichmann did read it—finding the whole gist of the play was to assassinate the officers of the Venetian Cabinet to save Venice.

Later that evening, Mary Surratt asked Weichmann if he would be kind enough to drive her to Surrattsville the following morning, Tuesday, April 11. He would have to take the day off at the War Department tomorrow to accommodate her, but he respectfully agreed to do this for his landlady.

26

"Now, by God, I will put him through."

> *"But thou, after thine hardness,*
> *and heart that cannot repent,*
> *heapest up as a treasure unto thyself*
> *wrath against the day of wrath,*
> *and of the declaration of the just judgment of God,"*
> —Romans 2:5 GNV

Tuesday, April 11, 1865—Washington, D.C.

A flurry of activity came rushing at Lincoln as soon as he awoke from his brief and fitful sleep. His attention could now be focused on solving post-war problems and returning the seceded states back into the Union. He could redirect the time and energy spent preparing battle plans toward the nation's re-unification and reconstruction. He was tired and sleep-deprived yet buoyed by the ending of the war.

The president consulted with General Benjamin Butler on the freedpeople problem. The personal bodyguard for the president, Marshal Ward Hill Lamon, and Secretary of the Interior, John Palmer Usher, called on the president, who sent Lamon to Richmond on business connected with the reconstruction convention. Lincoln wrote a pass for Lamon that stated: "Allow the bearer, W. H. Lamon and friend, with ordinary baggage to pass from Washington to Richmond and return."

Lincoln bodyguard
Ward Hill Lamon

Lincoln and his Cabinet convened for a meeting. The chief topic was the cotton industry—one of the world's largest industries. At that time, most of the world's supply of cotton came from the American South. Indeed, it was the South's economic backbone.

This industry, fueled by the labor of slaves on plantations, generated huge sums of money for the United States and influenced the nation's ability to borrow money in a global market. When the Southern states seceded from the United States to form the Confederate States of America in 1861, they used the cotton industry to provide revenue for their government, arms for their military, and the economic power for a diplomatic strategy for the fledgling Confederate nation.

How would the relationship between foreign consumers and the United States be restored while embracing Southern reconstruction *and* emancipating and replacing the slave labor that had driven the cotton industry in the agricultural South? In response, the president issued a proclamation closing certain ports of entry and a proclamation concerning foreign port privileges. It was a complicated dichotomy—like petting the irritable cow to get to her golden calf.

Mrs. Lincoln wrote General Grant that the president was ill but "would be very much pleased to see you this . . . evening . . . and I want you to drive . . . with us to see the illumination."

There was a grand celebration planned at the White House. A young and boisterous Tad Lincoln got caught up in the moment and waved a captured Confederate flag from the White House balcony, which incited a raucous cheer from the crowd assembled on the north lawn. Someone on the house staff quickly tugged him back inside by his trousers, eliciting a roar of laughter from the crowd.

Moments later, the president appeared at a window over the front door and Mrs. Lincoln at a neighboring window. Lincoln read his speech to the crowd on the north lawn. He discussed the status of the Confederate states and his plan for restoring them to their rightful place in the Union. He singled out Louisiana as the first state he'd like to see do so. Lincoln announced that he also wanted to see educated people of color and Black veterans given the right to vote.

Among the crowd, John Wilkes Booth and Lewis Powell stood on the White House lawn listening to the president's speech. Booth boiled at the idea of giving freedmen any sort of political power. He told Powell, "That means ni**er citizenship. Now, by God, I will put him through. That is the last speech he will ever make."

As part of the earlier plot in March to kidnap Lincoln, Booth, Atzerodt, and Herold had hidden two Spencer carbine rifles, ammunition, and some other supplies at Lloyd's tavern in Surrattsville. The cache was still there. On the morning of April 11, Mary Surratt requested Louis Weichmann to go to the National Hotel and ask Booth for the use of his horse and buggy for their trip to the Surrattsville tavern. Weichmann went to the hotel, found Booth in his room, and gave him Mrs. Surratt's message.

Booth answered, "I have sold my horse and buggy, but here is $10—go and hire one."

"I thought they were John's [Surratt] horses," replied Weichmann, as they were the same ones John Surratt claimed were his and had kept at Howard's Stables.

"No, they are mine," replied Booth.

After leaving Booth, Weichmann visited a local livery where he rented a horse and carriage and drove Mary Surratt to the Surrattsville tavern. On the way there, they were met on the road by the tenant of her property, John M. Lloyd, in the country near a small village, Mary Surratt's hometown, Uniontown. When the buggy stopped, Mrs. Surratt requested Lloyd come closer so they could speak.

Mary Surratt leaned out of the buggy and spoke to him in such a way that Weichmann could not hear the conversation. She was being very covert when she inquired about the items secreted at his tavern. At first, Lloyd didn't seem to know what she was referring to, but he came to understand her meaning. Mary Surratt became more assertive and inquired about the shooting irons.

Lloyd replied, "They are hidden far away in the back, and I'm afraid the house might be searched."

Mrs. Surratt said, "Get them out ready—they will be wanted soon."

She publicly stated that the reason she made the trip was to collect a debt owed to her by a former neighbor. Weichmann would later testify he witnessed no such transaction.

Dr. Charles A. Leale had been assigned to duty as the surgeon in charge of the Wounded Commissioned Officers' Ward at the General Hospital at Armory Square. Back in Washington, Dr. Leale took a brief break from his exhausting job and strolled down Pennsylvania Avenue for some fresh air. He noticed a large crowd of people headed toward the White House. He fell in and walked with the crowd for a closer look. He discovered Lincoln giving a public address, unaware that it would be his last.

The doctor was intrigued by the president's facial expression and features. He noticed the dark circles under his eyes and the deepened lines on his face. The president appeared more haggard than ever before.

PART III

Sicarius

27

"Disturbing Dreams"

> *"...because I know, that the spirit of the holy gods is in thee, and no secret troubleth thee, tell me the visions of my dream, that I have seen, and the interpretation thereof."*
> —Daniel 4:6 GNV

> "I slept no more that night; and although it was only a dream, I have been strangely annoyed by it ever since."
> —Abraham Lincoln

Wednesday, April 12, 1865

After Robert E. Lee surrendered the demoralized remains of the Army of Northern Virginia to Ulysses S. Grant on April 9, Lee stayed at Appomattox until the last of his troops had given up their arms and were paroled on April 12. Even then, Lee didn't race the one hundred miles home to Richmond. Along the way, he spent one final evening at the camp of his top commander, General James Longstreet, and another night at his brother's farm, where out of habit or solidarity with his dispersing army, he slept outside in his tent.

Private William Fies, 64th Ohio Volunteer Infantry, was captured at the Battle of Franklin on November 30, 1864. He and five other men from his company were sent to Andersonville via Cahaba. While confined at Andersonville, Fies was haunted by a recurring dream. In the dream, he heard what he believed was yelling and splashing, but it didn't make any sense. He had no idea what it could possibly mean.

At Camp Fisk, William Fies, William Lugenbeal, and Epp McIntosh were assigned to ward tents as soon as they had been cleared by a doctor. They were examined for contagious diseases and assessed before being issued bunks and quarters. Since Epp was the most malnourished of the three, he was given quarters furthest from the cookhouse. Overeating had been fatal to some of the inductees of Camp Fisk, as their digestive systems could not bear the sudden burden of large amounts of food.

Fies also had the recurring nightmare while at Camp Fisk. In his dream he heard the familiar yelling and splashing, only to wake up to the moans of the patients in his hospital ward, accompanied by the noise of a rainstorm blowing the tent's flaps. Unnerved, Fies sat upright in his cot until the fog of sleep cleared enough for him to know where he was—safely outside the walls of Andersonville. He calmed himself—unaware that very soon he would be suddenly awakened by screaming and splashing and the smell of burning human flesh. And unfortunately, it would not be a dream.

It was in that bewitching hour, the hour between three and four in the morning, when dreams seemed to have their way in the mind. Sometimes, pleasant dreams inhabited the hippocampus. But sometimes, dreams were of a different nature. The kind that disturbed sleep and the sleeper.

Perspiration beaded on his upper lip. His closed eyes rolled and fluttered beneath the lids. The man asleep had a fitful night of slumber, interrupted by images that troubled him. He mumbled incoherently to no one except possibly the cohabiter in his dream. His voice was low and monotone. His eyes continued to vacillate indicating rapid eye movement. Then the tall man stopped breathing momentarily, perhaps a half minute or more before sitting bolt upright, gasping for air. He sat there inhaling deeply, panting with eyes wide.

Abraham Lincoln placed his large hands on the mattress next to his hips and tried to control his breathing and calm himself. His heart was pounding in his chest like a jackhammer. He looked around the room to confirm where he was and that it was only a nightmare. The president wondered if his reactions had inadvertently awakened Mary or his son. He listened for any movement or activity coming from the adjacent bedrooms.

His pulse rate was beginning to level off, and respiration was slowly returning to normal. Lincoln coughed and swallowed hard. He had broken into a sweat, and the back of his nightshirt was wet. He swung his body around ninety degrees and put his feet on the floor of the White House bedroom, wiping his face with his bare hands, smoothing his hair.

Just three days before his death, Abraham Lincoln told his personal bodyguard, Ward Hill Lamon, that he had a dream about a funeral that took place in the East Room of the White House.

In the dream, Lincoln walked through an eerie White House until he encountered a soldier posted near the casket, surrounded by mourners. Lincoln asked the soldier "Who is dead?" The soldier replied, "The president, killed by an assassin!" The president also told Lamon, "Then came a loud burst of grief from the crowd, which woke me from my dream. I slept no more that night; and although it was only a dream, I have been strangely annoyed by it ever since."

Thursday, April 13, 1865

Washington D.C. was in the mood to celebrate as the effects of the Civil War wound to a close. The city had been putting on grand shows with fireworks, bonfires, and torchlight parades. Almost everyone had reason to be in a good mood, except for disappointed secessionists like the disgruntled actor—John Wilkes Booth.

The president didn't sleep well the night before, following his disturbing dream, and since he had risen early, he visited the telegraph office before daylight. Lincoln exchanged pleasantries with the telegraph operator, Charles A. Tinker, and went to Secretary Stanton's office. Lincoln interviewed General Grant and Secretary Stanton on military problems. The president conferred again with Secretary Gideon Welles regarding the re-establishment of authority in the Confederate states.

With little concern for his personal safety, Lincoln rode alone on horseback about a mile out of D.C. to the Summer White House at the Soldiers' Home. He discussed various topics with Assistant Secretary of the Treasury Maunsell B. Field. During their encounter, Field observed that the president appeared weary and sad despite the celebrations that surrounded him.

Abraham Lincoln wrote a check to "Self" for $800, but he would never cash it.

Vicksburg, Mississippi

There were many people involved in the process of freeing former POWs and sending them home. Captain Frederick Speed was a staff officer at Vicksburg, eager to facilitate their rapid shipment. The officer properly charged with managing the prisoner movement, Captain George Williams, happened to be away from his post consulting with superiors when the Confederate Commissioner's message about releasing the prisoners came through. Captain Speed volunteered to act in absentia during Williams's absence.

On April 13th, Speed took over Williams's job processing the former POWs. Even with everyone sharing a sense of urgency, necessary administrative steps required time, especially drawing up accurate rolls to ensure that the soldiers were properly logged as they passed through the system.

As fast as a sizable group of men were organized, generally sorted by state unit to simplify their movement, Speed turned them over to the Quartermaster Department for transportation. Although Speed felt his intentions were honorable throughout, the situation soon spun out of control, causing the officer to make some hasty decisions with disastrous consequences.

At 1 a.m. on Good Friday, April 14th, the *Sultana* pulled into a berth at the Cairo wharf and tied off. At first light, the Cairo newspaper *The War Eagle,* was trumpeting that the "regular and unsurpassed passenger packet" *Sultana* would depart for New Orleans by 10 a.m. the next morning.

28

April 14, 1865 - Good Friday

*"Be angry, but sin not:
let not the sun go down upon your wrath,
Neither give place to the devil."*
—Ephesians 4:26 – 27 GNV

"Great God! I have no longer a country!"
—John Wilkes Booth

April 14, 1865—Good Friday

Early morning, there was a slight fog, but as the day wore on gray skies gave way to cloudy blue. At 10 a.m., a dapper John Wilkes Booth entered the National Hotel dining room. He was always a late riser and the last patron to break his fast before the staff prepared for the lunch crowd.

Booth was impeccably dressed in a dark suit of clothes and a tall silk hat. On his hands, he wore kid gloves of a subdued color. Over his arm hung a light overcoat, and he carried a cane as a fashion accessory.

His fiancé, Lucy "Bessie" Hale, and her friend Miss Carrie Bean, were meeting Booth for a late breakfast in the dining room.

New Hampshire Senator John P. Hale

The Hale family—Senator John P. Hale, wife Lucy, and daughter Bessie—took up residence at the National Hotel in Washington, D.C., while the senator finalized his appointment as Minister to Spain. It was likely here at the National Hotel where Bessie first met and began her relationship with John Wilkes Booth.

Not one to be short of female companionship, Booth fell captive to Bessie's beauty and charm at first sight. He sent her an anonymous letter expressing his fascination and interest in meeting her. He showered her with gifts of beautiful flowers, leading to a steamy courtship and a proposal of marriage. Her parents did not approve.

Bessie and Booth had a conversation while they ate. Booth considered how he should best break off his relationship with her. After all, his future plans had little room for such encumbrances as romance. Besides, with her father's recent appointment as Minister to Spain, she would be soon leaving for Europe. Seldom at a loss for words, Booth fumbled for them now.

The time didn't appear to be right for such discussions, especially publicly. Maybe later would be more suitable. He had a lot on his mind, and he needed time to think. After breakfast, Booth excused himself, left the hotel, and went for a grooming at the barbershop—unaware it would be his last haircut.

Freshly groomed, Booth walked up 6th Street to H Street for a quick stop at the Surratt Boardinghouse. From there, he went along H to 10th Street and was seen approaching by Harry Ford, who was standing in front of the theater with some gentlemen. Upon seeing Booth's approach, Ford turned to his companions and said, "Here comes the handsomest man in the United States."

Lucy Lambert "Bessie" Hale

Booth smugly walked past the men, went inside to the box office, got his mail, came back outside, and sat on the front steps to read his correspondence. One of the letters was so lengthy that it drew the attention of Harry Ford and his companions.

When Booth finished reading his mail, he finally acknowledged their presence and asked Ford, "What's on tonight?"

"*Our American Cousin*, and we are going to have a big night," replied Ford. "The president and General Grant are going to occupy the presidential box, and General Lee is going to have the adjoining one." Ford playfully attempted to annoy Booth.

Booth paused and responded bitterly, "I hope they are not going to do like the Romans—parade their prisoners before the public to humiliate them."

Harry Ford told Booth that he was only kidding about Lee's attendance, but the president and Grant would certainly attend, as a note had been sent from the White House, engaging the box.

Later, some opinions would state that the plot to assassinate Lincoln originated then and there, that up until this point, the plot had been to kidnap and transport the president south for the ransomed exchange of Confederate POWs. But with the surrender of Lee, the evacuation of the Confederate capital in Richmond, the collapse of the Confederacy, and Jefferson Davis on the run, the kidnapping of Lincoln served no purpose for a forced prisoner exchange.

Now, the opportunity for the alternative—murder—presented itself on the steps of Ford's Theater. Booth was face-to-face with that opportunity. Immediately, he became noticeably distracted and left the theater hurriedly.

Booth met with John F. Coyle, editor for the *National Intelligencer*. Coyle, a liberal journalist who opposed Lincoln, was considered a warm friend to Booth. During this meeting, Coyle introduced Booth to a man named Donoho, who was well acquainted with Booth's father. They went to a neighborhood restaurant for conversation and "refreshments." Booth was considered a social drinker, but following the collapse of the Confederate army, he increased his alcohol intake considerably.

During the conversation Booth posed the question, "Suppose Lincoln was killed; what would be the result?"

"Johnson would succeed," Coyle replied, referring to the vice-president.

"But what if *he* was killed?"

"Then Seward," answered Coyle. The secretary of state was next in line.

Booth continued. "But suppose *he* was killed, what then?"

"Then anarchy or whatever the Constitution provides." Coyle laughed. "But what nonsense—they don't make Brutuses nowadays."

Booth shook his head and said, "No—no, they do not."

At 12:45 p.m., Davy Herold and George Atzerodt went to Naylor's stables to secure a horse from John Fletcher for Herold. Herold told Fletcher to hold the horse for him until he called for it around four. Herold paid $5 for the hire, also requesting a first-class saddle with English stirrups and a double-reined bridle.

Herold returned at 4:15 p.m. and retrieved the horse, inquiring how late he could keep the animal. Fletcher told him he could stay out with the horse no later than 8 or 9 o'clock. This horse, however, like Booth's, would never return to the stable.

At about 5 p.m., Davy Herold met Star Saloon restaurateur and musician Scipiano Grillo on 10th Street. Davy asked Grillo, "Have you seen John Wilkes Booth?"

Grillo answered, "Yes, I saw him this morning at the theater around eleven, and then again about four in the afternoon, when he stopped by for a drink."

Grillo and Herold walked up the street until they saw George Atzerodt sitting on the steps of the Kirkwood House. Herold stopped to talk to Atzerodt. Afterward, Herold and Grillo went into the Willard Hotel. There, Herold met two young men and chatted a while out of earshot of Grillo. Herold and Grillo then walked on toward Grover's Theatre. Grillo noticed that Herold was walking with a limp.

Grillo asked, "What's the matter? You are walking lame."

"Nothing. My boots hurt me," replied Davy.

When Herold pulled his pants leg up to fix his boot, Grillo noticed a big dagger, the handle protruding four or five inches above the top of his boot.

Grillo asked, "What do you want to carry that for?"

"I am going into the country tonight on horseback, and it will be handy there."

Grillo scoffed, "You ain't going to kill anybody with that."

That same afternoon, Harry Ford sent two employees, Ned Spangler, carpenter and scene shifter, and Joseph "Peanut John" Burroughs, errand boy and bill distributor, to the theater's presidential box to remove a partition, creating a larger space for the presidential party. There was an outer door to the box that opened to the inside of a vestibule; the vestibule opened to the balcony. As they worked on partition removal, Spangler said, "Damn the president and General Grant."

Burroughs asked, "What are you denouncing that man for—a man who has never done harm to you?"

Ned barked, "He ought to be cursed, he got so many men killed."

As Spangler and Burroughs continued their work, curiosity brought a man named Theodore Rhodes into the box to view the stage. While there, Rhodes heard someone behind him and turned to see a man with a piece of wood approximately three feet long and about the width of two of his fingers. The ends of the slat had been miter cut, slanting toward each end from the center.

Spangler noticed the intrusion of the nosy stranger and said,

"The president is going to be here tonight."

"He is?" Rhodes asked.

"We are going to fix up this box for his reception. I suppose there is going to be a big crowd here and we are going to endeavor to arrange it so he won't be disturbed."

Rhodes watched as Spangler attempted to affix one end of the piece of wood into a hole about the size of his thumb that had been bored into the presidential box. The piece, designed to block the door, did not properly fit, whereupon Spangler whittled the end a bit and carved the hole out a little larger. When he was satisfied with that, he placed the slat against the panel of the door and across to the wall, forming a triangle. He asked Rhodes if he thought it would hold tightly. To Rhodes, it looked like the improvised wood slat would indeed secure the box from anyone outside attempting to enter.

By nightfall, almost all the arrangements for the assassination were in place. Horses had been secured, weapons purchased, and liaisons established. Escape routes had been carefully planned with discreet contacts strategically dotting the road leading south.

That same day at Camp Fisk in Vicksburg, Sergeant John Clark Ely recorded in his diary:

"Today Major Anderson again raises the same old flag over Sumter and today the North rejoice over their victories and today came an order from General [Napoleon] Dana for us to be paroled and sent North. Bully, may we soon see our sweethearts."

Union General William T. Sherman received a communique from Confederate General Joe Johnston, requesting a meeting to discuss terms of "exterminating the existing war." Sherman responded immediately, planning to meet with Johnston on Monday the 17th at an old ramshackle, roadside, frame house near Durham, North Carolina, belonging to a local farmer named James Bennett.

Just days prior to delivering his famed Gettysburg Address, President Abraham Lincoln had watched a performance by Booth in a play called *The Marble Heart* at Ford's Theatre. As a famous and popular actor who had frequently performed at Ford's and who was well known to its owner, Booth had free access to all parts of the theater, even having his mail sent there. He used his privileged theater access to his advantage.

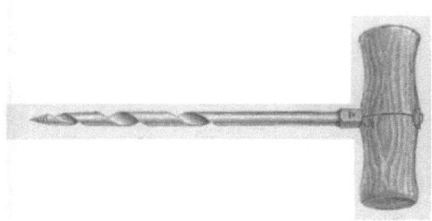

Gimlet Tool

By boring a small spy hole into the door of the presidential box that day, Booth could check that his intended victim had made it to the play and observe the box's occupants. He used a small gimlet to create the hole in the angle of a door panel leading to the box. It wasn't that noticeable. He cleaned up wood shavings and other evidence. Booth pressed his face to the door with his eye aligned with the hole. He checked the peephole for optimum viewing access. Satisfied, Booth went directly from Ford's Theatre to Pumphrey's livery stable and made arrangements to procure a horse for his escape.

James W. Pumphrey was an acquaintance of conspirator John Surratt Jr., and it was Surratt who introduced Booth to him. Pumphrey's stable was located near the National Hotel, Booth's Washington residence. Previously, Booth had been hiring one horse in particular, one he preferred, from Pumphrey. Booth told Pumphrey that he would be back to get the horse at around four o'clock that afternoon.

At the hour agreed upon, Booth arrived at the stable. Pumphrey informed Booth that the horse he was familiar with and wanted was not available, but he had another horse for him to hire. Consequently, Booth got a swift, little bay mare with a white star on her forehead and a black tail and mane. Pumphrey warned Booth that the horse was high-spirited, and she would break her halter if left unattended.

Booth told Pumphrey he was going to Grover's Theatre, as he had to write an important letter. He added that he planned afterward to stop for a drink and then take a leisurely ride. Unwittingly, the stable owner had just agreed to provide Booth with a means of escape from the theater. This would be the last time Pumphrey would ever see John Wilkes Booth or the mare. Booth took the horse with him and placed her in the stable at Ford's Theatre.

John Wilkes Booth did write a letter, but not at Grover's Theatre. He wrote the letter at the National Hotel. It was written to the editor of the *National Intelligencer*, John Coyle. Booth explained that his plans had changed from kidnapping President Lincoln to assassinating him. In addition to signing his own name, he also added the names of his co-conspirators: Lewis Powell, George Atzerodt, and David Herold.

Later, Booth did get a drink at Peter Taltavull's Star Saloon located next to Ford's Theatre, but he definitely did not go on a pleasure ride. Instead, he approached stagehand Ned Spangler with the request to hold the reins of the skittish mare that he had hired, while he briefly attended to some business within Ford's Theatre.

The business he referred to was murdering President Lincoln.

Booth next informed Powell, Herold, and Atzerodt of his intention to kill the president. Booth called on George Atzerodt at the Kirkwood House where he was boarded and instructed him to murder Vice-President Andrew Johnson, who was staying in the room directly below Atzerodt's. He assigned Powell to assassinate

Secretary of State William H. Seward at home in his sick bed. David Herold would assist in their escape into Virginia.

Two colored women, Mrs. Mary J. Anderson and Mrs. Mary A. Turner, reported seeing Booth at 3 p.m., standing in the rear door of Ford's Theatre, talking to an unknown woman and pointing down the alley. What Greenback Saloon barkeeper James P. Ferguson saw was Booth standing near his saloon, adjacent to the theater, talking to James L. Maddox, property manager at Ford's and also a bit-part player.

Booth remarked to Maddox, "See what a fine horse I have got—now watch, she can run like a cat," spurring the mare and tearing off down the street.

Booth was seen joining Maddox, Ned Spangler, and a young man named John Mouley for drinks at the Greenback Saloon.

At 4 p.m., Booth met with fellow actor John Matthews on Pennsylvania Avenue between 13th and 14th Streets. About that time, the officers of General Lee's army passed.

Matthews asked Booth, "Johnny, have you seen Lee's officers just brought in?"

"Yes, Johnny, I have." Booth placed his hand on his forehead and exclaimed, "Great God! I have no longer a country!"

John Matthews

Noticing the paleness, nervousness, and agitation in his friend, Matthews remarked, "John, how nervous you are! What is the matter?"

"Oh, no, it is nothing." Booth regained his composure and continued, "Johnny, I have a little favor to ask of you; will you grant it?"

"Why, certainly, Johnny, what is it?"

"Perhaps I may leave town tonight and I have a letter here which I desire to publish in the *National Intelligencer*. Please see to it for me unless I see you before ten o'clock tomorrow—in that case I will see to it myself."

At that moment, an open carriage carrying General Grant, Mrs. Grant, and their luggage rode by.

"Why, Johnny, there goes Grant. I thought he was going to the theater this evening with the president."

"Where?" Booth asked.

Matthews pointed toward the carriage, whereupon Booth grasped Matthew's hand tightly to stop the point, then galloped off down the street following the carriage. As General and Mrs. Grant drove down Pennsylvania Avenue, Booth quickly rode past at a gallop, then wheeled his horse. He rode back, peering into the carriage as he passed again. The curiosity of the rider did not elude Mrs. Grant.

Julia Grant leaned into her husband and said, "That is the very same man that sat near us today at lunch with some others and tried to hear our conversation. He was so rude, you remember, as to cause us to leave the dining room. Here he is again riding after us."

Lewis Powell ordered an early dinner from the landlady of the Herndon House, Mrs. Murray, telling her that he was going to Baltimore. He paid his bill and was served in advance of the usual dinner hour of 4 p.m.

29

"...and your old men shall dream dreams."

> *"And it shall be in the last days, saith God,*
> *I will pour out of my Spirit upon all flesh,*
> *and your sons, and your daughters shall prophesy,*
> *and your young men shall see visions,*
> *and your old men shall dream dreams."*
> —Acts 2:17 GNV

> "...moving with great rapidity
> toward a dark and indefinite shore,"
> —Abraham Lincoln

April 14, 1865

It was Good Friday, and Abraham Lincoln was busy with a flurry of activities typical of the commander-in-chief—signing papers, conducting meetings, and composing correspondence. Early spring in D.C. was agreeable, especially now with the war concluding. Captain Robert Todd Lincoln arrived in Washington from the scene of General Robert E. Lee's surrender at Appomattox in time to enjoy an early breakfast with his father, the president.

During the morning, President Lincoln conferred at length with Speaker of the House Congressman Schuyler Colfax of Indiana, who was preparing to visit the West Coast. The president interviewed former Senator John P. Hale of New Hampshire, the newly appointed Minister to Spain.

Lincoln went for a short drive with General Grant, in town for a Cabinet meeting. Grant begged off on the invitation to attend the play at Ford's Theatre with the Lincolns, wanting to instead have a quiet evening with his wife before heading for their departure at nearby Union Station. The truth was, however, that the wives disliked one another. Mrs. Grant had convinced her husband that if he didn't figure out a way to decline the invitation, she would, and probably without the diplomacy and tact that the general was known for. Julia Grant had no intention of revisiting Mary Lincoln's embarrassing behavior witnessed a few weeks ago at City Point, Virginia.

On March 23rd, the president and the first lady visited General Grant's military headquarters at City Point for a meeting with Generals Sherman, Grant, and Admiral Porter to plan what was deemed to be the final stages of the war. As part of the visit, there had been a scheduled visit with the troops bivouacked in the area. President Lincoln would ride to the review on horseback with the military hierarchy, while Mary Lincoln and Julia Grant would follow and ride in an army ambulance through the muddy camp.

First Lady Mary Todd Lincoln

When the two wives arrived on the scene, the wife of Fifth Corps commander General Charles Griffin was spotted riding horseback alongside the president. Mary Lincoln considered this a serious breach of protocol and became visibly agitated and extremely upset. Mary Lincoln found it intolerable and was having none of it. In her excited state, she attempted to climb out of the ambulance. Attendants had to restrain her from jumping into the deep mud that surrounded them. Julia Grant was embarrassed and humiliated.

The following day, the entourage visited the camp for a review of the Army of the James. After lunch, the president rode on horseback two miles to the parade ground while the wives followed again in the ambulance. Mary Ord, the attractive wife of General Edward Otho Ord, rode on horseback behind the president and the generals. Upon arrival at the parade ground, an aide accompanying Mrs. Ord had her join the president and the generals as they rode by in review of the troops. Mary and Julia arrived just in time to see Mary Ord riding next to the president. Mary Lincoln immediately became upset. When Julia tried to calm her, she turned on her and accused her and her husband of coveting the White House and wanting to replace the Lincolns.

Mary Lincoln screamed, "I suppose you think you will get to the White House yourself?!" Mary's tirade wasn't over yet. When Mary

Ord saw the ambulance arrive with the two wives, she broke away from the group on horseback to join them—unaware of what she was about to ride into. Mary Lincoln again flew into a rage, calling her vile names in the presence of Julia Grant and the officers.

"How dare you ride beside the president! The men in ranks might think you're his wife—while here I am behind the scenes in an ambulance mired down in the mud!"

Mary Ord broke down in tears while the mild-mannered Julia Grant tried to diffuse the situation. Mrs. Grant graciously continued to try and calm Mary Lincoln. For Julia Grant, it was a humiliating experience that she never wanted to repeat—especially in a public setting such as the theatre.

The president returned to the White House and received many members of Congress who called on him to congratulate him on the successful conclusion of the war. He interviewed William A. Howard, a Detroit lawyer, who in the 1860 and 1864 elections supported Lincoln's bid for the presidency.

Lincoln wrote an appreciative note to General James Henry Van Alen: "I thank you for the assurance you give me that I shall be supported by conservative men like yourself, in the efforts I may make to restore the Union, so as to make it, to use your language, a Union of hearts and hands as well as of States."

Next, the president visited the cipher room of the War Department and told General Thomas T. Eckert of his plans to attend the theater, inviting him to come along. In 1862, Eckert was sent to Washington, D.C., to organize and administer the War Department's military telegraph. Eckert devised ciphers that enabled him and his fellow telegraphers to send and receive secret messages. Eckert was well respected by Secretary Stanton and President Lincoln for his organizational skills and discretion; they charged him with important missions that went beyond his formal duties as a telegrapher. Eckert thanked the president for the offer, but respectfully declined the president's theater invitation.

At about 10 a.m., Governor Thomas Swann of Maryland and Senator John Creswell, also of Maryland, presented a memorandum to the president concerning his Maryland appointments. At 11 a.m., the Cabinet met. Grant reported on the surrender of Confederate forces at Appomattox, and Secretary Stanton presented a draft of the plan for reestablishing authority in the former Confederate states.

Thomas Eckert

The president told several Cabinet members about his recurring dream of a ship "moving with great rapidity toward a dark and indefinite shore" that presaged Union victories. The Cabinet meeting lasted from 11 a.m. until 2 p.m. There were informal discussions relative to what should be done about President Jefferson Davis and other leaders of the Confederacy. Secretary of War Stanton would later confess "that he had never felt so sensible of his deep affection for Lincoln as he did during their final interview."

Secretary of the Treasury Hugh McCulloch later reflected that on this morning, "I never saw Mr. Lincoln more cheerful and happy. The burden which had been weighing upon him for four long years and which he had borne with heroic fortitude, had been lifted; the war had practically ended—the Union was safe."

Between 2 and 3 p.m., the president lunched with Mrs. Lincoln in a private parlor. Edward D. Neill, White House employee, met with the president about a signed commission. Lincoln interviewed Vice-President Johnson at three o'clock.

Major Henry Rathbone and his fiancé, socialite Clara Harris, accepted the Lincolns' invitation to the play at Ford's Theatre. They were invited after several others declined. Rathbone was the son of a well-to-do businessman, born in Albany, New York, in 1837. Rathbone's father became Albany's mayor. When Henry was seventeen, his father died, and he inherited a substantial fortune in the amount of $200,000 (nearly $ 7 million in today's money). Rathbone studied law at Union College and worked in an Albany law partnership before entering the Union Army at the start of the Civil War. Initially serving as a captain he gained respect as a brilliant and brave young officer and by the war's end, he had attained the rank of major.

Clara's father was a Lincoln crony and Clara had become acquainted with the president and Mrs. Lincoln. Henry Rathbone became engaged to Clara Harris, who was also his stepsister, as his widowed mother had married Clara's father, New York Senator Ira Harris, who had also lost his wife.

Later that afternoon, Mrs. Nancy Bushrod, a Washington Black woman, pushed past White House guards and sought to speak with the president regarding her husband's pay. Lincoln heard the commotion outside his office and interceded on her behalf.

"I'm here," Lincoln said to Mrs. Bushrod. "Tell me what you want. I have time for all good people who need to see me." The president instructed the security detail to allow the woman to pass. "Let the good woman come in."

Lincoln invited her into his office. She informed the president that she and her husband, Tom, had been slaves at the Harwood Plantation outside Richmond until they were freed by the Emancipation Proclamation. Her husband was off serving with the Union Army of the Potomac while she raised their three children—twin boys and a baby girl—here in Washington. She further explained to Lincoln that she had been receiving her husband's pay, but that it had stopped for some reason, and she had been unable to find work. Her cupboard was bare, and the crying of her hungry children that morning had driven her to desperation. She herself had not eaten in two days, but she summoned the strength to make the five-mile trek to the White House. She had charged right past the first group of guards, but the next group stopped her. Her mission seemed to be ending in defeat when Lincoln appeared and invited her in.

"You are entitled to your soldier-husband's pay," Lincoln told her. "Come this time tomorrow and the papers will be signed and ready for you." Assured by the president's words, Mrs. Bushrod thanked Lincoln and triumphantly strode out of the White House. Abraham Lincoln would be shot just seven hours after she left him.

30

"Hail to the Chief"

> *"Rejoice with the wife whom thou hast loved*
> *all the days of the life of thy vanity,*
> *which God hath given thee under the sun all the days of thy vanity:*
> *for this is thy portion in the life, and in thy travail wherein thou laborest*
> *under the sun."*
> —Ecclesiastes 9:9 GNV

April 14, 1865

Lincoln had more work to do before he could enjoy an evening at the theater with the First Lady and their guests, Major Henry Rathbone and Clara Harris. Mary Lincoln suggested they cancel their theater plans and have a quiet night at home instead. The president felt it would disappoint folks if they didn't show up, after letting it be known that the president and First Lady would attend.

That afternoon, Lincoln put into practice his liberal policy toward the rebel leaders. Intelligence had reached Secretary Stanton at the War Department that "a conspicuous secessionist," Jacob Thompson, was en route to Portland, Maine, where a steamer awaited to take him to England. Operating from Canada, Thompson had organized a series of troublesome raids across the border that left Secretary Stanton with little sympathy for the Confederate marauder.

Upon reading the telegram, Stanton didn't hesitate a moment. "Arrest him!" he ordered Assistant Secretary Charles Dana. As Dana was leaving the room, however, Stanton called him back. "No, wait; better to go over and see the president." Assistant Secretary Dana reported to the president at 4:30 p.m. Dana described the situation, explaining that Stanton wanted to arrest Thompson, but thought he should first refer the question to the president. Should Jacob Thompson be arrested or allowed to leave the country?

"Well," said Lincoln, "when you have got an elephant by the hind leg, and he's trying to run away, it's best to let him run."

Late in the afternoon, the president and Mrs. Lincoln went for a drive in their carriage. They stopped at the Navy Yard to view three monitors damaged in a Fort Fisher, North Carolina engagement. These monitors would become prison cells shortly, but Lincoln would never know that. As they rode, the Lincolns talked of a future—a time after his term was over when they could enjoy travel—when they could go back to Illinois and live quietly.

The president and Mrs. Lincoln returned from their drive at about 6 or 7 p.m. Mrs. Lincoln began dressing for the theater, while the president met Governor Richard J. Oglesby of Illinois with other Illinois friends at the White House. After supper, the president interviewed Speaker of the House Congressman Schuyler Colfax of Indiana, accompanied by California Congressman Cornelius Cole.

Dr. Charles Leale, Union Army surgeon, learned that President Lincoln was going to Ford's Theatre to see *Our American Cousin*. After completing his duties, Dr. Leale changed into civilian clothes and rushed to the theater. Intrigued, he went not singularly to just see the play, but to get a closer look and study President Lincoln's face and facial expressions.

As Lincoln shrugged on his suit jacket, former Massachusetts Congressman George Ashmun tried to meet with him at 8 p.m. regarding cotton claims against the government. The president gave him an appointment as follows: "Allow Mr. Ashmun and friend to come in at 9 a.m. to-morrow." (Ashmun considered this Lincoln's last autograph.) The president's valet assisted with his coat, handed him his stovepipe, and advised Lincoln that he was going to be late for the theater. Lincoln jokingly asked if he was in trouble. The First Lady scoffed and told the valet to tell the president he should hurry.

Simultaneously, at 8 p.m., Booth met with Lewis Powell and George Atzerodt at the Herndon House. He told Powell that the time for action had come, handing him a revolver, a knife, and a bogus package of medicine. Booth instructed him to do his duty and meet him beyond the Anacostia Bridge. Booth stated that he would murder Lincoln and Grant and that Powell should kill Secretary Seward. Atzerodt was instructed to assassinate Vice-President Andrew Johnson.

Dr. Charles Leale entered the theater just past showtime and asked for a seat in the orchestra section so he would have an unhindered view of the president. But because Leale arrived late, he was given a seat in the dress circle, or second or top level—near the front, same side, and forty feet away from the president's box.

The president exchanged a few words with former Congressman Isaac Arnold of Illinois, while getting into his carriage to go to the theater. Around 8:20 p.m., Major Henry Rathbone and Clara Harris met the president and First Lady at the Harris residence, on the corner of 15th and H Streets. Major Rathbone wore his dress Union Blues and Clara Harris was dressed in a beautiful white gown. From there, Rathbone and Harris rode in the carriage with the Lincolns to the front door of Ford's Theatre.

At approximately 8:30 p.m., the president, Mrs. Lincoln, Clara Harris, and Major Rathbone entered the theater to watch the play, featuring Laura Keene and Harry Hawk, which had already begun. As the president and his party made their way to the presidential box, the performance on stage stopped. Noticing the presidential party's entrance, the crowd began to cheer, and the orchestra struck up "Hail to the Chief." The audience gave the president a standing ovation. President Lincoln simply smiled, bowed, and continued toward his party's waiting box.

Ford's Theatre

He took his seat in a cushioned rocking chair near the door, and his wife Mary took the chair to Lincoln's right. Major Rathbone would be seated farthest away from the door on an upholstered walnut sofa with Miss Harris to his left.

Dr. Leale could see the full face of the president; he stood only a few aisles away from Lincoln. What was to be a short observation of the president's face would later turn into nine hours of close doctoring for Leale.

Lincoln's main bodyguard, Ward Hill Lamon, did not attend the play to provide personal security as he normally would for the president. He had been sent to Richmond on an assignment by the president. Instead, John Parker, a police officer well known for his love of whiskey, had been assigned guard duty to protect Lincoln. Parker would leave his post outside the presidential box during intermission to satisfy an alcoholic craving.

With Lincoln's bodyguard imbibing at the Star Saloon, no one would see a man peeping through a hole in the door of the presidential box. No one in the theater suspected that the play would end abruptly in a few minutes.

Former Mosby's Ranger and current Booth conspirator, Lewis Powell was given the task to kill Secretary Seward. Unfamiliar with the streets of Washington, D.C., Powell was assisted by Davy Herold, who would guide Powell to Seward's home and keep the horses at the ready for their escape. Powell would fail his assignment, however, managing to only severely injure Seward, and Herold would flee before Powell could exit the Seward home. As a result, Lewis Powell would lose his way in the capital city and wind up returning to the one place with which he was familiar—Mary Surratt's boardinghouse.

31

"Sic Semper Tyrannis!"

"All that are proud in heart, are an abomination to the Lord: though hand join in hand, he shall not be unpunished."
—Proverbs 16:5 GNV

"Sic Semper Tyrannis!"
—John Wilkes Booth

A little before 9 p.m., John Wilkes Booth appeared in the alley behind the theater. He was wearing boots and spurs when he rode up to the rear door of Ford's Theatre—fully prepared and committed to carry out the most sensational assassination in United States history. And it would remain so until 1963, when John F. Kennedy was assassinated in Dallas, Texas, in broad daylight.

Booth was seen in front of the theater, having a brief and private conversation with two or three people. He then quickly ducked into the Star Saloon next door for a dose of liquid courage. He then returned to the rear of Ford's Theatre.

Booth called out to Ned Spangler from the rear entrance of Ford's Theatre to hold his horse. "Ned, you will help me all you can, won't you?" Booth left the reins to the mare in the hands of Spangler and entered the backstage door.

Assigned to hold Booth's horse, Spangler was called in to shift the stage scenery. He asked another stagehand, Joseph "Peanuts" Burroughs, to take over holding the reins of Booth's horse. Spangler then re-entered the backstage door as well.

Once inside, Booth grabbed the iron ring in the backstage floor, lifted the trap door, and quickly descended a set of steps leading to the dirt floor basement beneath the stage. He could hear the activity and the floor squeaking above. The smell of the dank earth was powerful enough to taste. He felt his way and crossed to the opposite side of the stage, emerging unseen on the other side of the stage—the side that corresponded to the president's box. Inside the theater, it was nearly the end of the second act.

The presidential box at Ford's Theatre was situated to the right of the stage. One must pass through an outer door, then an inner door to access the box's interior seating. The theater was splendidly decorated with flags and bunting to celebrate the war's end and acknowledge the president's attendance. The crowd was in a festive mood—ready to celebrate peace at long last.

Booth slipped into the outer hallway of the theater and walked up to the dress circle to the right and near the president's box, where he paused and steadied himself against a wall. He reached into his pocket and took out a small pack of visiting cards, selected one, held it in his hand, and put the rest back into his pocket. As Booth neared the president's box, Charles Forbes, a personal assistant to the president, stopped him. Booth calmly showed Forbes something, most likely the visitor card. Booth was allowed to pass.

During Act 3, Scene 2 of the play at about 10:10 p.m., Booth quietly sneaked into the presidential balcony box as silently as he could and wedged the piece of wood left by Spangler between the outer door and the inner wall. This piece of wood would prevent anyone else from entering the outer door. Booth then peered through the hole bored into the inner door to determine the president's position and to observe Lincoln's undivided attention on the stage.

Booth was familiar with the play. He knew which line got the biggest response, and timing was critical in his plan. He also knew that soon, there would be only one actor—Harry Hawk, onstage. This moment not only cleared his path for his escape but gave him the stage and the audience's undivided attention.

He drew his weapon from his pocket and pulled the hammer back until it is latched—cocking the Derringer. He crept up behind Abraham Lincoln, stealthily positioning himself just behind the president's left shoulder. He leveled the pistol at the back of Lincoln's head and took careful aim. His heart was pounding like a locomotive.

Booth's derringer

On stage, actor Harry Hawk recited his famous line that normally received a burst of loud laughter. As expected, the crowd burst into laughter, and at that very moment, 10:13 p.m., Booth fired his single shot .44 caliber Derringer pistol into the back of the president's head at point-blank range. The pistol report was more of a "poof" than a loud "pop." The audience heard it, grew silent, and froze. The bullet, less than one-half inch in diameter, entered slightly above and between Lincoln's left ear and the median of the back of his head, and lodged close behind the right eye, fracturing his orbital socket. The president slumped forward in his chair, and then backward, never to regain consciousness.

The black powder smoke from Booth's gun filled the presidential box, but Major Rathbone was still able to see the assassin. As Rathbone attempted to apprehend him, Booth pulled a dagger and slashed Rathbone's left arm from the elbow to the shoulder. Rathbone again grabbed at Booth as the assassin prepared to jump from the sill of the president's box.

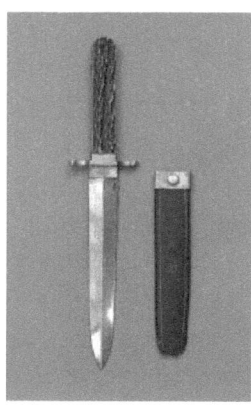

Booth's dagger

Booth jumped twelve feet to the hardwood stage below Lincoln's box seat, catching his boot spur on the flag, ripping it, and landing awkwardly on his feet. Rathbone pointed and cried out, "Stop that man!" Major Rathbone then turned his attention back to the president.

Ever the actor, Booth got to his feet, ran to the back of the stage, stopped, and delivered his last line: "Sic Semper Tyrannis!" (Thus always with tyrants!)

As he ran toward the north-side exit of the theater, Booth passed between actors Laura Keene and William J. Ferguson. Major Joseph B. Stewart, a lawyer, who was six-feet, six-inches tall and probably the tallest man in Washington, sat in the front seat of the orchestra section on the right-hand side. Startled by the shot, he looked up and saw Booth tumbling onto the stage. Rising instantly, Stewart climbed over the orchestra pit and footlights, and pursued Booth across the stage, shouting several times, "Stop that man!"

With adrenaline and alcohol coursing through his veins, Booth exited the stage and ran down a narrow aisle that led to the rear door of the theater. Unexpectedly, he bumped into William Withers Jr., the orchestra leader, who was just coming off a break. Booth slashed at Withers twice with his knife, cutting his coat and knocking him to the floor. Upon exiting the building, Booth grabbed the reins of his horse from Joseph "Peanuts" Burroughs, hitting him in the head with the butt end of his knife and knocking him to the ground. At that moment, Major Stewart burst through the backstage door and spotted Booth hoisting himself astride the bay mare. Stewart sprinted toward the horse reaching for the reins, but Booth quickly spun the mare in a tight circle and spurred her into a full gallop pounding the ground in a frenzy of hooves.

Booth tucked tight in the saddle and rode off in a full gallop up the alley, then left on F Street, fleeing into the darkness.

Many in the audience recognized the assassin as the actor John Wilkes Booth, so the Army was soon in hot pursuit, initiating the nation's largest manhunt in U.S. history. Booth would remain at large for the next 12 days.

32

"Oh! My husband's blood!"

"A man that doeth violence against the blood of a person, shall flee unto the grave, and they shall not stay him."
—Proverbs 28:17 GNV

The frozen theater crowd watched actor John Wilkes Booth's scene play out on stage. Many theatergoers claimed they at first thought Booth leaping from the presidential box was part of the performance. Others, first alerted to the trouble by Booth making his noisy escape, fell completely into chaos when they saw what was happening in the president's box.

Major Henry Rathbone noted that Lincoln had not changed positions, but his head was "slightly bent forward and his eyes were closed." Rathbone began to feel the effects of his injury. Blood saturated his sleeve and was pooling on the floor. Suddenly, the room swam in his vision. Weak from blood loss, his knees buckled and he crumpled to the floor. Clara Harris and Mary Todd Lincoln began to scream.

Clara was unhurt. She was, however, covered with her fiancée's blood as she tried to stop the bleeding with a handkerchief. Mrs. Lincoln was inconsolable, mistaking the major's blood on Miss Harris's dress for her husband's. Major Rathbone regained consciousness and assumed Lincoln's wound was mortal, so he struggled to the door of the presidential box to seek medical aid. The door, Rathbone discovered, had been barred shut by the assassin with a piece of wooden plank.

Clara Harris

Rathbone could hear people on the other side of the door pressing against it, trying to get in but were unable to gain access. Spangler's trick with the plank had served its purpose.

Maj. Henry Reed Rathbone

Rathbone, after several attempts of trying to remove the plank, finally succeeded when he was able to persuade those pushing against the door to stop and managed to get the door open. The screaming from the box extended to the rest of the theater. The doctors in the house were located and rushed to the president's aide. Several tried to gain entrance. One of them was Dr. Charles Leale, the first doctor to reach President Lincoln. At the time, Leale was a 23-year-old surgeon. Six weeks earlier, he had graduated in medicine from Bellevue Hospital Medical College in New York City.

Dr. Leale saw Lincoln slumped in his rocking chair, supported by Mrs. Lincoln, who was crying frantically. Leale received permission to take charge of the situation. He found the president unresponsive, barely breathing, and with no detectable pulse.

Upon the first look at Lincoln, Dr. Leale thought the president was dead. He would later testify, "His eyes were closed, and his head had fallen forward. He was being held upright in his chair by Mrs. Lincoln, who was weeping bitterly."

Dr. Leale then placed his finger on the president's right radial artery checking for a pulse. He was unable to feel any movement from the artery. Leale made the decision to remove Lincoln from his chair and place him on the floor, hoping this would help revive him. After he laid Lincoln out, he searched for the wound.

Dr. Charles Leale

The doctor recalled seeing Booth as he ran across the stage with a bloody dagger in his hand. With this remembrance and seeing Major Rathbone's injury, Leale thought it possible that President Lincoln may have been stabbed. He related: "While kneeling on the floor over his head, with my eyes continuously watching the president's face, I asked a gentleman to cut the coat and shirt open from the neck to the elbow to enable me, if possible, to check the hemorrhage that I thought might take place from the subclavian artery or some other blood vessel."

He didn't find an injury. He lifted Lincoln's eyelid. From the look of the eyes, Leale determined Lincoln had a brain injury. Dr. Leale then ran his fingers through Lincoln's hair and found the bullet wound. He was able to remove some of the clotted blood in the wound, and when this happened, pressure on the brain was relieved, and Lincoln had a pulse. Dr. Leale's quick efforts temporarily saved President Lincoln's life, which allowed him to live until the next morning.

While Dr. Leale was attempting to save President Lincoln, two other doctors, Army surgeons Dr. Charles S. Taft and Dr. Albert F. A. King, arrived to render assistance. The three doctors quickly figured it was best to remove the president from the theater, but he was too badly wounded for transport and would not survive a carriage ride across the rough cobblestones back to the White House. Instead, they decided to move the president to a boardinghouse across the street—the Petersen House, 453 10th Street NW, so that he could be placed in a bed.

They carried the president up the curving entrance steps and down a hall to a small, first-floor bedroom. They laid the president diagonally across a single bed pulled out from the corner of the room, his extreme height not permitting any other position.

Despite his serious wound, Henry Rathbone escorted Mary Lincoln and Clara Harris across the street to the Peterson House. Mary Lincoln immediately went to the room where the president had been placed. Every time Mary looked at Clara's blood-stained dress, she lamented, "Oh! My husband's blood!" Although the blood was most likely Rathbone's, that did not register with Mrs. Lincoln. Clara concluded it would be inappropriate and pointless to correct the First Lady.

Dr. Leale and the other doctors began making a complete examination of the president and asked some people, including Mrs. Lincoln, to step out of the cramped bedroom. Shortly thereafter, Rathbone passed out again due to blood loss.

When a surgeon who had been attending Lincoln finally examined Rathbone, he determined the wound was more serious than initially thought. Booth had cut him nearly to the bone and severed an artery. Clara sat in the floor and cradled Major Rathbone's head in her lap while he lay semiconscious. Rathbone was then taken to the Harris home for medical attention. For a while, Clara remained with Mary Lincoln as the president lay dying over the next nine hours.

Throughout the night Cabinet members, physicians, and distinguished men of Lincoln's inner circle helplessly watched at Lincoln's bedside. All the Cabinet officers were there, except Secretary of State William H. Seward, who was recovering from an earlier fall from a carriage.

Moments after Booth shot the president, Seward himself would suffer a savage attack by Lewis Powell.

33

"Murder! Murder!"

> *"Again he said, 'What hast thou done? The voice of thy brother's blood crieth unto me, from the earth.'"*
> —Genesis 4:10 GNV

> "I'm mad! I'm mad!"
> —Lewis Powell

The D.C. streets were wet with a spray of misty rain. At about 10:30 p.m., David Herold escorted Lewis Powell to Secretary Seward's residence on Lafayette Square near the White House. Local newspapers had reported that Seward was at home convalescing, so Powell and Herold knew exactly where to find him. Powell was armed with a Whitney revolver and a large knife. Wearing clothes purchased by Booth, black pants, a long overcoat, a gray vest, a gray dress coat, and a hat with a wide brim, Powell walked up to Seward's front door. Herold waited outside at the curb, holding the reins of Powell's horse.

Powell knocked and rang the bell. Seward's butler, William Bell, answered the door. Holding up a small bottle, Powell claimed that Seward's physician, Dr. T. S. Verdi, sent some medicine to the house. Bell was suspicious, as Dr. Verdi had departed the home only an hour earlier and left instructions for Seward not to be disturbed. Bell asked Powell to wait, but Powell pushed past him and began mounting the stairs to the second-floor bedrooms.

Frederick Seward

Hearing the commotion, Seward's thirty-five-year-old son Frederick appeared at the top of the steps in his nightclothes and ordered Powell to stop. Seward's daughter, twenty-year-old Fanny, stuck her head out of her father's bedroom door and whispered,

"Be quiet—father is sleeping." She then returned to the bedroom, closing the door.

Powell repeated to Frederick, "I'm here to deliver medicine."

Frederick put his hand out and said, "give me the bottle."

Powell handed over the bogus medicine bottle, pulled out his revolver, pressed the barrel against Frederick's chest, and pulled the trigger. The revolver misfired. Powell then pistol-whipped Frederick about the head over and over, crushing his skull. William Bell, the butler, fled the house screaming, "Murder! Murder!" and raced next door to the office of General Christopher C. Augur for help. Terrified at the ruckus, Herold tied Powell's horse to a tree and fled the scene on his own steed.

With Frederick dispatched, Powell drew his knife and burst through Seward's bedroom door. Inside were Seward, his Army nurse Sergeant George F. Robinson, and his daughter Fanny. Powell slashed Robinson on the forearm, and the soldier fell to the floor. He punched Fanny in the face and leaped onto the bed straddling Secretary Seward.

He began savagely knifing Seward in the head and throat. Seward, however, was wearing a metal and canvas splint on his jaw, which deflected most of Powell's blows. Powell managed to cut through Seward's right cheek and along his right throat, causing a large amount of blood to flow. Believing Seward to be dead, Powell hesitated. Seward's other son, 38-year-old Augustus, burst into the room. Powell stabbed him several times.

George F. Robinson – Seward's Army nurse

Fighting back, Augustus dragged Powell onto the floor. Augustus and Robinson wrestled with the strong and uninjured Powell. Powell stabbed Robinson in the chest and shoulder and slashed a portion of Augustus's scalp from his head. Powell got to his feet and shouted, "I'm mad! I'm mad!" and fled the room.

He was confronted by State Department messenger Emerick "Bud" Hansell in the hallway. A curious Hansell had arrived at the house moments earlier and found the front door ajar and a noisy commotion inside. As Hansell turned to flee, Powell stabbed him in the back, then ran out of the house and threw his knife in the gutter of the street. Inside the Seward house was a ghastly scene—blood was everywhere.

Powell's eyes darted around looking for his accomplice and quickly realized Herold had abandoned him. With almost no knowledge of the streets of D.C., and without Herold's guidance, he had no way to find his escape route. He mounted his horse and began spurring the animal. The horse did not respond to the urgency, walking away from Seward's home at an unhurried pace north on 15th Street. Secretary Seward's butler spotted him, pursued him on foot, screaming that he was the assailant until Bell was out of breath and gave up the chase. Powell eventually wound up in the far northeast part of the city near Fort Bunker Hill, where he discarded his bloody overcoat.

He had dropped his hat at the Seward home during the altercation. During much of the Victorian era, it was considered unseemly for any man, even a menial laborer, to be seen in public without a hat. Powell would have been viewed with suspicion had he tried to enter the city without one. Ripping the sleeve from his undershirt, he placed it on his head in the hope that people would think it was a stocking cap. To complete his disguise as a common laborer, he stole a pickaxe from a farmyard. Lewis Powell then headed for the one place he knew he would find sanctuary—Mrs. Surratt's boardinghouse.

Dr. Leale gave control over the president's medical care to the Lincoln family physician, Robert K. Stone, and the commander of the Armory Square Hospital, D. W. Bliss. Clara Harris left to care for her fiancée.

At the Harris residence, Dr. G. W. Pope was called to attend to the wounded Major Henry Rathbone. Due to the loss of blood, Henry became delirious and continued talking about the shooting of Abraham Lincoln. Rathbone later recalled that he was horrified at the anger on Booth's face. The assassination of the president would become something that literally haunted and cursed Rathbone for the rest of his life.

Robert Todd Lincoln and the president's personal secretary John Hay came to the Peterson House from the White House. Dr. Stone grimly told Robert he was sorry, but there was no hope. Family members and others close to the president began their long night vigil, waiting for death to overtake Abraham Lincoln.

Booth galloped toward a bridge that crossed the Anacostia River, the first point of a pre-planned escape route to the south. Booth's mare had been ridden hard and had sweated up a lather from the physical exertion. He reined in the horse as he approached the bridge, slowing her canter. Steam rose from the high-spirited mare. Army sentry Sergeant Silas Cobb, who oversaw guarding the Navy Yard Bridge that led out of D.C. toward Virginia, raised his hand and stopped the assassin at the gate blocking the wooden bridge.

"Sir, why are you riding so late?", asked Cobb.

Booth responded, "I've been in the city on an errand, and I got a late start going home—to Charles County."

Booth's sweaty mare skittered and pranced. Cobb took hold of the bridle in an attempt to steady the horse.

"And where is home? What town do you live in?"

"I do not live in a town," Booth replied. Cobb thought the rider seemed to be in a hurry.

Cobb continued, "You must live in some town."

"Southern Maryland, near Beantown. It is a dark road and I thought if I waited 'til now that I would have the moon to help me," Booth offered.

"What is your name, sir?"

"John Wilkes Booth."

Inexplicably, Booth volunteered information that would shortly prove invaluable to his pursuers. If Booth failed to cross this bridge, his escape was over. He was ahead of the news of Lincoln's assassination, but that advantage would not last. Whether or not Booth's fame or name recognition could have possibly influenced Cobb's decision here is unknown. Sergeant Cobb hesitated, then nodded to the private who opened the gate. Despite a citywide curfew, Sergeant Cobb had allowed him to pass.

Cobb said, "All right, you may pass, but you cannot come back across before daybreak."

"I have no intention of returning," Booth said over his shoulder as he crossed.

Less than ten minutes later, Davy Herold arrived at the same bridge. Identifying himself as Smith and giving his address as White Plains, Maryland. Herold somehow also convinced the sentry to let him pass. Shortly thereafter, Herold caught up with Booth. He noticed Booth appeared to be in pain and a spur was missing.

Davy asked, "What happened?"

"My horse lost her footing and fell. My left foot was still in the stirrup, and I think I sprained my ankle," Booth said.

Herold regarded Booth's horse and noticed that one side of the mare was muddied, and her left knee was bloody. The two then headed southeast toward Lloyd's Surrattsville Tavern.

They rode like thunder until they arrived. There, they were supposed to pick up a cache of supplies previously left for them. Mary Surratt had visited Lloyd earlier that day. She told Lloyd to have the shooting irons ready for pickup and handed him a wrapped package from Booth.

Herold quickly dismounted and pounded on the Surrattsville Tavern door until a sleepy and hungover Lloyd finally answered. Lloyd noticed that Booth seemed to be in great pain. He also noted that Booth did not dismount, unlike Herold, who knocked on his door to awaken him. Booth told Lloyd he thought he had broken his leg when his horse fell. At Lloyd's, the two fugitives collected the cache, and Booth attempted to drown the throbbing pain of his leg with a bottle of whiskey.

Just before Booth and Herold wheeled around and rode off, Booth yelled to Lloyd, "We have killed President Lincoln and Secretary Seward!"

34

"Now he belongs to the ages."

*"Unto the hope of eternal life,
which God that cannot lie,
hath promised before the world began:"*
—Titus 1:2 GNV

Louis Weichmann, an old school friend of John Surratt, Jr. and boarder at the Surratt boardinghouse since last November, currently worked as a clerk in the War Department with Major Daniel Gleason. After moving in with the Surratt's, Weichmann informed Gleason of the goings-on there.

It would eventually be Louis Weichmann's trial testimony that would seal the fate of those conspiring to murder the president, the vice-president, and the secretary of state.

Saturday, April 15, 1865

Around 2 a.m. in drizzling rain, members of the D.C. police visited the Surratt boardinghouse, seeking John Wilkes Booth and John

Surratt, Jr. War Department employee Daniel Gleason alerted federal authorities to the underground Confederate activities centered at the Surratt house.

Following the crime, numerous troop detachments were sent out to scour the countryside in search of the assassin. A young baby-faced Union private named John W. Millington of the 16th New York Cavalry was on guard duty when news came that President Lincoln had been shot at Ford's Theatre. Millington was ordered to form part of a cordon around the city to prevent the assassin from escaping.

Into the cold, rainy night, they rode. The whiskey and adrenaline had started to wear off, and Booth could no longer ignore his pain. Booth and his accomplice, David Herold, made their way across the Anacostia River and headed toward southern Maryland. Looking for a doctor to tend to his injured leg, Booth later wrote in his diary that he "rode sixty miles that night, with the bones of my leg tearing the flesh at every jump." The doctor the two men were looking for was Booth's friend and Southern sympathizer, Dr. Samuel Mudd.

About thirty miles from D.C. in Charles County, Maryland, they awakened the doctor around 4 a.m. When the two men arrived at the Mudd farm, Herold dismounted and knocked loudly on the front door. When Dr. Mudd answered, he observed the two men who appeared to be in distress and in need of assistance.

Dr. Samuel Mudd's house

Mudd hesitantly let them in to treat Booth's broken leg. Once Booth was guided inside to a settee in the front parlor, Mudd lit a match to a coal-oil lamp. He thumbed the wick screw, adjusting the flame for the brightest illumination. The doctor and patient instantly recognized each other without a word spoken.

Dr. Mudd examined Booth's broken leg, cut off his tight riding boot to relieve the pressure due to swelling, isolated and stabilized the tibia and fibula, and wrapped the left leg in a pasteboard cast made from a hat box. He provided Booth with a set of crutches and a single shoe loosely fastened to replace the boot. While the two weary fugitives slept in Mudd's home, Dr. Mudd made his way to Bryantown to run some errands. When Booth awakened from his slumber, he shaved off his trademark mustache to disguise himself.

In town, the doctor was immediately confronted with the explosive news that Lincoln had been shot and that the Army was searching for John Wilkes Booth. Realizing his complicity in the heinous crime and the consequences to follow, Mudd hurriedly returned home and ordered Booth and Herold off his property. They grudgingly left Dr. Mudd's farm. Dr. Mudd would later testify that even though he was acquainted with Booth, he did not recognize him as he set his leg. Though Mudd swore to this on the witness stand during his trial, his claim was ludicrous, as the two were old friends and had celebrated the recent Christmas holiday together.

In the bedroom at the Peterson House, the death vigil lasted throughout the night, until well after sunrise, when Abraham Lincoln breathed for the last time at 7:22 a.m. There was not a dry eye in that small boardinghouse bedroom as silver dollars were placed over the president's eyes, a custom of the day. Stanton stood solemnly still, sobbing, and said, "Now he belongs to the ages."

In the gloom of a cold, misty rain, Andrew Johnson walked the few blocks from Kirkwood House to the Petersen House. As he approached the Peterson House, Johnson saw a massive crowd gathered in the street, filling it from sidewalk to sidewalk.

Andrew Johnson was admitted to the bedroom where the Cabinet and military leaders were gathered around the president's deathbed. Johnson stood with his hat in his hand, looking down, saying nothing. He then looked up and spotted Robert Lincoln. Johnson took Robert's hand and whispered a few words to him. He briefly conversed with Secretary of War Stanton, and then went to the parlor to pay his respects to Mary Todd Lincoln.

He exited the Peterson House in stunned silence and walked somberly back to his room at Kirkwood House. There, in his parlor at 10 o'clock that morning, Johnson took the oath of office from Chief Justice Salmon P. Chase. Andrew Johnson placed his left hand on the Bible, raised his right, and was gravely sworn in as the 17th president of the United States.

PART IV

The Journey Home

35

Easter Sunday Photos

*"Behold, I come shortly:
hold that which thou hast,
that no man take thy crown."*
—Revelation 3:11 GNV

In the turmoil that followed Lincoln's assassination, scores of suspected accomplices were arrested and thrown into prison on the order of Secretary of War Edwin Stanton. Stanton vigorously pursued the apprehension and prosecution of the suspects involved in the assassination. All the people who were discovered to have had anything to do with the plot or anyone with the slightest contact with Booth or Herold on their flight were put behind bars.

Saturday, April 15, 1865

As Robert E. Lee rode along on Traveller toward home, he took in the war's destruction and the nation's devastation—from burned-out farmhouses to downed bridges to animal carcasses strewn along the road. His army had destroyed the two bridges over the James River into Richmond, so when Lee reached the former capital of the Confederacy, he crossed a pontoon bridge put up by his recent enemy.

The ruins of Richmond

It had rained all that morning, and both Lee and his horse were soaked and spattered with mud. With him were two of his three sons, some aides, servants, and a seriously wounded Confederate officer. They first passed through the part of Richmond that burned when the Confederates fled, the streets bisecting piles of charred rubble.

When they reached beyond the fire line, word quickly spread that General Robert E. Lee was back, and the people came out to greet him. Historian and biographer Douglas Southall Freeman (1886-1953) wrote in his biography: "Along a ride of less than a mile to the residence at 707 East Franklin Street, the crowd grew thicker with each block. Cheers broke out, in which the Federals joined heartily." Lee acknowledged these displays of affection and respect by doffing his muddy hat.

When he arrived at the rented brick house where Mrs. Lee was living, he had trouble getting down from Traveller, overcome either by the emotion of the moment or an old soldier's weariness of the years of war. One woman who looked on felt that his body simply would not do what he asked of it. Once dismounted, Lee struggled through the crowd of well-wishers who surrounded him, touching him and shaking hands. He then entered the house and his new life as a civilian.

General Robert E. Lee atop his horse, Traveller, after the end of the American Civil War.

Famed Civil War photographer Mathew Brady had been in Richmond for several days. He'd made nearly sixty photographs of the ruined city. He got wind of Lee's return and asked an old acquaintance, Confederate Colonel Robert Ould, to appeal to the general to have his photograph taken. Brady said in a newspaper interview late in life that both Ould and Mrs. Lee had helped him persuade the general to submit to the camera, although as Brady put it, "It was supposed that after his defeat it would be preposterous to ask him to sit." But, Brady continued, "I thought that to be the time for the historical picture." Apparently, the reluctant Lee, or perhaps

Mrs. Lee, agreed, because it was arranged that Brady could come to the house and make his pictures.

Custis Lee, Robert E. Lee, and Walter Taylor

The next day, Easter Sunday, Brady took six photographs in all: four of Lee alone and two of him with his aide, Colonel Walter Taylor, and his oldest son, Major General Custis Lee who had been captured three days before the surrender.

Brady posed the officers beneath the overhang of the back porch on the basement level because the light was best there. Lee's youngest son, Rob, wrote years later of his father: "I believe there were none of the little things in life so irksome to him as having his picture taken in any way."

But Lee had a fine sense of history—for example, wearing for his surrender his best uniform and a dark red silk sash. Ulysses Grant said in his memoirs that "General Lee was dressed in a full uniform which was entirely new and was wearing a sword of considerable value."

Despite how much Lee disliked posing, on this Easter Sunday morning, he once again put on a clean uniform and wore well-shined black shoes, but he left aside the sash and the sword and the boots. The results were an undeniably iconic portrait—one of the best remembered visual records of General Robert E. Lee.

In the wake of Lincoln's death and the charges that the South was responsible, Lee might also have chosen to pose in the domestic setting of his home—a leader still in his uniform, but sans sash, braid, sword, and boots, visibly morphing into a civilian—as a symbol of stability and responsibility in those very dangerous and uncertain hours.

Grant wrote in his memoirs that at Appomattox he had "suggested to General Lee that there was not a man in the Confederacy whose influence with the soldiery and the whole people was as great as his." Lee was a beloved figure, and not only in the South. "The people of Virginia and of the entire South were continually giving evidence of their intense love for General Lee," Rob Lee wrote. "From all nations, even from the Northern States, came to him marks of admiration and respect."

But these photographs—in which the physically and emotionally exhausted general, grizzled at age 58, summoned the strength of his unusual personal dignity for Brady's camera, showing no trace of the humiliation of defeat, but only a self-possessed seriousness—gave the South a hero to cling to in those dark days of ruin and rebuilding after the war, and for decades to come.

36

"I was a stranger..."

"For I was an hungered, and ye gave me meat:
I thirsted, and ye gave me drink:
I was a stranger, and ye took me in unto you."
—Matthew 25:35 GNV

"I guess I have mistaken the house."
—Lewis Powell

Easter Sunday, April 16, 1865

After leaving Dr. Mudd's farm before daylight, Booth and Herold headed east of Zekiah Swamp but got lost in the foggy darkness. Eventually, they found the home of Oswell Swann, a half-African American, half-Piscataway Indian tobacco farmer near Hughesville, Maryland. Booth offered to pay him $2 to lead them to William Burtle, a Confederate agent, who lived just west of Swann. Swann also provided them with foodstuffs of milk, bread, and whiskey for another $5. On the way to Burtle's, Booth changed his mind and gave him another $5 to take them to the home of Confederate sympathizer, Colonel Samuel Cox.

Cox, unwilling to let them stay, directed the fugitives to a hiding place in the woods and sent for his foster brother, Thomas A. Jones, another Confederate agent. By mid-morning, Jones arrived and instructed the men to lay low. Herold and Booth spent an uncomfortable Easter Sunday in a pine thicket near the Jones home.

Jones kept Booth and Herold hidden and supplied with food and water for six days, while he waited for a chance to put the two men across the river into Virginia.

The end of suffering and starvation was in sight. The war and risk of death far from home were about to be over. During the first five days in April, Epp McIntosh and about 340 other prisoners were sent by railroad, wagons, or marched, and finally delivered to Camp Fisk, where arrangements were being made for their transportation home. He was little more than skin and bones, suffering from his many days in captivity.

The staff doctor at Camp Fisk wrote Epp's weight on the acceptance form as 80 pounds. He could not stand for long or walk without help, and then for only a short distance. Pictures of the time define Epp, barely out of his teens, as "the living skeleton" —an example of the inhumanity at Andersonville.

The paroled prisoners were all given new uniforms, and were given beans, sowbelly, and hardtack to eat. The new uniform hung on Epp's emaciated frame like a scarecrow. Epp later said that "if anyone would have told him how good hardtack and sowbelly could taste, he'd have called them liars."

Epp spent a week at Camp Fisk, eating, sleeping, and making sure he woke up every morning. Some nights, he had nightmares that reminded him of his days in Andersonville.

In the dreams there was nothing but a vast darkness, and he could not see the men—he could only hear their cries and plead for God to help them. He thanked God for answering his prayers, with the knowledge that the war and his torment were finally over and better days were ahead.

The "Living Skeleton" Epp McIntosh

Monday, April 17, 1865 – 7 a.m.

Detectives entered John Wharton's Sutler store at Fortress Monroe and informed Samuel Arnold that he was under arrest. Arnold seemed more relieved than surprised. He cooperated with authorities when questioned, giving them the names of co-conspirators Booth, O'Laughlen, Atzerodt, and John Surratt.

Mid-morning in the pine thicket, Thomas Jones whistled a secret melody to let Booth and Herold know he was not the enemy. Jones came bearing food, whiskey, and newspapers, which Booth was eager to see. He wanted to know how the country reacted to his "good deed." The newspapers were not kind to Booth or his conspirators. Jones told them they must wait a little longer to cross the Potomac into Virginia. He could hear Union troops and patrol boats in the distance. Moving from their hiding place now would be dangerous.

The *Sultana* chugged onward, headed south for New Orleans, draped with black crepe and flying her flags at half-mast. The people aboard the *Sultana* shared the devastating news of Lincoln's assassination with citizens during their stops along the waterway.

Tuesday, April 18, 1865 – 2 a.m.

After Lewis Powell's attempted assassination of Seward, he wandered the backstreets of D.C., hiding here and there, before deciding to return to the one place in the city where he would be accepted, housed, hidden, and fed. He had no other place to go. He'd been there several times before and was confident he could find his way back. He still had the "sleeve hat" on his head and carried a stolen pickaxe as part of his disguise.

Major Henry W. Smith and two detectives, Ely Devoe and William Wermerskirsh, had been ordered by Colonel Henry Wells to visit the Surratt boardinghouse and arrest all the inhabitants there and anyone visiting. They were additionally ordered to make a thorough search of the premises, collecting all possible evidence, such as correspondence, documents, and photographs. After rousting the occupants of a wrong house nearby, they corrected course and arrived at the Surratt boardinghouse.

Mary Surratt was taken into the parlor and informed that she was under arrest. Major Smith ordered Devoe to procure a carriage for Mrs. Surratt, her daughter Anna, Honora Fitzpatrick, and Anna's cousin, Olivia Jenkins, for transportation to General Christopher C. Augur's headquarters for questioning.

"They can walk," Devoe suggested.

Smith wouldn't hear of it. He noticed how sick and shaken Anna had become due to their presence. Smith insisted the ladies would be treated kindly as long as they were in his charge. He repeated the order to acquire a carriage. Devoe exited the Surratt house to procure one while Mary Surratt tried to calm her crying daughter.

"Do not behave so, baby," she said.

"You are already so worn out with anxiety that you will make yourself sick."

Anna cried, "Oh, Mother! To be taken for such a thing!"

"Hush, now. Get ready to go out into the chilly night."

Mary knelt in prayer while they waited for the carriage. They heard footsteps approaching the front door and assumed it would be Devoe announcing the carriage was ready.

Anna Surratt

The well-lit parlor of the Surratt house was a welcome sight as Lewis Powell walked up the sidewalk to the front door. He rang the doorbell and knocked. Major Smith and Detective Wermerskirsh took cautious positions before they opened the door to a tall, dark-haired man with a pickaxe over his shoulder. Powell was taken aback at being greeted by strangers.

"I guess I have mistaken the house," said Powell.

"No, you have not. Whose house are you looking for?" Smith asked.

"Mrs. Surratt's."

Smith slowly reached for his pistol. "This is the house. Come in at once."

It was too late to back out now. Powell hesitantly stepped forward and crossed the threshold. Wermerskirsh pushed the door shut behind him. The questioning continued.

"What do you come to a private house for at this hour of the night?"

"I came to get directions from Mrs. Surratt about digging a gutter tomorrow morning."

Smith was skeptical of the man's story. It didn't make sense to show up at this time of night for such work.

"I think you are a spy." Smith pointed to a chair.

"Sit down. Your story does not hang together."

Smith stepped into the parlor and called, "Mrs. Surratt, will you step in here a minute?"

Mary Surratt came into the foyer in full view of Powell.

"Do you know this man? Did you hire him to come dig a gutter for you?"

Mary looked at Powell, raised her right hand, and solemnly declared, "Before God, I do not know this man and have never seen him before, and I did not hire him to dig a gutter for me. I am so glad you officers came here tonight, for this man came here with a pickaxe to kill us."

All the inhabitants, including Lewis Powell, were taken into custody and promptly transported to General Christopher Augur's headquarters.

Tuesday, April 18, 1865 – 3 a.m.

Seward's butler, William Bell, was nervously waiting in a room in General Augur's office. He had been brought here to possibly identify the man who had assaulted everyone at the Seward home.

The detectives escorted a group of men into the room and closed the door. The detectives watched Bell closely as he eyed the men as they entered. Bell scanned their faces, examining each one, exchanging glances. Suddenly, Bell froze—eyes widening. He fixed his gaze on the tall muscular dark-haired young man in the room. Bell stood and moved in closer without breaking eye contact. Without saying a word and standing face-to-face with the fearsome giant, he slowly raised his hand and pointed his index finger in the face of the suspect. Lewis Powell's face broke out in a big grin.

With Lewis Powell identified as the man who assaulted Secretary Seward, he was formally charged and imprisoned aboard the monitor *USS Saugus*, anchored in the Anacostia River at the Washington Navy Yard. A second identification came around mid-morning when Secretary Seward's son, Augustus Seward, wounded and patched with bandages, visited the monitor and positively identified Powell as the man who attacked him and his father.

On the same day, Michael O'Laughlen and Ned Spangler were also arrested.

Edmund "Ned" Spangler

Lacking the manpower to track him down in Baltimore, Provost Marshal James McPhail asked for assistance from city police to apprehend O'Laughlen. O'Laughlen expected to be arrested. He wanted to spare his mother the grief and embarrassment of seeing him taken away in handcuffs, so he arranged his surrender at his sister's house.

Spangler had been in and out of police custody since the assassination, brought in with numerous Ford's Theatre employees for questioning and released. He was asleep in an upstairs bedroom of a boardinghouse at the corner of 7th & G Streets when his landlady's daughter knocked and told him through the door that two men were downstairs waiting to speak to him. He had been expecting them and knew why they were there.

"Let's take a little walk," said one of the detectives. Their walk ended at 1st & A Streets—at Carroll Prison. He would be transferred to an ironclad for added security.

The most important prisoners were kept aboard the monitors moored in the Navy Yard to prevent escape, as well as any outside effort to free them. Imprisoned along with Powell on the *Saugus* were Arnold, O'Laughlen, and Spangler.

The April 18th edition of *The New York Times* reported improvement in the condition of Secretary Seward and his son Frederick. The newspaper also gave John Wilkes Booth's description, as follows:

"28 years old, 5'8" tall, 160 lbs., compact build, wears a mustache with jet black hair—inclined to curl, of medium length, eyes—black and heavy—wears a large seal ring on his little finger, when talking inclines his head forward and looks down."

The paper also gave the description of Lewis Powell:

"22-23 years old, 6'1" tall, thick straight black hair, no beard, face round and moderately full, cheeks red on the jaws, eye color unknown and not prominent, straight nose with chin pointed and prominent, hands soft and small—show no sign of hard labor—vulgar manner, small thin voice inclined to tremor, wears overcoat with pockets on the sides and over the breast, black pants, new heavy boots."

With the knowledge that Booth was suffering from a broken leg—information supplied by Lloyd—detectives immediately set about looking for doctors in the area. The troopers started scouting through the country, searching all the houses and buildings, rousting out the occupants, and making a thorough search of the area. The search area widened to include the road leading south to Surrattsville and beyond, to the home of Dr. Mudd in Bryantown.

At every port along the Mississippi, there was chatter among the crews. James Cass Mason, captain of the *Sultana*, caught wind of the amassed multitude of paroled former POWs gathered at Vicksburg, readying for transport. Mason was also aware that his boat was presently heading in the wrong direction to cash in on the opportunity—south to New Orleans. His fear was that the *Sultana* and more importantly, the boat captain himself, would miss out on the windfall profits from transporting these soldiers.

After the *Sultana* docked at Vicksburg, Mason went into town on an urgent quest for passengers for his boat's return trip. Major General Napoleon Dana, the Union Commander for the Department of the Mississippi, had ordered that the soon-to-be paroled prisoners at Camp Fisk be sent northward on privately owned steamboats moored at the Vicksburg docks.

Major General Napoleon Dana

In the quartermaster's office, Captain Mason reminded the major general and all present that his boat belonged to a transport cooperative that enjoyed a contract with the federal government for just such services. Other steamers were not part of this deal, and therefore, should not be entitled to engage in the services of supplying transportation for paroled POWs. After stating his case, Mason was even more determined to complete his run to New Orleans and return as quickly as possible to Vicksburg for his fair share of the lucrative government pie.

While the soldiers were still at Camp Fisk, word reached them that President Lincoln was dead. Since all telegraphic communications between the North and South had been cut off by the order of Secretary of War Edwin Stanton, the sad news was brought to Vicksburg by way of the *Sultana*.

Stanton issued a reward poster for the capture of John Wilkes Booth, David Herold, and John Surratt Jr., with a total monetary amount of $100,000—$50,000 for Booth, $25,000 each for Herold and Surratt. The poster displayed pictures of all three conspirators. Another $10,000 was added to the reward by Colonel Lafayette C. Baker, a Union spy and investigator employed as an agent of the War Department.

The vainglorious murderer Booth scoffed at what he was later told was the price on his head. He thought *it should be a half-million*.

Twenty-four hours later, Thomas Jones came back to the pine thicket and whistled the signal, a three-note tune. He brought more whiskey and food. Jones instructed Herold to dispose of the horses at once. They were neighing too loudly and drawing too much attention, and besides, the horses were no longer needed. Herold took the horses—Booth's bay mare from Pumphrey's and Herold's horse rented from Naylor's—to a nearby quicksand morass and shot them in the head. Herold stood and watched as they slowly sank into the mire.

37

"Darkness favors us."

"The way of the wicked is as the darkness: they know not wherein they shall fall."
—Proverbs 4:19 GNV

"…darkness favors us."
—Thomas Jones

Wednesday, April 19, 1865

Taking advantage of southward Mississippi River currents, Captain Mason was determined to make it to his destination as soon as possible. The quicker he could finish his business in New Orleans, the quicker he could return to Vicksburg to cash in on his government transport contract, hauling the newly paroled POWs.

Mason knew the *Sultana* was not the only boat poised to cash in. The captain wasted no time, arriving in the Crescent City ahead of schedule. The *Sultana* remained in New Orleans for two days before heading back to Vicksburg with approximately 250 passengers and crewmen aboard.

Despite the conclusion of government inspectors following an April 12th inspection in St. Louis, crew members aboard the vessel grew concerned about the condition of the steamer's massive boilers. The report stated that the "*Sultana* may be employed as a steamer upon the waters herein specified, without peril to life from imperfection of form, materials, workmanship, or arrangement of the several parts or from age or use."

Meanwhile, Confederate authorities had begun to parole prisoners waiting at Camp Fisk. Major General Dana ordered that muster rolls listing the men's names be prepared as quickly as possible, so the soldiers could be immediately transported by train to Vicksburg to board steamers tied up at the docks.

The officer in nominal command of the prisoner exchange was Captain George Williams. A graduate of the United States Military Academy at West Point, Williams was a veteran of more than 13 years of service in the regular Army but had never risen above the rank of captain.

While serving as the provost-marshal at Memphis in 1864, he was dismissed from service because of "excessive cruelty to prisoners and gross neglect of duty." He was saved from disgrace by the intervention of General Ulysses S. Grant, whose written testimonial helped persuade the Army to reverse his dismissal.

For better or worse, Captain Williams would not be available at the Vicksburg wharf to see that his responsibilities were carried out. He would be at the other end of the logistical quagmire—Camp Fisk.

Thursday, April 20, 1865

At dusk, Thomas Jones came back to the makeshift campsite and again whistled the familiar three-note tune. Booth struggled to stand on his one good leg, wincing in pain. For a man accustomed to luxury and the finer things in life, being reduced to his current state of affairs was both uncomfortable and humiliating.

Thomas Jones

As Booth and Herold approached Jones, he told them, "Darkness favors us." With Booth hobbling on crutches, they walked three and a half miles to the Potomac River making a pit stop at Jones's house. He didn't allow them inside but brought them food and whiskey. After hiding the fugitives in the pine thicket for 5 days, Jones got the chance he was waiting for and sent Booth and Herold off in a rowboat.

In the inky pitch black, the fugitives cast off and ventured out into the Potomac River, aiming for the Virginia shore. They again got lost due to the darkness and fog and ended up landing on the bank of the wrong river, a tributary, Nanjemoy Creek, in Maryland.

On the day of the assassination, Booth had rented a room for George Atzerodt in the Kirkwood House, the same hotel where Vice-President Andrew Johnson was staying, to make it easier to murder the vice-president. Atzerodt had tried to drink up enough courage to go through with the plot but had chickened out.

George Atzerodt

Atzerodt was identified as one of the conspirators and was quickly tracked down and arrested. His cousin, Hartmann Richter, who had harbored Atzerodt for 4 days, was also taken into custody. Atzerodt was found to be in possession of weapons and property connecting him to Booth and was promptly charged with conspiracy.

Friday, April 21, 1865

Booth and Herold made landfall and concealed the boat. By now, a week after he had shot the president, practically the entire civilized world was aware of John Wilkes Booth and the manhunt to capture him.

The two wanted men, on the wrong side of the Potomac, walked to Indiantown, a farm owned by Herold's friend Peregrine Davis, a verbose character in Charles County, described as "one of the noisiest" rebels in the area. There, they found Davis's son-in-law, John J. Hughes. Hughes agreed to feed the fugitives, but they must hide somewhere else. Booth and Herold would spend about 36 hours hiding on the Indiantown property.

The answers given by Dr. Samuel Mudd during initial questioning didn't seem to add up. Detectives were sent back to the Mudd farm to follow up on the investigation. One of the detectives, Lieutenant Alexander Lovett would later testify:

"On Friday, the 21st of April, I went to Mudd's farm again, for the purpose of arresting him. When he found we were going to search the house, he said something to his wife, and she went upstairs and brought down a boot. Mudd said he had cut it off the man's leg. I turned down the top of the boot, and saw the name, 'J. Wilkes' written in it." Mudd was taken into custody.

The *Sultana* left New Orleans with a contingent of paying civilian passengers, her crew, and numerous heads of livestock bound for market in the captain's hometown of St. Louis. The crew's concerns about the vessel proved justified when they discovered steam escaping from a crack in one of her four boilers. As the *Sultana* reached a point about ten miles south of Vicksburg, issues with the leaky boilers forced her to continue upriver at a greatly reduced speed. She hobbled into Vicksburg and stopped for some hasty repairs to her boilers. Captain Mason took on more passengers and arranged to haul a load of one thousand bushels of coal. The forty-ton load of coal was stowed in the lower cargo hold.

The *Sultana's* chief engineer, Nathan Wintringer, and second engineer, Samuel Clemens (no relation to the famous author), found that the two-year-old boilers had bulges and were leaking. Fearing the crack posed a significant threat to the safety of the steamboat, Wintringer declared that he would not proceed beyond Vicksburg until necessary repairs were made.

One crewman, who disembarked only two hours before the *Sultana* left New Orleans, later reported that the boilers had been patched or repaired at Natchez, Mississippi, and at Vicksburg on the two previous trips. Captain Mason suggested yet another temporary patch be installed.

Private John W. Millington's unit, Company H, 16th New York Cavalry, was ordered to Washington, D.C., where they would serve as an escort at Abraham Lincoln's funeral. After the service, Lieutenant Edward P. Doherty instructed the unit they were to be held in the city and quartered in the J Street barracks awaiting further orders. Riding with the 16th New York Cavalry was a former hatter and street preacher named Sergeant Boston Corbett.

President Lincoln's funeral train departed Washington for its final destination, Springfield, Illinois, for the scheduled burial on May 4th. The funeral train consisted of nine cars and carried three hundred guests. The train also carried the small casket of Lincoln's son, Willie, who had died three years earlier. Mary Todd Lincoln had decided that he should also be buried in the family plot in Springfield.

38

Camp Fisk

> *"Promising unto them liberty,*
> *and are themselves the servants of corruption:*
> *for of whomsoever a man is overcome,*
> *even unto the same is he in bondage."*
> —2 Peter 2:19 GNV

Saturday, April 22, 1865

After dusk, Booth and Herold pushed off from the Nanjemoy Creek shores, leaving John J. Hughes and his Indiantown farm behind. Failing in their first attempt, they finally made their way across the Potomac to Virginia. They expected a warm welcome. Instead, they were grudgingly given food by various Virginians and told to move on.

Lewis Powell repeatedly banged his head into the iron walls of his cell aboard the *Saugus*. Whether this was a genuine suicide attempt (as his jailers believed) or not, it deeply alarmed military officials.

They fashioned padded canvas hoods with only a slit for the mouth and nostrils. Powell and the other prisoners aboard the monitors were forced to wear them 24 hours a day, 7 days a week, to prevent suicide attempts. The only conspirators not required to wear the hoods were the ones being confined at the Old Capital Prison—Mary Surratt and Dr. Mudd.

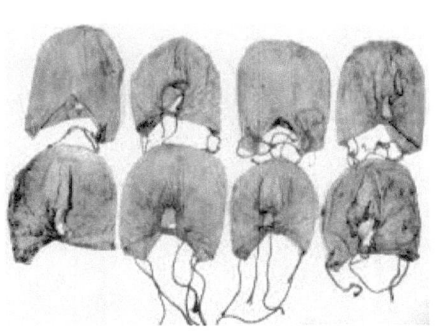

Padded prisoner hoods

Powell cried when the hood was placed on him. The hoods were hot, claustrophobic, and uncomfortable, and within the humid confines of the monitors in the steaming and humid Washington spring, the prisoners suffered immensely.

As Confederate forces folded their flags in surrender, lines of authority were broken, leaving rebel soldiers scattered and without definitive leadership to guide them through end-of-war transition. Within the Confederacy, many of the telegraph lines were down, leaving east-west communications spotty at best. The Union-held city of Vicksburg became the western center for prisoner exchange. Union POWs were quartered and cared for at Camp Fisk, awaiting exchange for an equal number of Confederate soldiers a mile away at Camp Townsend.

The system had broken. More federal soldiers were accumulating at Camp Fisk than could be swapped for rebel soldiers on a one-for-one basis. At last, a message made it through from the Confederate official in charge of prisoner exchange. The message authorized the release of Union prisoners without a corresponding match in place, though rolls were to be maintained toward a future accounting.

Captain Frederick Speed

What had been an orderly and measured exchange arrangement became a hastily improvised operation, intended to quickly move the federal POWs to northern areas for better care. And with no real government controls over safety, and comfort issues ignored, the river merchants knew they would be able to pack the former prisoners aboard their ships without regard to peacetime load limits and reap windfall profits. It was a situation ripe for corruption.

During the third week of April, Major General Napoleon Dana ordered Captain Frederick Speed to prepare rolls of the prisoners to be paroled and shipped out of Camp Fisk. He was assisted by two former POWs in preparing the rolls. Two steamers—the *Henry Ames* and the *Olive Branch*—were docked at Vicksburg, ready to help transport soldiers home.

Captain Speed got angry over not being informed in due time about the arrival of the *Olive Branch*. He stormed into Dana's office, demanding that Captain Kerns be arrested for not supplying timely information. Plus, it made him look bad. There was no arrest, but friction arose between the man sending the soldiers from Camp Fisk and those charged with placing them aboard transports.

Captain Speed became convinced that one quartermaster officer had solicited a bribe to ensure a full load on the *Olive Branch* and personally complained to Major General Dana. The incident suggested a poisonous atmosphere among those responsible for helping return the prisoners to their homes. Dana stated the matter would be tabled for now and dealt with later, after the camp had been cleared.

Sunday, April 23, 1865

In his eight days at Camp Fisk, Epp McIntosh managed to gain five pounds on beans, sowbelly, and hardtack. Epp now weighed 85 pounds; he was still weak but improving. Epp and about 1,300 other paroled Union veterans boarded the steamboat *Henry Ames*, headed for Memphis, Tennessee, early in the morning of the April 23rd. An additional 619 soldiers plus crew followed aboard the *Olive Branch*.

Happy to be finally headed home, Epp and his comrades were excited to be aboard the *Henry Ames* when it cast off at Vicksburg.

As the *Henry Ames* steamed north, Booth and Herold touched down in Gambo Creek, Virginia. While Booth was thrilled to finally be in Virginia again, they were still in the wrong place. They were trying to get to Machodoc Creek and Mrs. Elizabeth Queensberry's house.

Fortunately for them, the large farm was only a mile southwest. Herold hiked there, while Booth, crippled and in agonizing pain, waited with the boat. Mrs. Queensberry had been expecting the fugitives, although days earlier. Upon meeting Herold, she sent for a Confederate agent named Thomas Harbin. Together, they all went back to Gambo Creek, fetched Booth, rode 8 miles to Cleydael, Virginia, and arrived at the home of King George County's wealthiest resident, Dr. Richard Stuart, around 8 p.m. Dr. Stuart gave them food and whiskey but refused to treat Booth or allow them to stay at his house. Instead, he directed Booth and Herold to the nearby cabin of a Negro couple, William Lucas and his wife. Booth was insulted and angered by Stuart's rebuff.

The *Sultana,* in need of repairs, was docked at Vicksburg early Sunday evening of the 23rd. Arriving so soon after the departure of the steamers *Henry Ames* and *Olive Branch*, the *Sultana* almost did not get any former prisoners to carry north.

Captains George Williams and Frederick Speed traveled to Camp Fisk. The two officers agreed that Speed would remain at the parole camp to supervise the loading of the men onto the trains, while Williams would ride on the first train back to Vicksburg, where he would keep count as the veterans boarded the *Sultana*. The tired but excited former prisoners, grouped according to their native states, quickly climbed onto the first train. The train cars were loaded with as many passengers as possible, packed in shoulder to shoulder, standing room only.

Brigadier General Morgan L. Smith

Speed, aware that the rolls of only 300 of the remaining soldiers had been prepared, reported to Major General Dana that no prisoners would be shipped on the *Sultana*; he said he could not complete the remaining paperwork before the steamer's scheduled departure on the following day.

Captain Mason was furious when he learned the *Olive Branch* and the *Henry Ames* had been loaded with POWs and the *Sultana* was now poised to get none of the prisoners promised him. Mason immediately stormed into Vicksburg and met with Chief Quartermaster Colonel Reuben Hatch, Brigadier General Morgan L. Smith, and Captain Frederick Speed.

Smith diffused a tense situation when he promised Captain Mason a full load of soldiers for his upriver journey. Mason got a similar promise from Colonel Reuben Hatch—a man whose military record was tarnished by evidence of corruption.

39

"Windfall Profits"

> *"For they that will be rich,*
> *fall into tentation and snares,*
> *and into many foolish and noisome lusts,*
> *which drown men in perdition and destruction."*
> —1 Timothy 6:9 GNV

The office was neat and orderly. Military decorum demanded it. Colonel Reuben Hatch took compliments and credit for the state of affairs carried out by his office with methodical precision, but he had very little to do with it. In fact, he had scant understanding of the office he had been duly sworn to occupy and execute. Hatch was surrounded by obedient underlings to carry out those menial tasks for him. He had more important things on his mind. The armies were folding up their tents and going home. Hatch decided he had to strike now while the iron was hot—never let a good crisis go to waste.

Hatch knew Captain Mason needed the money, so he suggested that if he could guarantee Mason a full load of soldiers on the *Sultana*, Mason would in return guarantee to give Hatch a kickback of $1.15 per man. Mason, influenced by greed and having rationalized the risks, readily agreed to Hatch's scheme of the offered bribe.

Hatch sat at his desk doodling in a notebook. He was calculating and figuring mathematical possibilities. He sketched out more on the paper and smiled at what he saw.

The arrangement was set. Mason, captain and part owner of the steamship, would take on far more passengers than practical, despite there being several other northbound riverboats docked in Vicksburg that could have taken their share. The going rate of the government transportation contract was $5 per enlisted man and $10 per officer, although some accounts suggest Mason received less per man; nevertheless, he took on far more men than normal to make a higher net profit.

Colonel Reuben B. Hatch

With a long history of ineptness and exploitation, Reuben Hatch managed to keep his job because of his family's many political connections. Throughout the war, he had shown gross incompetence as a quartermaster, but skill as a thief—he had on multiple occasions bilked the government out of thousands of dollars. Although brought up on court-martial charges, Hatch was able to get letters of recommendation from noted authorities including President Lincoln, Secretary of War Edwin Stanton, and General Ulysses S. Grant.

With Captain Mason demanding as many men as his boat could carry as soon as possible, Captain Speed felt pressure to expedite clearing out Camp Fisk. At first, Speed refused to place any of the soldiers on the *Sultana* until the necessary rolls were completed. However, Captain George Williams convinced Speed there was no need to prepare the rolls before the soldiers boarded the steamer. Williams suggested the rolls could be made up at the boarding platform rather than in the camp. In the interest of expediency, Speed agreed to this plan, although he most likely underestimated how difficult it would be to maintain an accurate accounting in the chaotic conditions at the wharf. According to Williams, the men could merely be checked off as they went aboard the vessel, and the rolls could be completed after the departure of the boat.

Captain Speed reported to Major General Dana all the prisoners remaining at the parole camp and in the hospital at Vicksburg would be shipped as planned on the *Sultana*. He also informed Dana the total number of prisoners would be between 1,300 and 1,400. Speed believed the number would not exceed 1,400 men. Speed and Williams both assured Dana the load was not too large for the boat, referring to loads already headed north on the *Henry Ames* and the *Olive Branch*, and that the men appeared comfortable and not overcrowded.

A nearby non-contract steamboat named the *Pauline Carroll* remained empty at the docks. Evidence suggested one of Colonel Hatch's officers, Lieutenant William Tillinghast, stood to make money if some of those coming from Camp Fisk could be diverted to the *Pauline Carroll*. Still believing the estimated 1,400 soldiers would all fit reasonably on the *Sultana*, which had a federal contract, Speed refused to consider such a transfer when Tillinghast proposed it.

The actions of the three senior officers at the scene that day were remarkable for what they failed to do. Major General Dana, Brigadier General Morgan L. Smith, and Colonel Reuben Hatch neglected to even visit the wharf to see for themselves what was going on, even though concerns had been brought to their attention and they were headquartered nearby. Afterward, none would be questioned about their failures to supervise the loading process that resulted in so many former POWs being placed aboard the *Sultana*.

Captain Speed's decision to place all the remaining prisoners on one vessel was opportunistic and unwise. Since the *Sultana* had a total legal carrying capacity of only 376 persons (passengers and crew combined), even his estimate would have been far too many for the steamer to hold. In reality, Speed had grossly underestimated. Instead of his estimate of 1,400 prisoners awaiting transport, there were more than 2,000.

At first, the system seemed to work. The steamboat *Henry Ames* departed Vicksburg on April 22nd, carrying 1,315 soldiers bound for the Benton Barracks in St. Louis. It was followed by the *Olive Branch*, which left for the same destination with 619 liberated prisoners. Therefore, it seemed not only possible but logical that other steamboats could carry large numbers. And after all, the men were eager to get home.

Reuben Hatch, for his part, was already counting on the windfall profits coming his way. With the war now over and the process drawing to a close, there would be fewer opportunities for Hatch to exploit in the future.

40

"No, they can all go on one boat."

> *"For whosoever shall keep the whole Law,*
> *and yet faileth in one point,*
> *he is guilty of all."*
> —James 2:10 GNV

> "No, they can all go on one boat."
> —Captain Frederick Speed

The city of Vicksburg sits atop a high wooded bluff with her streets sloping down steeply to the Mississippi waterfront. Known as the "Gibraltar of the Confederacy", the rugged hills that overlook the river and her docks made it a prized natural defensive position for whoever held it. By 1860, Vicksburg was a major transportation hub, catering to Mississippi steamboats and the railroad nearby. Boats departed from her docks daily for connections to all the major towns and cities dotting the riverbanks. With a population of nearly 5,000 Vicksburg was second only to Natchez.

A view from the top of the Court House to the southwest features the tall spire of St. Paul's Catholic Church. To the west, a small railroad line begins at Monroe, Louisiana and terminates at the river's docks at Vicksburg. From there, passengers and freight are brought into the city on ferry boats and sent to all points east. Vicksburg was the funnel that passengers and goods flowed through in 1865. As a result of the war, the steep banks below the famous Shirley House were Swiss-cheesed with hillside caves dug during the siege by locals for bomb-proof dwellings. Below the caves the docks were occupied with an assortment of ironclads, paddlewheels, and fishing boats. One of those paddlewheel steamers docked there that day was the *Sultana*.

The hillside caves at Vicksburg

Captain Mason knew the timing was vital. If the *Sultana* did not leave on April 24th, some other steamboat would carry the remaining troops from Vicksburg, and he would miss out on a profitable opportunity. Therefore, the leaking boiler that had slowed the steamer's return from New Orleans had to be repaired quickly.

A local boilermaker, R. G. Taylor, summoned to the docks to examine the problem, told Mason his boat needed extensive repairs. Those extensive repairs meant replacing the scorched and leaking boilers, and that would take days to complete—days Mason didn't have. Mason implored Taylor to patch the leaking boiler again, so the steamer could leave Vicksburg on schedule. Although he initially refused and left the dock, for reasons unknown Taylor returned and finally agreed to place a small metal patch over the area that was leaking steam. After completing the job, Taylor warned that the repairs were only temporary. Mason assured him the work would be completed and the boat properly repaired when the *Sultana* reached St. Louis.

The confidence that Captains Williams and Speed had in the ability of the *Sultana* to carry all the remaining prisoners was not shared by Captain William F. Kerns. Kerns had tried in vain to convince Speed to place some of the men on the *Lady Gay*, a steamboat then docked at Vicksburg that was even larger than the *Sultana*. Speed refused to divide the prisoners and continued to maintain that they all could travel on one boat. The *Lady Gay*, consequently, headed north from Vicksburg without a single paroled prisoner aboard. A few minutes after the departure of the *Lady Gay*, Captain Williams and the first trainload of former POWs, an estimated 570, pulled into Vicksburg.

This trainload of men joined 398 soldiers already aboard the *Sultana*, who probably came from the nearby military hospital. By then, the vessel already exceeded her carrying capacity by more than 600. Among this first contingent of passengers was Sergeant John Clark Ely. He noted in his diary that the "*Sultana* [was] a large but not very fine boat."

As the day wore on, two more trainloads of men arrived and boarded the *Sultana*. Captain Williams, whose responsibility was to count the soldiers as they went aboard the steamer, was not at the dock when the second group of men walked across her two four-foot-wide gangplanks. Therefore, 400 more soldiers now aboard were not added to his tally.

It became apparent there were significantly more passengers than originally assumed. Three trains arriving from the parole camp disgorged hundreds upon hundreds of former POWs, but the Vicksburg officials only made record of two of the trains. Hordes of soldiers limped or were carried onto the *Sultana*.

After this second load of soldiers boarded, Captain Kerns warned Colonel Hatch that too many prisoners were being placed on the one steamer and tried to have some men sent north on the recently arrived *Pauline Carroll*. Hatch sent a telegram to Speed at Camp Fisk asking if there were more prisoners than could go aboard the *Sultana*. Speed, still convinced that there was no more than a total of 1,400 to be shipped that day, replied: "[No,] they can all go on one boat." With that assurance, Hatch refused to divide the men between the two vessels.

Equally certain that his assessment was correct, Captain Kerns approached General Smith, pleading with him to "interpose his influence and have part of the prisoners go on the *Pauline Carroll*." Smith, like Hatch, did nothing.

The third and final train arrived at the riverfront late on the afternoon of April 24th, carrying the remaining approximately 800 paroled prisoners. As the long column of soldiers from the train snaked toward the *Sultana*, Captain Kerns once again implored Speed and Williams to reconsider and place some of the men on the *Pauline Carroll*, which was still docked beside the *Sultana*. Both officers refused Kerns' request.

Captain Williams, who had been aboard the *Sultana*, declared there was plenty of room on her decks for the men to be comfortable. A little while later, Captain Kerns watched in dismay as the *Pauline Carroll* steamed away from Vicksburg with a total of 17 passengers.

Dr. George S. Kemble, the medical director of the Department of the Mississippi, who visited the *Sultana* after the second trainload of men had boarded, shared Captain Kerns' view. Concluding the steamboat was too crowded for the comfort and safety of the sick men, Kemble sought and received permission from General Dana to remove 23 men who were confined to cots from the decks of the *Sultana*. He also redirected a column of 278 soldiers who came from the hospital. Dr. Kemble's actions would potentially save over 300 lives.

Major William Fidler of the 6th Kentucky Cavalry and the highest-ranking former Union prisoner of war at the dock, also disagreed with Captain Williams' assessment. As the last detachment of men boarded the steamer, Fidler complained to Mason that there were too many passengers aboard the ship. Fidler could have been more assertive, but probably didn't have the energy for the fight. Unfortunately, he would hobble across the gangplank and board the *Sultana* despite his objections. And he would never make it home.

Major William Fidler, 6th Kentucky Cavalry.

41

"Boots and Saddles"

"When the wicked rise up, men hide themselves:"
—Proverbs 28:28 GNV

Monday, April 24, 1865

An eyewitness watching from another boat recalled chatter among the last group of soldiers to be herded onto the *Sultana*. They complained "there was no room for them to lie down, or any place to attend to the calls of nature. There was much indignation." They also said they were not going to be "packed on the boat like damned hogs."

Captain James Cass Mason, having received many more troops than even he desired, became concerned about the stability of his boat. Although he "thought he could carry them through," Mason protested any further loading. He, too, was ignored, and the loading continued.

While the exact number of people loaded onto the *Sultana* on April 24th remains unknown, there can be no question that the steamer was grossly overcrowded. The human load was so great that it was necessary for the crew to install even more supports for the upper decks, for fear that the sagging floors might collapse. Captain Speed was shocked when informed by Captain Williams that he had counted 1,996 men boarding the boat, several hundred more than his estimate. And that tally did not include the unaccounted trainload of passengers already aboard the *Sultana*.

Booth and Herold arrived at the William Lucas farm around midnight, exhausted and angry. Booth expected more assistance and cooperation from those sympathetic to the Cause. He was now forced to run like a hunted animal—groveling and dependent on the charity of strangers. Angered by their reluctance to assist and what Booth viewed as dismissive disrespect, he threatened Lucas and his wife, forcing them from their own home at knifepoint. The Lucas' were driven to sleep in the yard. To temporarily escape the pain in his broken leg, Booth drank all of Lucas's whiskey and dozed off.

While a nationwide manhunt ensued, they slept in the cabin at Lucas's farm that night. Eager to be rid of their unwelcome guests, the next morning Lucas' son Charlie, took Booth and Herold ten miles down the road in a wagon to Port Charles.

Assistant Adjunct General A. R. Sewell sent an order to the Commander of the 16th New York Cavalry, Captain Joseph Schneider, to assign a reliable and discreet commissioned officer with 25 men to report to Colonel Lafayette C. Baker at once. Captain Schneider selected Lieutenant Edward P. Doherty to lead the group.

Doherty's regiment was assigned to the defense of Washington, D.C., for the duration of the war, where he distinguished himself as an officer.

One of Doherty's men, Private John Millington, returned from a patrol in the city. He put his horse into the stable, leaving him saddled. He fed the horse and went to the barracks to get something to eat. Before he could finish eating, "Boots and Saddles" was sounded by the bugler, and there was a rush to the stables.

Lieutenant Edward P. Doherty

Millington's regiment was ordered to fall in as they led out, disregarding company formation. Since his horse was already saddled, Millington slipped on his bridle, led him out of the stable, and mounted. He was next on the left of the sergeant, Boston Corbett. The company was ordered to count off in fours.

They rode in a column west on Pennsylvania Avenue and north on 14th Street, about opposite the old Willard Hotel. They halted and dismounted in front of the office of Colonel Lafayette C. Baker, chief of government detectives and scouts in the War Department.

42

"JWB"

> *"Can any hide himself in secret places,*
> *that I shall not see him, saith the Lord?*
> *Do not I fill heaven and earth, saith the Lord?"*
> —Jeremiah 23:24 GNV

He stared at the ceiling again, looking at the same spot where the paint had cracked, and wondered what day it was. He was unable to turn his head; the brace restricted his view. William Seward's new injuries didn't really add to his discomfort. The dull ache in his jaw held his attention for the moment, and that was a good thing.

The secretary didn't want to think about the truth—the overwhelming reality that someone had wanted him dead and had plotted to accomplish it. He inventoried in his mind every disagreement and enemy he could recall, personal or political, and kept coming up empty. And it was that emptiness that fueled his depression.

It seemed an unlikely miracle, but Seward would recover. He was not told of President Lincoln's death. He deduced from clues seen through his bedroom window and what he knew in his heart. After the attack, Seward wondered why his friend had not dropped by to visit as he knew he would. Then he saw the flag at half-mast.

Without being told, Seward remarked to his nurse, "The president is dead. If he was alive, he would have been the first to call on me, but he has not been here, nor has he sent to know how I am, and there's a flag at half-mast." He could not appreciate the dark desperate intensity in the hearts of others.

But the thing that hurt him most, the mental anguish burning him to the core, was the *knowing*. Knowing that the ones he loved the most were savagely attacked because of him. He did not think his wife Frances would ever get over the shock, and life as they knew it would never be the same. Frances Seward would be dead in two months.

The drapes had been opened, so he knew it was morning. Dust mites twinkled and danced in the angled sunbeam streaming through his bedroom window. Peach, cherry, and apple trees were in bloom in Washington, pink and white signifying new birth—new growth. Spring was in the air. Although a crispness accentuated the mornings, the days were warming up nicely into the low sixties. The April showers had let up, and the sky was a beautiful azure with puffy clouds. Birds were chirping, busily building their nests for the next generation.

Surrounded by trees in bloom along Pennsylvania Avenue, Lieutenant Doherty sat on a bench across from the White House conversing with another officer. The arrival of a messenger interrupted the conversation. The messenger carried orders directing Doherty to report directly to an agent of the War Department—Union spy and detective, Colonel Lafayette C. Baker. As ordered, Doherty dutifully reported in.

Luther Baker. Lafayette Baker, and Everton Conger

Based on a reliable tip, Doherty was given orders to lead a squad of Union cavalry into Virginia to search for the assassin. His detachment included Detective Luther Baker (double cousin of Lafayette C. Baker), Lieutenant Colonel Everton Conger, Sergeant Boston Corbett, John Millington, and about two dozen soldiers from the 16th New York Cavalry. Luther Baker and Everton Conger were detectives and civilians at the time, which left Lieutenant Doherty as the de facto military leader of the group.

Moments later, Doherty and the two detectives exited the building, mounted up, and Doherty gave the order to march. They rode to the wharf of the Navy Yard on the east branch of the Potomac (the Anacostia River), where they boarded the propeller-driven steamer, the *John S. Ide,* and started down the Potomac River.

En route, Doherty showed everyone in the company a photograph of John Wilkes Booth and stated that Booth had reportedly crossed the Potomac near Port Tobacco. The detachment arrived at Belle Plain, Virginia, near Aquia Creek, which was right at the border of King George and Stafford Counties. They went ashore about 10 o'clock that night. It had taken Booth and Herold nine days to reach King George County. The troops had made it there from D.C. in only four hours.

Doherty and his detachment proceeded in the direction of Fredericksburg, and after they advanced about three miles, they turned southwest and struck the Rappahannock River about 12 miles above Port Conway. There they met two fishermen who informed them of several surgeons living in the vicinity. They visited the surgeons and searched their premises, making such inquiries and examinations as Doherty thought necessary.

This being accomplished and no trace found of the assassin or his accomplice, Conger requested Doherty to furnish him with four men and a corporal, which he did. Conger's unit moved down the Rappahannock River, following its course. Doherty moved out with the remainder of his command and made a detour of some 15 miles by the way of King George Court House, forming a junction with Conger's unit at Conway's Ferry at 2 p.m.

William Storke Jett— "Willie", as he was known—spent less than one year in Confederate service. He joined the 9th Virginia Cavalry on June 16th, 1864, at the age of 17. Just 13 days later, he received a severe wound when he was shot in the abdomen during the First Battle of Reams Station. The wound so incapacitated Willie that he never returned to active duty with the regiment.

By his own account, once he recovered from his wound, he served the remainder of the war as a commissary agent in Caroline County, Virginia. When he learned of the surrender of Robert E. Lee and the Army of Northern Virginia, Willie made his way to meet up with his brother, Lucius, who was a private in Mosby's 43rd Battalion Virginia Cavalry.

Jett traveled to Loudoun County, where he learned that Mosby's command had already disbanded. At that point, Willie was determined to return home to Westmoreland County, believing the war was over. First however, he would pay a visit to friends in Caroline County, especially his girlfriend, Izora Gouldman, whom he had met and fallen in love with during his convalescence.

Willie Jett's name would most certainly have been forgotten in history if not for a chance encounter on his trip home. On the afternoon of April 24th, Willie, in the company of two other former Confederates, waited for the ferry along the Rappahannock River at Port Conway. There, they made the acquaintance of a couple of men also waiting for the ferry—the most wanted men in the country—John Wilkes Booth and David Herold.

As the two groups waited together, they fell into conversation, and Herold attempted to curry favor and assistance with Willie and his associates. Herold offered them a drink. They declined.

Herold claimed that he and Booth were brothers and Confederate soldiers under General Ambrose P. Hill's command, using the aliases David E. and James William Boyd. While Herold had a conversation with Willie and his two associates, Mortimer B. Ruggles and Absalom R. Bainbridge, Booth observed them from a distance—pointing and gesturing in his direction. Herold told the trio that the crippled man with him was injured in the war effort during a prison escape. Convinced, and unrightly so, that Herold had divulged their true identities, Booth hobbled over to the group on his crude crutch in evident pain to join the conversation.

"I suppose you have been told who I am?" Booth asked.

Thinking he meant Herold had told them they were Confederate soldiers, escapees from prison, Ruggles answered in the affirmative.

Instantly, Booth dropped his weight upon his crutch, drew his revolver, and said sternly, "Yes, I am John Wilkes Booth, the slayer of Abraham Lincoln, and I am worth just $175,000 to the man who captures me."

Upon learning this, Jett, Ruggles, and Bainbridge were astonished. They, however, admired Booth's coolness of manner, yet could tell he was in great pain, his face pinched with much suffering. He had shaved off his trademark mustache. He had a ten-day growth of beard. Booth and Herold both appeared to be the worse for their exposure and hardships of the past few days.

Booth wore a black soft hat, dark clothes, and one cavalry boot—the one on his wounded left leg having been cut off and replaced by a shoe. His weapons were a carbine, two revolvers, and a knife, the blade of the latter bearing the stain of blood, for with it he had wounded Major Rathbone.

Ruggles noticed that Booth's wounded leg was greatly swollen, inflamed, and dark, as from bruised blood. It seemed to have been wretchedly dressed, the splints were just pasteboard, rudely tied around it. That he suffered intense pain all the time there was no doubt, though he tried to conceal his agony, both physical and mental. From the visual examination made of his broken leg and aided by some experience he'd had with wounds, Ruggles felt confident that amputation would have been necessary to save Booth's life, perhaps even that would not have prevented a speedy death.

While Booth held the revolver on them, the trio confided that news reports were that Lincoln's assassin had already been captured in Washington and, even though they did not necessarily sanction his actions, they were not men who would take blood money and would still honor the promise made to Herold in getting them safely across the river. After their conversation, Booth relaxed and put his weapon away.

The wind lulled after they had waited a long time, and the ferryman came over for them. Captain Ruggles helped Booth mount his horse and carried his crutch. The two parties were poled across the river on a scow from Port Conway to the village of Port Royal, a distance of about 300 yards. The ferryman, Jim Thornton, eyed the group very closely with little being said. Booth sat squarely on Ruggles's horse, looking expectantly toward the opposite shore, and when the boat finally struck the wharf, he lost no time in landing. Despite his constant pain, all could see that his spirits were improving, and Booth laughed heartily when they all surrounded him in a group.

Booth exclaimed, "I'm safe in glorious old Virginia, thank God!"

Once across the river, Herold asked Willie to help find a place for Booth and himself to stay and rest. The group rode a couple of blocks south from the ferry landing to the home of attorney Randolph Peyton, an acquaintance of Willie's. Mr. Peyton was not home, but his two sisters, Sarah Jane and Lucy were, and they let Booth into the house, under the impression that the assassin was a wounded Confederate soldier.

William Storke "Willie" Jett

Sarah Jane had second thoughts, however, on allowing Booth and Herold to stay the night in the house with two unmarried women.

She thought it would be "inappropriate", so she asked Willie Jett to take them away. Willie crossed the street to seek shelter at the home of George Washington Catlett. The Catletts were not at home either, so Sarah Jane suggested they might find accommodations down the road at tobacco farmer Richard H. Garrett's place, a 500-acre farm known as *Locust Hill*.

"Now, boys," said Jett, "I propose to take our friend Booth up to Garrett's house. I think they'll give him shelter there and treat him kindly."

"Jett understands this country," said Captain Ruggles, "and I think that it will be well to act as he directs."

"I'm in your hands," said Booth. "Do with me, boys, as you think best."

"I think our plan is to escort Mr. Booth up to Garrett's . . . and trust to their hospitality to see him kindly cared for until such time as he sees fit to seek other quarters," Jett said.

With the decision made, the group mounted their horses and rode toward Garrett's farm, Booth on Ruggles's horse. Jett rode his own horse with Herold behind. Ruggles rode behind Bainbridge. They went two miles to Garrett's farm, between Port Royal and Bowling Green. During the ride, Booth told Jett he would not be taken alive.

He declared, "If they don't kill me, I'll kill myself."

At the gate leading to the Garrett Farm, Herold got down from behind Jett and waited there, while Booth, Ruggles, Bainbridge, and Jett rode on to the farmhouse.

Captain Willie Jett made the introductions. He said to Garrett, "Here is a wounded Confederate soldier that we want you to take care of for a day or so—will you do it?"

"Yes, I certainly will," replied Richard Garrett.

News of the president's assassination had spread, but it had not yet reached the rural community of Port Royal. For the moment, the Garretts were unaware of Lincoln's assassination.

Booth was helped to dismount the horse. In an attempt to divert suspicions regarding the India ink tattoo "JWB" on his left hand, Booth was introduced as James W. Boyd, a Confederate soldier who had been wounded in the Battle of Petersburg and was returning home.

Richard H. Garrett

With Booth delivered to the Garrett farm, the rest of the group returned to the gate and retrieved David Herold. They rode on to the home of Bainbridge's friend, Joseph Clark. Coincidently, Herold had known Clark for quite some time as well and stayed there for the night. Jett and Ruggles rode on three more miles beyond to a hotel owned by the father of Jett's current girlfriend, Izora Gouldman—the Star Hotel in Bowling Green.

The following morning, Herold and Bainbridge arrived at the hotel and picked up Ruggles. The trio rode back to Garrett's farm, where Herold reunited with Booth.

Meanwhile, when news reached the former POWs at Camp Fisk that the war was officially over, they knew that at long last they were out of harm's way and would shortly be released. Sergeant John Clark Ely, a former prisoner at Andersonville, was heading home. Confederate captors had finally released Ely and the other half-starved, sickly survivors of his company for prisoner exchange. Ely later wrote of their exodus out of Andersonville on the first leg of the long way home:

Sgt. John Clark Ely

"Coming like cattle across an open field were scores of men who were nothing but skin and bones; some hobbling along as best they could, and others being helped by stronger comrades. Every gaunt face with its staring eyes told the story of the suffering and deprivation they had gone through, and protruding bones showed through their scanty tattered garments. One might have thought that the grave and sea had given up their dead."

Ely boarded the first train out of Camp Fisk, happy to be headed to the loading dock to board the *Sultana*. He would never make it home.

43

"...the greatest trip ever made on the western waters."

"But he that obeyeth me, shall dwell safely, and be quiet from fear of evil."
—Proverbs 1:33 GNV

Monday, April 24, 1865

Though the rolls were incomplete and the exact number of people aboard was unknown, the *Sultana* carried as many as 2,100 soldiers, approximately 100 civilian passengers, and 85 crewmen for a possible total of more than 2,300 people—more than six times the *Sultana's* legal limit.

William J. Gambrel, first clerk and part-owner of the vessel, told one soldier that "if we arrived safe at Cairo it would be the greatest trip ever made on the western waters," as there were more people aboard than were ever carried on one boat on the Mississippi River.

The *Sultana* was the last to leave the docks at Vicksburg since the loading of the boat took considerable time. In addition to the number of passengers already loaded, two companies of armed soldiers came aboard. Altogether, there were now possibly close to 2,400 souls aboard. They packed the steamer from top to bottom hull, cabins, Texas deck, and even on top of the pilothouse.

People were packed into every available space, including on the open decks. Ohio Sergeant William Fies muttered they were loaded "more like so many cattle than men," while Corporal Erastus Winters likened their experience to "something like a flock of sheep or a drove of hogs." Such was the extra weight that the hurricane deck began to sag and had to be braced with temporary stanchions.

In the *Sultana's* engine room, the crew threw lumps of coal the size of a man's head onto the top of the plates under the boilers, heating the water inside the steamer's four giant tubular boilers. As the coal turned to ash, the crew banged the shaker plates to flake off the ash and allow the coal to burn more hotly.

At 9 p.m., the *Sultana* slowly backed away from the wharf at Vicksburg and headed north on the flood-swollen Mississippi River. The enormous weight of the passengers and cargo on the decks of the steamer worried her crew. Gambrel warned Major Fidler that any sudden movement by the passengers could cause the decks to collapse. He also expressed concern that too many men crowding to one side of the deck could result in the boat capsizing.

Tuesday, April 25, 1865

Around daybreak, Doherty and his 16th New York Cavalry detachment arrived at the home of Dr. Horace Ashton, the last doctor on their list. Like the other doctors in the area, Dr. Ashton had neither seen nor heard anything regarding a man with a broken leg.

When they arrived at the Rappahannock River, the detachment split into two groups, each tracing a different route south to Port Conway on the Rappahannock. Doherty and most of the detail took the main road to Port Conway, passing through Office Hall. Unbeknownst to Doherty's men, they were now on the trail of Booth and Herold, as the pair had also passed through Office Hall on their way between Cleydael and Port Conway, just 24 hours before.

Luther Baker, Everton Conger, and four troopers took a less traveled route following the east bank of the Rappahannock, making sure that either route south would be covered. Both groups patrolled their routes and eventually met up again in Port Conway around lunchtime.

Up until this time, Doherty and the men in his detail had found no physical trace of Booth or his accomplice, Herold. Doherty's men had not eaten since leaving Washington, and the horses needed feeding and watering too. They were lucky enough to find hospitality at the home of a wealthy planter named Carolinus Turner. Orders were given to "fall out and rustle some rations." They stopped, fed the horses and themselves, and discussed their next move.

Turner's large and beautiful home was called *Belle Grove* and had the distinction of being the site of President James Madison's birthplace. About half of the troopers were served lunch at *Belle Grove*, with the rest being fed elsewhere. After lunch, Conger, exhausted and suffering from the long and arduous ride, fell asleep in the hall of the *Belle Grove* mansion. Doherty's group pressed on, traversing the road following the Rappahannock River toward Port Conway.

While Conger slept, Luther Baker and some of the detachment accompanied Doherty to the ferry at Port Conway, arriving about 2 p.m. and started interviewing the inhabitants. It was here, in little Port Conway on the Rappahannock River, that the 16th New York Cavalry finally got their first real lead on Booth's whereabouts.

Doherty's detachment met a group of Negro men who had been fishing. The fishermen stated that a closed hack had passed a few days before with two men in it and one of them had been into Mr. Rollins's house. The fishermen's animated testimony continued, adding that a Confederate captain was in charge, who warned them not to come near. Doherty showed the fishermen a photograph of Booth. They nodded in agreement that one of the men in the wagon resembled the man in the photograph. Doherty determined they would push across on the ferry.

Baker and Doherty proceeded to the house of Mr. Rollins, the owner of the ferry, and after exhibiting the photographs, concluded they were on Booth's track. William Rollins stated he had seen Booth, Herold, and three Confederate soldiers as they waited to cross the Rappahannock the day before. Mrs. Rollins identified the three soldiers as Captain Willie Jett and Lieutenants Mortimer Ruggles and Absalom Bainbridge. Even more helpful, Rollins's wife not only recognized the Confederate soldiers who ended up crossing the ferry with Booth and Herold but also knew one of them, Willie Jett, was courting Izora Gouldman, whose father owned the Star Hotel in Bowling Green.

Mr. Rollins informed Doherty the two men were brought to his house from Mathias Point by a Negro, to whom they had paid $15, and wanted to engage him to take them to Orange Court House. Rollins refused to go that far, but the two paid him to take them to Bowling Green for $10.

Rollins stated these two men showed great anxiety to get across the river and wanted to use his small boat and they would pay him extra. Rollins also stated that the man they had identified as David Herold had told him he and Booth were brothers and Booth had been wounded at Petersburg. Rollins informed the two men they could not use his small boat because he was using it to put out his fishing net.

It was at about this time, Rollins said, three Confederate soldiers came up and shook hands with one of them. Herold came to the house and apologized for not taking the horse and wagon he had inquired about, and said he had met an old schoolmate, and they were going to ride double together.

With this information in hand, Doherty dispatched three men in a small boat to bring over a scow, which was on the other side of the Rappahannock River. He also dispatched one of his men to ride back and awaken Conger and inform him they had a track of the assassins and to come down to the ferry immediately. The whole posse began the task of crossing the river. William Rollins offered his services as a guide for the posse.

When Conger returned with four comrades, they saw some of the detachment crossing the river in a scow about 20 feet long and 3 feet wide. It took a while, as this small ferryboat could only hold 10 men with horses per trip. By the time the entire group had made it across the river, it was close to 6 pm and the detachment set about galloping at full speed toward Bowling Green. They had traveled three miles and were approaching Garrett's farm when they met a man on horseback, who turned and fled. Some of the unit pursued, but the man darted into the forest of young pines and as it was nearly dusk, he escaped.

On the road, three miles from Port Royal, Doherty met a Negro on horseback. Wishing to not lose time, Doherty rode ahead of the column and directed the man to turn back and ride beside him. Doherty learned from him the party of the three men in question had all returned except Captain Willie Jett. Proceeding along they arrived at a house 7 miles from Bowling Green. Here, Doherty learned some of John Mosby's men had been along the day before and had taken three horses from three Union soldiers.

Conger and Baker entered the house and were informed the party who had passed there the preceding day had all returned except Captain Jett, confirming the previous report. The house of Mrs. Clark some four miles distant was spoken of as a place where some of the party might be. Doherty decided, however, to push on to Bowling Green and secure the aforementioned Captain Willie Jett. The detachment spurred their mounts into a full gallop, as they knew they were closing in on the assassin.

Earlier in the day, Richard Garrett's eldest son John paid a visit to Port Royal, where he learned President Lincoln was dead. At the dinner table that evening, John Garrett shared the tragic news the president had been assassinated. The news seemed to shock everyone at the table except the Garrett's nonchalant guest, James W. Boyd.

44

"missed the boat"

"For nothing is secret, that shall not be evident: neither anything hid, that shall not be known, and come to light."
—Luke 8:17 GNV

Tuesday evening, April 25, 1865

After supper, the dishes were collected and washed. The men stepped outside for a smoke and some fresh air. It was still light. The sun rested just above the treetops in the western sky. In the hours before the standoff, David Herold and Richard Garrett's son, John, stood in Garrett's front yard. They watched as a company of cavalrymen thundered past on their way to Bowling Green to follow a hot lead on the whereabouts of the assassin and accomplice, not knowing they had just ridden right past them.

The first night, Richard Garrett was hospitable toward Booth—gave him a meal at his table and a bed in his house. But Richard's sons, John and William Garrett became suspicious of their two guests. John Garrett, convinced the Boyd brothers were plotting to steal their horses during the night while the family slept, wanted them gone and decided to inform them they were no longer allowed to sleep in the house. The Garrett brothers were also keenly aware they must tread lightly—their guests were armed and anxious. There were women and children in the house to consider.

The Garretts did not yet know Booth and Herold's true identities. The two fugitives were still using the aliases John W. and David E. Boyd. John Garrett sensed that the Boyds were trouble. He had no idea of the magnitude.

As the sun set on the Garrett farm, cantaloupe and fushcia streaked the evening sky. Booth signaled to Herold it was time to go inside and retire for the evening. Herold helped Booth to his feet and handed him his crutch. John Garrett stood blocking his path to the front door of the house.

John Garrett asked, "Where do you think you're sleeping?"

"Why, in the house, of course," Booth replied.

"No, gentlemen, you can't sleep in my house."

Booth was incensed. He had slept on the cold, damp ground enough already, and the warm, cozy bed upstairs where he slept last night was much more to his liking. He considered threatening the Garretts as he had done at the Lucas cabin. *Teach these boys some damned manners...*

"We'll sleep under the house then," Herold interjected, eager to keep the peace.

"Impossible, the dogs sleep under there and would bite you. Maybe even attack you in your sleep," John Garrett replied.

Herold tried again to diffuse the obvious tension, "Well, what's in the barn then?"

"Hay and fodder," answered Garrett.

"We'll sleep there then," said Herold.

John Garrett reluctantly agreed to allow the fugitives to sleep in the tobacco barn. Herold humbly accepted the accommodation. Booth took it as an insult and considered the weight of the gun belt around his waist. He decided tonight would be their last night at the Garrett farm. They were better rested and fed. They would leave in the morning.

John and William Garrett walked the pair to the barn and opened the door. After Booth and Herold entered, the Garrett brothers closed the door behind them. John Garrett whispered to his brother, "We had better lock those men up." John Garrett listened at the barn wall for conversations inside, while William Garrett, quiet as a mouse, turned the key in the iron padlock—snicking the locking mechanism closed without alerting the barn's occupants.

Booth and Herold were now trapped. The Garrett brothers decided to sleep in the nearby corncrib tonight so they could keep an eye on their two guests.

The detachment arrived in Bowling Green at 11 o'clock that night. Among those hunting Booth was a former hatter and current soldier of questionable mental stability, Boston Corbett.

Arriving within half a mile of the town of Bowling Green, 10 men were ordered to dismount and quietly accompany Luther Baker into town. In Bowling Green, the detachment found out Jett was sleeping in the Star Hotel. Conger, Rollins, and Doherty rode ahead and positioned themselves around the hotel. The dismounted men arrived shortly afterward and by the time they had the hotel and outhouses surrounded it was nearly midnight.

The officers knocked at each door without receiving a reply. Finally at the hotel, Mrs. Gouldman opened the front door. Doherty entered and inventoried the inhabitants and discovered they were all female.

He asked, "Where are the men in the hotel?"

"My son is upstairs," she replied.

"Show me."

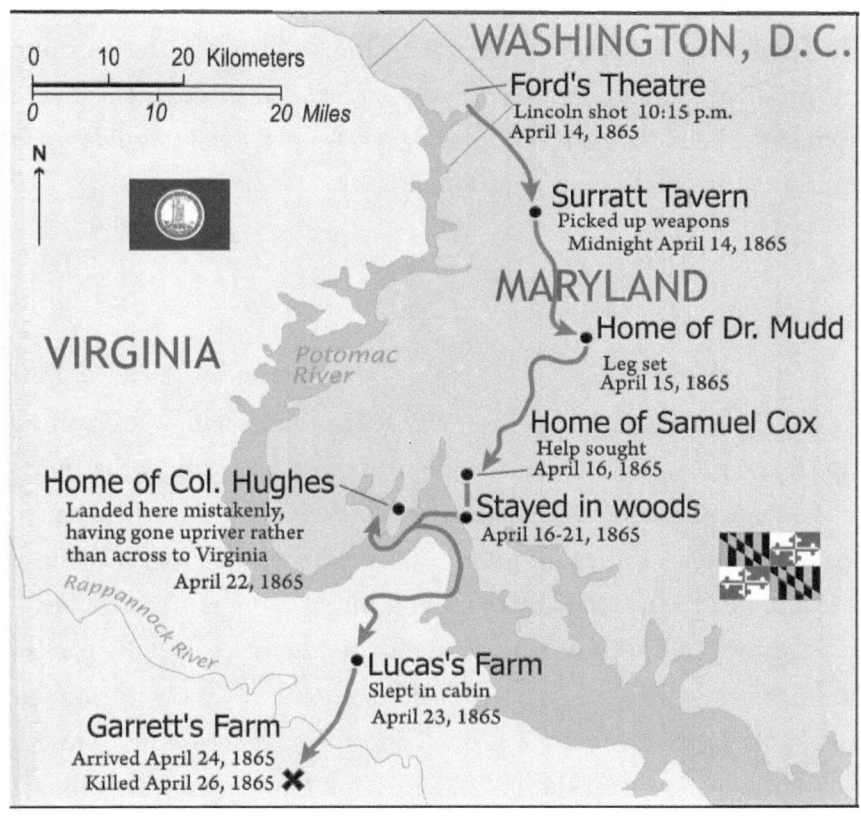

Booth's escape route

Mrs. Gouldman reluctantly showed them upstairs, finding Willie Jett in one bed and her son in another. Jett was taken downstairs and informed of the business at hand. Doherty told him if he did not divulge where the men they sought were, he would suffer—there would be no negotiations. Jett requested that two of the party withdraw, leaving him with one, and he would then make a full statement of what he knew of the assassin's whereabouts. This request was granted. Baker and Doherty had scarcely left the room when Jett told Conger he would show them the place where Booth and Herold were hiding.

The troops, with Willie Jett now in tow, galloped 12 miles back to the farmhouse of Richard Garrett, arriving at 2 a.m. on the morning of April 26th. Unknown to Doherty, Jett had made a covert deal with someone else in the posse—Luther Baker. If Jett agreed to guide them to Booth, he would not be held in custody.

Wednesday, April 26, 1865

The *Sultana* got clear of the Vicksburg wharf and went puffing upstream, breasting a current made stronger than usual by the river's flood stage. Captain Mason was a bit worried. He cautioned the men not to crowd to one side of the boat when a landing was made because there were so many of them it might cause serious trouble.

Save for the discomforts of such a large number of people packed into so little space, the first leg of the *Sultana*'s voyage was trouble-free. The early spring air was cool, and the soldiers—many without any cover—endured a slight, chilling rain. Those in the steamboat's rear section had to jockey for space with the regular cargo of nearly 100 mules and horses. Stored in the hold of the *Sultana* were 300,000 pounds of sugar and 90 cases of wine.

The *Sultana* docked at Helena, Arkansas

The paddlewheel steamed upriver against the fierce current, pausing at Helena, Arkansas. The stone-faced first clerk and part owner of the ship, William J. Gambrel, warned that if the passengers collectively got too close to one side of the ship, it could capsize. That horrifying scenario almost played out when the *Sultana* docked at Helena.

Word quickly spread among the passengers that a photographer had set up his camera on the riverbank. The excited soldiers hoping to be caught on film, quickly moved to the port side of the boat, causing the *Sultana* to list dangerously. The resulting famous photograph, where T. W. Bankes snapped his now iconic image of the doomed and overcrowded boat, was the last picture taken of the steamer—as well as the passengers aboard.

The *Sultana* moved on toward Memphis. The steamship *Henry Ames*, on its way to Cairo, also loaded with former POWs, arrived and docked at Memphis ahead of the *Sultana*. One of the passengers on the *Henry Ames*, Epp McIntosh, decided to go into the city to have a meal at the military commissary, look around, and buy some things—personal items to make his ride home more enjoyable. After being a captive in Andersonville for months, Epp was pleased to finally be free—a free man allowed to go and come as he wished. This decision to go get a meal and shop in the city of Memphis would become a decision that would forever change his life.

As the *Sultana* continued upriver nearing Memphis, Sergeant John Clark Ely wrote his diary post for that day—his last entry: *"Very fine day, still upward we go."*

The steamship arrived in Memphis that evening at 6:30 p.m. Sugar was unloaded from the bottom hull with assistance from the newly released POWs, allowing them to make a little extra money. The removal of the load from the hull made the boat even more top-heavy.

That evening in Memphis, more men crowded onto the northbound vessel. The first ones to reach the boat could hear banging noises from below as repairs were being completed on her cracked boiler. A Buckeye private from Ohio named William Boor convinced his friends to find a spot away from the power plant, warning them if it did explode, they would "go higher than a kite."

Epp's timing was off a bit. It could have been that he couldn't walk very far and certainly not very fast. He thought there would be ample time to visit the city of Memphis, get a hot meal, and be back in time before the boat's departure. He literally "missed the boat" when the *Henry Ames* sailed without him. A weak and befuddled McIntosh stood on the Memphis wharf and pondered his next move.

He would have to find another ride to Benton Barracks. Shouldn't be a problem, he thought. *There are other boats here that are likely headed* to Cairo. With the massive crowds cramming on the boats, one more passenger shouldn't be noticed or be a problem.

While the *Sultana* was at the Memphis docks, several officers from a nearby US gunboat paid a courtesy visit. "Some of the men [on board the *Sultana*]," noted one of them, "were too weak to walk without being supported by more fortunate comrades. Others were compelled by sheer weakness to lie on cots or blankets spread upon the decks."

When Epp boarded the *Sultana*, he soon learned it was difficult to find a space unoccupied. There was hardly a spot on any of the decks for a foot to trod without stepping on a body. Epp did find a spot however and settled in on the hurricane deck for the ride to Cairo. He was eager to catch up with his friends aboard the *Henry Ames*.

After the discharge of the sugar, cases of wine, and a few paying customers (including an opera troupe), a few men took the opportunity to briefly stroll the streets of the riverfront city prior to departure. Some would observe that the weight of the sugar had provided a ballast to counterbalance the immense weight of the overcrowded decks above.

Leaving Memphis and following a short coaling stop in nearby Hopefield, Arkansas, where the boat took on a thousand bushels of coal, the *Sultana* continued northward into the night.

45

"Trapped"

> *"Then they cry because of the violence of the wicked,*
> *but he answereth not."*
> —Job 35:12 GNV

Wednesday, April 26, 1865 – 2 a.m.

In the dull darkness, the only sounds were crickets and the occasional howl of a canine in the distance. It was a cool night with the temperatures dropping down into the lower 50's. All was quiet on the Garrett farm. Like most working farms, bedtime was around when it got dark, and the time to get up was just before sunrise. Richard Garrett and the rest of his family had gone to bed hours ago.

Booth and Herold were fast asleep in the tobacco barn. Herold had fallen asleep first. The pain in Booth's leg kept him awake a little longer, but both were exhausted from the journey. Booth had consumed whiskey until the pain subsided enough for him to finally get some rest. Faint noise was approaching, probably a mile distant.

The barking dogs and the clanking, rumbling sound finally woke Booth. Recognizing the unique music of cavalry on the move, the assassin knew he had only a minute or two to react. He woke Herold. They snatched up their weapons. "We went right up to the barn door and tried to get out," Herold would recall, "but found it was locked." Booth and Herold then went to the back of the barn where they attempted to kick out a board or two to make their escape. Their efforts proved unsuccessful.

When the search party reached the gate to the Garrett farm, Willie Jett was assigned a couple of guards and instructed to stay there. Lieutenant Edward Doherty and his squad scanned the area and dismounted. He ordered his command to surround the house, and as a precautionary measure, instructed six of his

The Garrett farmhouse – Port Royal, Virginia

men to cover the rear of the barns and outbuildings. They walked their horses up the dirt driveway to the two-story home of Richard Garrett. Private John Millington and Sergeant Boston Corbett were with the party sent to surround the barns. Doherty and Conger quietly and confidently walked their horses to the front of the farmhouse.

The lieutenant knocked loudly at the farmhouse front door, rousting the dogs. Richard Garrett walked downstairs in his nightclothes and answered the door, stepping out onto the front porch. Doherty immediately seized him and asked him where the men were—the ones who had fled to the woods when the cavalry passed the previous afternoon.

Garrett nervously replied, "I know nothing about any men being here."

Conger barked first, "Where are the two men who stopped here at your house?"

Startled, Richard Garrett replied, "They have gone."

"Gone where?" Conger demanded.

"Gone to the woods," said Garrett.

"What!" Luther Baker interrupted. "A lame man gone into the woods?"

"Well, he had crutches," Garrett pointed out.

"Will you show me where they are?" Baker continued.

"I will," Garrett promised, "but I want my pants and boots."

Garrett's interrogators refused to let him back into the house to dress, so his family passed his clothes to him through the door. Some of the soldiers entered the house and searched it. Conger told one of his men, "Bring in a lariat rope here, and I will put that man up to the top of one of those locust trees."

A soldier went to get the rope. While Richard Garrett legged his pants, Conger continued his interrogation. John Garrett emerged from the corn house, walked up to the nearest cavalryman, and asked whom they were pursuing.

"That I cannot tell you," the trooper answered, and told another soldier to take John to the house.

Soon, one of the soldiers sang out, "O Lieutenant! I have a man here I found in the corncrib!"

When they got near the house, John Garrett saw Doherty, Conger, and Baker on the front porch manhandling his father. Spotting John Garrett, Conger bellowed to his soldier escort,

"Where did you get this man from?"

"Found him in the corncrib," answered the soldier.

John Garrett asked, "What do you men want?"

Doherty said, "We want the two men who are stopping here and at once."

"That is what I want to know," added an irritated Conger. "Where are they?"

John Garrett advised his father to tell the men what they wanted to know. A terrified Richard Garrett stuttered nervously while being roughed up.

"Don't hurt the old man. He is scared. I will tell you where the men are you want to find," John Garrett offered.

Before John had time to answer, Doherty seized Richard Garrett by the collar, pushed him down the steps, then put a revolver to his head and ordered him to tell where the assassins were. Conger not only held a gun to Richard Garrett's head during the raid, but he threatened to hang Garrett if he didn't cooperate.

"In the barn!" John Garrett cried out.

"Not good enough!" warned Conger. "Which of the three barns?"

"In the tobacco barn," Garrett quickly replied.

Leaving a few men around the house, the posse ran toward the barn. Booth and Herold heard the soldiers rush and surround the barn. In the darkness, Booth and Herold were sitting up, quietly listening, and holding their weapons. Booth reached out and laid a hand on Herold to calm him to stay silent.

"Don't make any noise," Booth whispered. "Maybe they will go off thinking we are not here."

Conger heard someone moving around inside, rustling the hay. Doherty kicked on the door several times without receiving a reply. The ruckus stirred up the hounds again, barking and howling in the darkness. Baker summoned the fugitives to surrender. Meanwhile, William Garrett emerged from the cover of the corn house and joined his brother near the tobacco barn.

The barn door had been secured with a padlock, and William carried the key. He pulled it from his pocket and surrendered it to Baker. Baker unlocked the padlock and again told the inmates of the building to surrender. John Garrett was ordered to get a candle, which he immediately did and returned to the barn.

Luther Baker summoned John Garrett to his side and pointed to the barn door. "You must go into the barn and get the arms from those men."

Garrett objected violently to the suicidal plan.

Baker went on, "They know you, and you can go in."

Baker stepped forward and shouted to Booth, "We are going to send this man, on whose premises you are, in to get your arms, and you must come out and deliver yourselves up!"

Booth said nothing.

Baker grabbed John Garrett and half-guided, half-pushed him through the barn door and closed it behind him. Garrett was now standing alone and unarmed in the dark, holding a candle, at the mercy of the cornered pair.

Garrett nervously told them, "The barn is surrounded, resistance is useless, and you'd better come out and deliver yourselves up."

Herold told Booth, "I'm willing to surrender." Booth accused Herold of being yellow and hissed, "You coward! You have betrayed me! Get away from me before I kill you!"

After some delay, Booth finally addressed his pursuers. "For whom do you take me?"

Tired, yet boosted on adrenaline, the troopers held weapons at the ready.

Then a voice from inside the barn bellowed three questions:

"Who are you? What do you want? Whom do you want?"

It was the voice of Booth. The assassin stepped to the front of the tobacco barn and peered through a space between two boards, mistaking his counterpart for an Army captain he knew.

"It doesn't make any difference who we are," Doherty answered, "But we know who you are. You had better come out at once."

"We want you," Baker added, "and we know who you are."

"Give up your arms and come out!"

Booth stalled. "Let us have a little time to consider it."

Surprisingly, Luther Baker agreed. "Very well."

Sergeant Boston Corbett asked for permission to enter the barn alone. Doherty refused Corbett's request. Ten or fifteen minutes elapsed. The cavalrymen maintained a keen vigil on all four sides of the barn walls to ensure their prey did not slip out unnoticed.

Doherty finally said, "It doesn't make any difference. Come out."

Booth said, "I am a cripple and alone."

Doherty answered, "I know who is with you, and you had better surrender."

Booth replied, "I may be taken by my friends, but not by my foes."

"If you don't come out, I'll burn the building."

Doherty directed a corporal to pile up some hay in a crack in the wall of the barn to set the building on fire. As the corporal was picking up the hay and brush, Booth threatened,

"If you come back here, I will put a bullet through you."

Doherty motioned to the corporal to desist, deciding to wait for daylight and enter the barn and overpower the assassins. Booth said in a drawling voice, "Oh Captain! There is a man here who wants to surrender awful bad."

"You had better follow his example and come out."

"No, I have not made up my mind; but draw your men up fifty paces off and give me a chance for my life."

Doherty replied that he had not come to fight, that he had fifty men and could take him.

Booth, vowing not to be taken alive exclaimed, "Well, my brave boys, prepare me a stretcher, and place another stain on our glorious banner!"

Booth defiantly remained inside, ignoring the threat to burn the barn if he didn't surrender. At this moment David Herold reached the door. Doherty instructed him to hand out his arms.

David Herold

"I have none," Herold pleaded. Doherty didn't believe him. "Hand out your arms, and you can come out."

"I have no arms," Herold whimpered. "Let me out."

Doherty stated that he knew exactly what weapons he had.

Booth replied, "I own all the arms and may have to use them on you, gentlemen."

Doherty said to Herold, "Let me see your hands."

Herold put his hands through the partly opened barn door and was grabbed by the wrists. He proclaimed his innocence and was followed out the door by John Garrett. After tying Herold to a locust tree with a picket line rope,

Doherty handed him over to Private John Millington and ordered him to guard Herold.

Millington said to Herold, "Who was in the barn with you? Was it Booth?"

"Yes, Booth is in the barn," Herold replied.

"Booth told me when he asked me to help him, that he was going to kidnap Lincoln—

he didn't tell me he was going to kill him."

"When you learned that Booth had killed Lincoln, why'd you help him escape?"

"Booth threatened to kill me if I didn't help him get away."

As the officer in charge, Lieutenant Doherty continued to try to negotiate with Booth. Meanwhile, Conger, tired of the ongoing parley, set fire to the back of the barn. After he lit some straw, fire quickly spread throughout the structure.

Peering through a crack in the barn, by the light of the flames, Doherty saw in one hand Booth held a Spencer carbine rifle, with a Colt pistol in the other. On his crutch, Booth at first moved toward the fire, possibly considering extinguishing the flames, then turned and hopped toward the barn door.

46

"Useless, useless!"

> *"Thy fear, and the pride of thine heart hath deceived thee,*
> *thou that dwellest in the clefts of the rock,*
> *and keepest the height of the hill:*
> *though thou shouldest make thy nest as high as the eagle,*
> *I will bring thee down from thence, saith the Lord."*
> —Jeremiah 49:16 GNV

Sergeant Boston Corbett positioned himself at a large crack in the side of the tobacco barn. Viewing the scene lit by the burning hay, Corbett thought Booth was leveling his Spencer carbine at either Herold or Doherty. Corbett fired his Colt revolver through the crack, attempting to disable Booth by hitting him in the arm. But Booth made a sudden move, and the aim erred. The bullet struck Booth in the back of the head near the base of the neck—about an inch below the spot where Booth's shot had entered the head of Mr. Lincoln.

Booth fell like a dropped marionette. His spinal cord was severed, paralyzing him from the neck down. Doherty rushed into the burning barn, followed by some of his men, and pulled Booth out of the barn and into the yard beneath a tree. From there, he was carried to the veranda of the Garrett house where he lingered between life and death.

Conger initially thought Booth had shot himself. After realizing he had been shot by someone else, Conger and Doherty asked which officer had fired the shot. Corbett stepped forward and admitted he was the shooter. Corbett claimed he saw Booth aim his carbine, prompting him to shoot, despite Secretary Stanton's orders that he should be captured alive.

When asked why he had violated orders, in his written statement, Corbett replied, "Providence directed me . . . I aimed at his body. I did not want to kill him . . . I think he stooped to pick up something just as I fired. That may probably account for his receiving the ball in the head. What a God we have! . . . God avenged Abraham Lincoln!"

Willie Jett was brought to the scene. Booth could hear Jett's voice. He opened his eyes, looked up, and recognized Jett standing nearby. Booth attempted to cough, then asked, "Did that man betray me? Did Jett betray me?" The question went unanswered.

Lying on Garrett's porch surrounded by the soldiers, Booth asked to see his hands. Doherty lifted them up before his eyes and Booth gasped, "Useless, useless!" His speech became harder to understand. He mumbled incoherently and struggled to breathe. He was given brandy and water, but he couldn't swallow it.

Able to speak only in a whisper, Booth said to Doherty, "Tell my mother I died for my country."

A soldier was sent to Port Royal for a physician. The doctor could do nothing for Booth when he finally arrived at daylight. After lingering for several hours, at about seven o'clock in the morning, John Wilkes Booth breathed his last.

Doherty acquired a wagon. Booth's body was wrapped and sewn up into an Army blanket and loaded onto a single horse-drawn wagon. Creaking and popping, the old wagon slowly rolled back toward the ferry. The jostling of the body caused the neck wound to open and effuse blood, dripping red through the wagon planks and onto the axle and dirt below.

Booth had on him a diary, some photographs (including one of Bessie Hale), a large Bowie knife, two pistols, a compass, and a Canadian draft worth 60 pounds.

After Booth's death, John Wilkes' sister Asia, and her husband John Sleeper Clarke, remembered a package of papers that had been stored in a safe in their Philadelphia home. Discovered among those papers was a letter by John Wilkes Booth that became known as the "To Whom It May Concern" letter. In an effort to distance themselves from the heinous crime and prove their innocence regarding the assassination plot, the Booth family decided to have the letter printed in the *Philadelphia Inquirer*. In this letter, Booth wrote his feelings of despair and commitment to the Cause:

Lucy "Bessie" Hale

For four long years I have waited, hoped, and prayed for the dark clouds to break, and for the restoration of our former sunshine. To wait longer would be a crime. All hope for peace is dead. My prayers have proved as idle as my hopes. I go to see and share the bitter end. . . .

Who thinks of argument or patience when the finger of his enemy presses on the trigger? . . . This country was formed for the white man and not for the black. . . . When I aided in the capture and execution of John Brown who was a murderer . . . and was fairly tried and convicted . . . of treason . . . I was helping our common country to perform an act of justice. But what was a crime in poor John Brown is now considered by themselves as the greatest and only virtue of the Republican Party. Strange transmigration. Vice is to become virtue, simply because more indulge in it.

Alas! poor country, is she to meet her threatened doom? Four years ago, I would have given a thousand lives to see her remain as I had always known her, powerful and unbroken. . . . How I have loved the old flag can never now be known.

A few years since and the entire world could boast of none so pure and spotless. . . . But no, day by day she has been dragged deeper and deeper into cruelty and oppression, till now in my eyes her once bright red stripes look like bloody gashes on the face of heaven.

The men were exhausted after riding for days with little rest. Doherty and the detachment rode to Port Royal, where they arrived at 9 a.m. and crossed the river in a scow. While crossing the river, Luther Baker, without authority, rode off with the body of the assassin, taking with him the two men who had been previously detailed as guards to the body, and one of the prisoners, Willie Jett.

Doherty took some time crossing. The detachment experienced some difficulty in bringing Herold and the two Garretts along, having only one horse to mount the three men. After proceeding some distance, they were able to obtain an additional horse.

Fearing some accident might happen to the body of the assassin and the prisoner, Doherty dispatched an orderly to tell Baker to halt. The orderly rode over four miles at full speed. When he caught up to Baker, he told him his orders were to halt until the column came up. Doherty's order fell on deaf ears. Baker continued to ride.

Doherty arrived at Belle Plain at 6 p.m. and found neither the corpse nor Baker had arrived. He felt great anxiety about this situation and was about to request from Major Bosworth, 16th New York Cavalry (who was at there with his command), a detachment of men to go in search of the body. Moments later, Luther Baker arrived. A furious Doherty immediately confronted him and asked Baker where the prisoner Willie Jett was. He replied he did not know—Jett had escaped.

After a short delay to calm tempers, the body of the assassin was placed aboard the steamer *John S. Ide*, which proceeded to Washington, where Doherty delivered the remains of John Wilkes Booth and the prisoners, David Herold and the Garretts, to Colonel Lafayette C. Baker at 3 a.m. April 27th.

Booth's body was delivered to Dr. George L. Porter by Lafayette and Luther Baker at the old penitentiary building on the government arsenal grounds. His remains were buried in great secrecy beneath the warehouse floor near the site where the gallows for the assassination conspirators would later be erected.

Meanwhile, Garrett's tobacco barn had gone up in smoke. The structure and all its contents were a total loss. Searching the ashes and glowing embers, a few soldiers discovered Booth's two ruined revolvers and his carbine.

In the aftermath, Richard Garrett petitioned the federal government to reimburse him for his losses: "a well-built barn framed on heavy cedar posts, furnished with all the fixtures for curing tobacco," and a long list of farm and personal items that were inside the tobacco barn at the time of Booth's capture. Garrett listed a wheat thrashing machine, two stoves, five hundred pounds of fodder, and five hundred pounds of hay in his petition, claiming a loss of $2,525 (roughly $48,267 in 2023 dollars).

The response from the Congressional Committee stated they doubted Garrett's claim that he didn't know who Booth was until after the assassin's death. The report went on to declare that Garrett was undoubtedly disloyal to the country and was not entitled to any compensation whatsoever.

Sergeant Boston Corbett was arrested and briefly held as a possible accomplice in Lincoln's death, and for disobeying orders, but was later released. For his part in Booth's capture, Corbett would receive a portion of the $100,000 reward money.

47

April 27, 1865

"Save me, O God:
for the waters are entered even to my soul."
—Psalm 69:1 GNV

"I don't think I ever saw a more earnest fight.
The mule finally gave up." —Andrew Peery

Thursday, April 27, 1865 – General U. S. Grant's 43rd birthday

Just after midnight, the *Sultana* chugged away from the docks at Memphis, headed north against the strong current. Many of the passengers, without even a place to lie down, continued to stand or sit with legs folded on the decks of the vessel. The excitement of returning to their homes and loved ones prevented sleep for some, while others slept due to pure exhaustion.

By 2 a.m., the *Sultana* was only a few miles north of Memphis. She was making progress, but it was slow. The current of the mighty

Mississippi was powerful, and the boilers were tired, plus the load was much greater than usual. The boat swung around a bend in the river and began to labor her way past a small cluster of islands known as Paddy's Hen and Chickens, where the river was more than three miles wide.

Passengers on the crowded decks slept as stokers shoveled coal to feed the four massive boilers. Above the boilers were the upper decks, constructed of light, flimsy wood that was coated with highly combustible oil-based paints. Seasoned pilot George Kayton carefully steered the *Sultana* toward the Arkansas side of the river, avoiding the first of the Chicken Islands.

Struggling to navigate the swift currents of the flood waters around the islands with her massive load, the top-heavy *Sultana* listed to one side, then the other. When the steamer reached about seven miles north of Memphis, the *Sultana's* troubled boilers exploded. Sounding like a howitzer, the first boiler blew, followed a split-second later by two of the remaining three boilers. They exploded with a volcanic fury that a witness on the shore later described as the thundering noise of "a hundred earthquakes." The blast was heard in Memphis.

The explosions ejected boiling hot steam and water in all directions from the center of the lower deck. Scalding water and clouds of steam covered everyone within reach.

The entire middle portion of the boat, including the Texas deck and the pilothouse with all the passengers atop, was hurled high into the air, catapulting screaming men, flinging live coals and splintered timber into the night sky like fireworks. With them went great chunks of twisted machinery, a shower of red-hot coals that hissed and spurted as they hit the river. Shattered fragments of wood, cabin furniture, railings, deck beams, and human body parts rained from the fiery sky. The blast scattered hot coals from the furnaces all over the midship section. There was a huge, gaping hole in the middle of the hurricane deck, where flames were taking hold.

The upper decks, already sagging under the tremendous weight of her passengers, collapsed when the blast ripped through the steamer's superstructure. Many of the prisoners, an estimated five hundred who lay sleeping near the boilers, were scalded to death instantly. Those who were not injured in the blast jumped overboard.

The swift brown water was ice-cold. Many of the men could not swim, and there was little wreckage to cling to. Men died by the hundreds in the water near the wreck. They had been half-starved for months and were in no physical shape to swim to safety, even if they had known how. It was over a mile-long swim to reach either bank of the river. Tragically, there were only seventy-six life preservers and two small lifeboats available.

On the ship the fire quickly spread. Flames swept through the cabin from the bow to the stern. Within twenty minutes of the explosion, the entire superstructure was ablaze.

Most of the pilothouse was gone. The twin smokestacks shuddered and then toppled, one forward, the other backward, snapping the support cables like banjo strings, pinning men under them and holding them for the flames. The elk antlers dangled to one side momentarily between the smokestacks and then toppled into the wreckage.

The collapsed deck sections crushed and trapped victims. Some had arms and legs broken and crushed ribs, others were scalded and screaming in agony. Those not fighting to survive in the water faced life-or-death decisions. Their choice was between drowning or burning to death.

"I saw men, while attempting to escape, pitch down through the hatchway that was full of blue curling flames, or rush wildly from the vessel to death and destruction in the turbid waters below," recalled Private Daniel Allen, a Tennessee soldier. The superstructure was falling in and the entire midship section was nothing but a floating bed of coals.

The Mississippi River for a mile around was full of frantic, thrashing people. The light of the burning wreckage illuminated a scene that had never before been witnessed. It was a scene no imagination could conceive. The screams of women, the groans of those who were wounded and thrown from the boat by the force of the explosion, the cries for help when there were none to help. It was a scene which would compel one to shudder with horror. Hundreds died within the first minute after the blast. Hundreds more died within the next few minutes.

The instantaneous blast and immediate destruction of the boat allowed no time for the passengers or crew to do anything. Confusion and pandemonium ensued as men tried to save themselves and others.

Ladies rushed forth from their berths in their night attire, and with wild screams, plunged into the angry flood and sank to rise no more. The pitiful children, cried as they rushed to the side of the wreckage and plunged into the water. Their innocent voices were mingled with the hoarser voices of men in a desperate struggle for life.

Husbands threw their wives into the river and plunged into the water after them, but sadly saw them sink to their deaths before they could help them. Some climbed onto doors and fragments of the wreckage and were able to stay afloat longer. Those who were swimmers struck for the shore, where they hoped to find trees and bushes to keep them above the surface. Some were carried downstream by the current until reaching Memphis, where their cries attracted the attention of people on the steamers docked at the wharf.

The paying passengers aboard the *Sultana* fared no better. Union officer Lieutenant Harvey Annis paid for a private cabin for himself, his wife Anna, and their seven-year-old daughter. When the boilers exploded, the lieutenant strapped a life belt on his and his wife's waist, picked up their daughter, and rushed to the stern. They shimmied down a rope to the lower deck and jumped overboard. Harvey Annis died along with his daughter. Miraculously, his wife Anna survived.

Many trapped below deck in the resulting wreckage could only wait for certain death as fire quickly spread throughout the hull. The swollen river current scattered the survivors along both sides of the Mississippi and downstream. Some held on to bits of flotsam until they grounded on dry land or were snagged by trees and clambered into the branches.

Hearing the screaming of victims being carried past, locals from nearby Mound City, Memphis, and small settlements in between, put boats out to help. Some of the rescuers were able to haul in gasping survivors suffering from hypothermia; others spent frantic, futile minutes trying to locate voices that grew fainter and then fell silent.

Survivors clung desperately to the bow and stern sections of the boat, which the fire had not yet reached, and among them, panic set in. Men who were yet unhurt began to throw themselves into the water, thrashing about frantically for some bit of wreckage that might help them stay afloat. Hundreds of horribly burned and scalded men remained aboard the drafting hulk. Some had the strength and presence of mind to wrench doors or window blinds from their hinges, toss them overboard, and jump in after them. Others simply huddled in the diminishing spaces that the flames had not yet reached and shouted, prayed, or screamed helplessly for aid.

For as long as they were intact, the side paddle wheels acted as jib sails, keeping the stern pointed downwind. But once the fittings burned loose and the wheels broke away, the hapless steamboat pivoted around 180 degrees. The blaze reversed course, relentlessly turning toward the bow, where as many as five hundred people were huddled. Within minutes all were either burned to death or forced into the swift turbid water.

The deck supporting the passenger cabins collapsed at one end, forming a steep ramp down; screaming men and a tangle of wreckage slid into the hottest part of the fire. The burning wreckage began to drift slowly downriver, as those aboard fought to survive.

William Luganbeal

One of the stranger sights reported during the disaster was when a Tennessee man named Andrew Peery, who while still on the remains of the *Sultana*, watched a fight between a soldier and a mule. "Several times, the mule almost capsized the craft," Peery said. "I don't think I ever saw a more earnest fight. The mule finally gave up."

Another story was of Private William Lugenbeal of Columbus, Ohio, on board the *Sultana* at the time of the explosion. He went down to the lower deck to find all the windows, doors, and shutters had been removed for use as flotation devices. Thinking quickly, Lugenbeal remembered the *Sultana* mascot.

Lugenbeal grabbed a bayoneted rifle and stabbed the steamboat's mascot, an alligator, in its crate. After he dragged the dead alligator from the crate, he removed all his clothing except his drawers. He then tossed the wooden crate overboard and followed the crate into the water. When he surfaced, he tried to get hold of the box but slipped and missed it, going under again. Coming up for air the second time, he was able to get a firm grip of the crate and wriggled inside it with his feet dangling out the open end. He would later say that "he was saved by an alligator."

The river was alive and teeming with people crying and calling for help. They were in sheer agony. Their cries were terribly heartbreaking. Men in a desperate struggle for life pawed and fought over bits and pieces of wreckage in a battle to stay afloat. In the hours before dawn, hundreds of soldiers and civilians struggled in the river as they awaited rescue. But help did not arrive until after 3 a.m., more than an hour after the explosion.

A military courier boat, the *General Boynton*, first reported the *Sultana's* disaster. The courier boat had stopped at Memphis and had begun its trip upstream when it encountered survivors in the river. It quickly returned to Memphis to make its report. Three steamers from Memphis were immediately sent out to assist.

In Memphis, the watch on the gunboat *USS Grosbeak*, saw the flash of light and heard the explosion. As soon as the boilers had attained pressure, the skipper ordered the crew to cast off the mooring lines, and the *Grosbeak* went pounding up the river. Other steamers on the Memphis waterfront did likewise, hurrying upstream against the strong current to give any help they could.

PART V

The Aftermath

48

"We cannot hold out any longer!"

*"When thou passest through the waters,
I will be with thee, and through the floods,
that they do not overflow thee.
When thou walkest through the very fire,
thou shalt not be burnt,
neither shall the flame kindle upon thee."*
— Isaiah 43:2 GNV

The pilot of the steamer saw a bright glow in the sky and assumed it was probably a forest fire. As they came closer to the disaster site, they rounded a bend in the river and discovered the source of the fire was the wreckage of the *Sultana*. One of the first boats on the scene was the southbound steamer *Bostonia II*, which overtook the burning wreck at about 3:15 a.m. and rescued scores of survivors.

The *Bostonia II* was steaming among the survivors as soon as the crew was awakened and on deck. She passed through the debris and people, anchored, and sent a boat out to begin retrieving those still alive. The *Bostonia II* collected about one hundred survivors before weighing anchor and steaming to Memphis with its rescued cargo, and hurriedly returning to the disaster site.

USS Tyler

Other vessels joined the rescue, including the steamers *Arkansas*, *Jenny Lind*, and *Essex*. The Navy side-wheel gunboats USS *Grosbeak* and USS *Tyler*, manned by volunteers, displayed great care and compassion in picking up drowning men. The USS *Tyler's* regular crew had been discharged days before. Yawls, skiffs, and every available small boat were put into immediate service and sent out into the river to pick up survivors. Lieutenant James Berry, ensign of the *Essex*, was awakened about four o'clock in the morning and informed that the steamer *Sultana* had blown up and was now burning—that the passengers were floating down the river and crying for help. The lieutenant jumped up immediately and responded.

When rescuers saw the burning, floating mass and heard the cries of the struggling multitude, they rushed to construct crude rafts of logs and put them into the stream. With these, they succeeded in saving the lives of nearly a hundred people. Lieutenant Berry, with the help of his crew, pulled over sixty men aboard.

Berry was horrified by the agonizing cries of the people in the river. He said that never in his life had he hear anything so dreadful and hoped it would never be his curse to hear such screams again. He immediately ordered the boats to be manned, which was done in quick order. The first man picked up was chilled to his bones. Seeing the condition the man was in, Berry generously stripped off his own coat and put it on the man. The second man they rescued died a few minutes after being taken aboard.

The men of the *Essex* picked up a woman out of some drift. She was making her last struggle for life. About the time she was rescued, a steamboat yawl arrived and picked up more survivors clinging to the flotsam. Berry later said it was impossible for him to give any description of the scene, that there were no words adequate to convey the horror of that night. He continually heard people cry out, "Oh, for God's sake, save us! We cannot hold out any longer!"

USS Essex

The dark morning was drizzling rain and very black. Out of range for the fires to illuminate the way, the rescuers could barely see more than twenty feet ahead through the fog and smoke. They had nothing to guide them but the shrieks and groans of the wounded and scalded survivors. Many citizens in the area worked tirelessly to save victims they saw floating by. Those who ended up in trees were nearly covered by the flooded river on the Arkansas shore, before they were fetched and brought aboard rescue vessels.

During the horrid scenes following the explosion, Captain Mason stood on the deck of the doomed vessel, throwing buoys or anything that would float into the water—encouraging others by his example. He was last seen after everybody else had left the burning wreck. Mason and most of his crew were lost. His body was among those that would never be found.

George Kayton, pilot, William Roberts, mate, and Samuel Clemens, the badly scalded second engineer, were the only officers of the *Sultana* reported to have survived. Samuel Clemens, the engineer on duty, was hauled in by a passing steamboat. He lived long enough to make a deathbed statement about what happened. He believed the boat's weakened boiler exploded because its exterior was exposed to too much water. The water would have never sloshed so much if the boat not been "top heavy and consequently inclined to careen over from side to side."

Another engineer, Chief Engineer Nathan Witringer, was lost. The two clerks, William Gambrel and William Stratton were missing. Harry Ingraham, one of the pilots, also perished. None of their bodies were ever found.

The burning mass of what had been the *Sultana* floated down with the current until within a few hundred yards of Mr. John Fogleman's residence, where it grounded on the Arkansas shore. The hull struck a small island where there was a little grove of trees, and some of those who were clinging to them jumped ashore with ropes and secured what was left of the steamboat. Slowly, the worst of the flames died down, and finally, with the mooring ropes still holding the burning wreckage, survivors managed to hold on against the swiftly flowing current.

When the cold dawn light came, survivors dotted the river all the way to Memphis, clinging to logs, rafts, spars, barrels, sections of railing, and other bits of wood. All the rescue crafts in Memphis launched to do what they could, hauling half-dead men out of the cold river, constant and nameless. Hundreds of men were found on both shores of the Mississippi, many of them badly burned and without clothing.

Fogleman's residence was converted into a temporary hospital for the victims. The number who had been brought into the makeshift hospital, rescued from the river by noon, was 110 enlisted men, ten officers, four ladies, and fifteen civilian men.

The fire on the *Sultana* died down enough that scores of survivors clinging to the boat's hull were able to haul themselves back aboard where they fought the lingering flames and tried to ignore the gruesome sight of blackened and shriveled bodies. The fire never quit though, eventually forcing those still aboard to take to rafts or clamber into the trees to escape.

The *Sultana* had burned completely to the waterline. What was left of her drifted to the west bank of the Mississippi River.

Eventually, the flames succumbed to the cold river waters that closed over the charred hull at approximately 9 a.m. on a sandbar near the tiny settlement of Mound City, Arkansas. The *Sultana* gave up the hopeless struggle and sank, with a great noise of hissing and a huge pillar of smoke and steam rising toward the sky.

The *Sultana* came to rest in about twenty feet of water—the jackstaff was standing up before the blackened hull. The boat was almost entirely consumed. The charred remains of several human bodies were found with the remnants of the *Sultana*, crisped and blackened by the fiery catastrophe and those who witnessed it would never forget it.

49

"Gruesome Cargo"

*"For how can I suffer and see the evil,
that shall come unto my people?
Or how can I suffer and see the destruction of my kindred?"*
—Esther 8:6 GNV

Rescue vessels cruised around the disaster site, picking up the lifeless bodies of victims who would never see home. Some more fortunate souls who had escaped a watery grave were rescued. A number were plucked from the tops of trees along the Arkansas shore.

All those who survived the disaster were located within 12 hours of the explosion. About 800 survivors were transported to hospitals in Memphis. As many as 300 of those rescued died from injuries, hypothermia, and exposure. Bodies of victims continued to be found downriver for months, some as far as Vicksburg. Newspaper accounts indicated that the people of Memphis felt sympathy for the victims, even though they had recently been enemies.

One of the survivors rescued about 10 a.m. was a naked Army private from Bloomington, Illinois. Already weak before the disaster and literally 85 pounds soaking wet, Epp McIntosh was totally exhausted by the time a couple of Black fishermen fetched him out of the water. He had watched the horrific disaster play out before his eyes—frantic men fighting over bits of wreckage and pulling each other under in a desperate struggle for survival. Epp spent eight hours clinging to life on a sandbar, clutching a sapling in the swift current. Hypothermia and fatigue nearly killed him, but after everything he'd been through, he was determined to hang on and see his home again.

Another survivor was taken to a nearby hospital after being fished out of the icy waters. Sergeant William Fies of the 64th Ohio Infantry, describing the grim sights in one of the hospital wards, wrote he "was placed in a ward with quite a number who were severely scalded, or otherwise badly injured, and such misery and intense suffering as I witnessed while there is beyond my power to describe. The agonizing cries and groans of the burned and scalded were heartrending and almost unendurable, but in most cases, the suffering was of short duration as most of them were relieved by death in a few hours."

Newspaper clipping from the Evansville Daily Journal, May 11, 1865.

For many days after the disaster, a barge was sent out each morning to harvest dead bodies. And each night, it would return to the Memphis docks with its gruesome cargo.

So, the *Sultana* was gone and all that remained was to count the dead, tend to the survivors, and find out why the disaster happened. No definite count of the casualties was possible. Since no accurate assessment of the number of passengers had been made prior to boarding, it was impossible to calculate the exact number. Both the military's estimate of 1,238 and the Customs Department's figure of 1,547 were based strictly on Captain Williams' tally of prisoners placed on the *Sultana* at Vicksburg and was therefore, too low. In reality, the death toll estimate stood at more than 1,700.

Major General Napoleon Dana and Brigadier General William Hoffman, the US Army Commissary General of Prisoners, each conducted investigations. Hoffman's findings were the most critical of the military's involvement in the *Sultana* tragedy. He concluded "the shipment of so large a number of troops (1,866 in his reported estimate) on one boat was, under the circumstances, unnecessary, unjustifiable, and a great outrage on the troops."

His report also pointed a finger of guilt at Brigadier General Morgan L. Smith, noting although he "had nothing officially to do with the shipment of the troops—yet as it was officially reported to him by Captain Kerns that too many men were being put on the *Sultana*, it was proper that Smith should have satisfied himself from good authority whether there were sufficient grounds for the report. And, if he found it so, he should have interfered to have the evil remedied. Had [Smith] done so, the lives of many men would have been saved."

The cause of the *Sultana's* destruction has always been in dispute. Initially, the disaster was rumored to be the act of a Confederate saboteur. A federal government inquiry exonerated the officers and determined the Confederates were not involved in the fate of the boat. Many Northern newspapers immediately blamed the tragedy on sabotage, a possibility discounted by all the various military investigations.

Within hours of the disaster, General C. C. Washburn, commanding officer at Memphis, appointed a military commission to investigate the tragedy. Three inquiries followed to:

(1) Investigate post-war suspicions that a Confederate bomb had been aboard,

(2) Review the state of poorly repaired boilers, and

(3) Investigate the impact that overcrowding had in the disaster.

Major General Napoleon Dana and Brigadier General Morgan L. Smith, both in Vicksburg during the overloading of the *Sultana*, failed to exercise sufficient oversight for the prisoner transfers, but after the tragedy they managed the investigations to ensure that no blame fell on them.

Vicksburg's Chief Quartermaster, Colonel Reuben B. Hatch, was well connected into the Illinois political power grid and seemed immune to legal prosecution. Reuben Hatch's older brother, Ozias Hatch, was a political crony of Abraham Lincoln's, and instrumental in Lincoln's 1860 and 1864 presidential elections.

At the start of the Civil War, Reuben was caught with his hand in the till—paying low prices for lumber supplies, charging the government a high price, and pocketing the difference. But friends in important places, including Abraham Lincoln, cleared him of any wrongdoing. The evidence of his guilt was overwhelming, but thanks to the Secretary of State for Illinois, Ozias Hatch, Reuben never appeared before the court-martial tribunal ordered to try him.

Secretary Hatch, along with Illinois Governor Richard Yates and Jesse K. Dubois, the state auditor, wrote to Lincoln proclaiming Reuben Hatch's innocence and sought the president's aid.

President Lincoln endorsed their letter and forwarded it to the judge advocate in Cairo, who handled the prosecution, and requested that if "the judge advocate has the means of doing so I will thank him to give me his opinion of the case." Lincoln also appointed a civilian commission to investigate the charges leveled against Reuben Hatch. Two of the three men on the commission were from Hatch's home state of Illinois, so it was not surprising the accused was cleared of all charges.

Following his exoneration at Cairo, Reuben Hatch continued his military career, rising to the rank of Lieutenant Colonel. In early 1865, a military commission competency board at New Orleans tested Hatch on his knowledge of the duties of an Assistant Quartermaster General, a position he had held for the previous four years—and found him "totally unfit" to discharge the duties of that post. Nonetheless, just ten days after the board released its findings, Hatch was inexplicably promoted to the position of Chief Quartermaster for the Department of the Mississippi and stationed at Vicksburg. That was his job title at Vicksburg in April 1865, when the *Sultana* was loaded with her doomed POWs.

After the disaster, Hatch refused three separate subpoenas to appear before Captain Frederick Speed's trial and give testimony.

50

"I want you to die quick."

"Because thou servedst not the Lord thy God with joyfulness, and with a good heart, for the abundance of all things. Therefore thou shalt serve thine enemies which the Lord shall send upon thee, **in hunger and in thirst, and in nakedness, and in need of all things:** *and he shall put a yoke of iron upon thy neck until he have destroyed thee."*
—Deuteronomy 28:47- 48 GNV

"I want you to die quick."—Captain Christian Rath

At the tip of a peninsula jutting into the confluence of the Potomac and Anacostia Rivers lies Greenleaf Point, the site of the Washington Arsenal. Established in 1791 on 28 acres, the Washington Arsenal included barracks, a hospital, a three-story prison, storage for artillery pieces, an ammunition factory, and a courtyard. A room on the northeast corner of the third floor was selected and converted into a courtroom, where the alleged conspirators would be tried. The conspirators were now held at the Washington Arsenal prison. President Johnson requested the accused be tried by a military tribunal, despite defense counsel's objections and requests for a civilian court trial were denied. In the opinion of Attorney General James Speed, he stated:

Prosecutors John A. Bingham, Joseph Holt, & Henry Lawrence Burnett

> "...if the persons who are charged with the assassination of the president committed the deed as public enemies, as I believe they did, and whether they did or not is a question to be by the tribunal before which they are tried, they not only can, but ought to be tried before a military tribunal. If the persons charged have offended against the laws of war, it would be as palpably wrong of the military to hand them over to the civil courts, as it would be wrong in a civil court to convict a man of murder who had, in a time of war, killed another in battle."

In short, the decision to try the accused before a military tribunal instead of a civil court was based primarily on the fact that Abraham Lincoln held the military title of Commander-in-Chief during a time of war. Therefore, as a representative of the highest office of the military, his assassins should be tried by a military tribunal.

Three days after the *Sultana* disaster and four days after Booth's demise, the federal government began to act. On May 1, 1865, President Andrew Johnson ordered the formation of a nine-man military commission to try the conspirators involved in the assassination of the president. Secretary of War Edwin Stanton appointed Joseph Holt as Judge Advocate General, along with John A. Bingham and Henry Lawrence Burnett as Assistant Judge Advocate Generals to lead the prosecution.

The following day, President Johnson offered a $100,000 reward for the capture of former Confederate President Jefferson Davis.

The trial for the alleged conspirators began on May 9, the same day that Jefferson Davis was captured in Irwinville, Georgia.

Mary Surratt was charged with "aiding, abetting, concealing, counseling, and harboring" her co-defendants.

Perhaps due to an agitated nervous condition, Mary Surratt suffered excessive menstrual bleeding and was so ill the last four days of the trial, she was permitted to stay in her cell.

According to Thomas Harris, a member of the Military Commission that tried her, the most damning evidence against her came from her tenant at the Surrattsville Tavern, John M. Lloyd. Lloyd testified that five or six weeks before the assassination John Surratt, Herold, and Atzerodt came to his tavern to drop off two carbines, ammunition, about twenty feet of rope, and a monkey wrench. Lloyd was asked to conceal the items until they were called for. He additionally stated that three days before the assassination, Mary Surratt told him the "shooting irons" would be needed soon and he should be ready.

Equally damning testimony came from another tenant of Mary

Surratt, Louis Weichmann. He testified that on the day of the assassination, Mrs. Surratt sent him to acquire a horse and buggy to drive her to the Surrattsville Tavern. On this trip she took along "a package, done up in paper, about six inches in diameter." This package proved to be part of the cache delivered and hidden for Booth at the Surrattsville Tavern. According to Weichmann, she stated the purpose for the trip was to collect a debt. He witnessed no such transaction. Weichmann's account described numerous private conversations in the Surratt boardinghouse between Mrs. Surratt, Booth, Powell, and several other alleged conspirators. The prosecution called 366 witnesses. The trial ended on June 28, 1865.

The military tribunal found her guilty on all charges but two. She was found guilty of aiding, abetting, and counseling—and found not guilty of harboring and concealing conspirators Samuel Arnold and Michael O'Laughlen. She was also found not guilty of conspiring with Edmund Spangler. A death sentence required six of the nine votes of the judges. Mary Surrat's trial would prove to be the most controversial of all and may explain why no known record of how the nine-judge commission voted exists today. Surratt was sentenced to death—the first woman ever to be executed by the federal government.

David Herold also stood trial before a military tribunal with Mary Surratt and two other conspirators: Lewis Powell and George Atzerodt, at the Washington Arsenal in Washington, D.C. During the trial, Maryland Representative Frederick Stone and General William T. Sherman's foster brother, Thomas Ewing Jr., appeared as defense counsels for Dr. Mudd and Herold. As Herold had already admitted his involvement in the assassination conspiracy, the only defense his lawyer Frederick Stone could offer was that Herold was feebleminded and under undue influence from Booth.

During testimony, Stone described Herold as "a weak, cowardly, foolish miserable boy. Such a boy, was only wax in the hands of a man like Booth." Stone went on to say that Herold was not guilty of murder, all he did for certain was help Booth escape. When the verdict was delivered, all four were found guilty, and all four were sentenced to be hanged on July 7, 1865. Absent from the court proceedings was Mary Surratt's son, John Surratt, Jr.

In Elmira, New York at the time of the assassination, John Surratt, Jr. fled to Montreal, Canada, and then Europe when he learned of the president's death. A world-wide manhunt ensued to bring the fugitive to justice, while his mother stood trial in America.

Fort Jefferson Prison – Dry Tortugas

In a separate trial, the defense was generally credited with helping Dr. Mudd avoid the death penalty by a single vote. The prosecution was able to prove that Mudd did not report Booth's visit to the authorities for twenty-four hours after he learned of the Lincoln assassination. This evidence appeared to link him to the crime, as did the various changes in his story under interrogation.

O'Laughlen was also tried along with Arnold, Spangler, and Mudd. The government attempted to prove O'Laughlen had stalked General Ulysses S. Grant on the nights of April 13th and April 14th with the intent to murder him. The prosecution was not able to prove this, but there was no doubt that O'Laughlen was a willing conspirator through late March. O'Laughlen, Arnold, Spangler, and Mudd were sentenced to life imprisonment at Fort Jefferson in the Dry Tortugas, the westernmost and most isolated archipelago of the Florida Keys—sixty-eight miles west of Key West, Florida.

On July 7 at 1:15 p.m., Surratt, Powell, Atzerodt, and Herold were taken through the courtyard and up the steps of the gallows. Mary Surratt wore a black alpaca dress, bonnet, and black veil that hid her face. Too weak to walk under her own power, she was assisted by an army officer on each arm. Likewise, the legs of Atzerodt and Herold appeared unable to support them. They were also assisted by army officers on each arm. Powell boldly strode tall and erect, past four pine boxes and four freshly dug graves, and up the steps to his destiny. Chairs had been placed on the platform where the condemned were to sit. Each prisoner's ankles and wrists were manacled. More than 1,000 people including government officials, members of the military, friends and family of the condemned, official witnesses, and reporters—watched from the arsenal courtyard and the tops of its walls.

John F. Hartranft

Famed photographer Alexander Gardner, who had photographed all the military dignitaries of the Civil War, including the conspirators two months prior, photographed the execution as it happened for the government.

Major General John Frederick Hartranft read the execution order while the condemned sat in the chairs. As the Provost Marshal of Washington Arsenal prison, Hartranft's responsibility was to signal the executioner to carry out the death sentence.

White linen cloth bound their arms to their sides and tied their ankles and thighs together. On Powell's behalf, the Reverend Dr. Abram Dunn Gillette, a loyal Unionist and pastor at the First Baptist Church in Washington, D.C., thanked the prison officials for their kindness and said a prayer for Powell's soul.

Powell's eyes filled with tears when he said, "Mrs. Surratt is innocent. She doesn't deserve to die with the rest of us."

The executioner, Captain Christian Rath, was a former sheriff with experience at hangings. Rath had come to admire Powell's pluck, and whispered to Powell, "I want you to die quick," as he prepared him for execution.

Captain Christian Rath

Powell replied, "You know best, Captain."

Captain Rath would not be successful, though. Lewis Powell would not "die quick."

The prisoners were instructed to stand and move forward a few feet to the nooses. A white bag was placed over the head of each prisoner after the noose was cinched in place. Mary Surratt's bonnet was removed, and the noose was fastened around her neck by an officer.

She complained, "the bindings about my arms hurt."

The officer preparing her for execution told her, "Well, it won't hurt long."

Her last words, spoken to the officer as he moved her forward to the drop were, "Please don't let me fall."

The chairs were removed from the platform. Lewis Powell said to Captain Rath through his hood, "I thank you. Goodbye." Atzerodt trembled as he addressed the crowd, "Gentlemen, take warn—", choking on the words. He regained his composure and stated, "Good-bye, gentlemen, who are before me now. May we all meet in the other world." A final adjustment was made to his noose, and he cried out, "Don't choke me!" All eyes were on the four condemned as they stood motionless, awaiting their fate. At 1:26 p.m., Captain Rath clapped his hands three times, and the soldiers under the gallows knocked the supports from under the drops. The doors fell with a loud slam, and the four bodies jerked violently at the ends of their ropes.

Mary Surratt, who had moved forward just enough to barely step onto the drop, lurched forward and slid partway down the drop, her body snapping tight at the end of the rope, swinging back and forth.

Mary Surratt and George Atzerodt seemed to die quickly. David Herold and Lewis Powell struggled for nearly five minutes. Herold's bladder emptied as he struggled against the noose. Powell's body swung about wildly, and once or twice his legs came up so that he was almost in a sitting position. The fall from the gallows did not break his neck. He slowly strangled to death.

The execution of (L-R) Mary Surratt, Lewis Powell, David Herold, & George Atzerodt.

51

"It Was Murder!"

> *"The gathering of treasures by a deceitful tongue,*
> *is vanity tossed to and fro of them that seek death."*
> —Proverbs 21:6 GNV

The official cause of the *Sultana* explosion was determined to be a combination of mismanagement of water levels in the boilers, the top-heavy ship's listing back and forth in the water due to severe overcrowding, and the faulty repairs made to the boilers days before the disaster. Amazingly, the inquiry further stated that the soldiers aboard were the party most responsible. Although Captain Mason had objected to the overcrowding, the soldiers defiantly stormed aboard, refusing to wait for other boats to transport them, trying to get home as soon as possible.

Three different military commissions were ordered to investigate the disaster. Each tended to limit its area of authority, and none probed too deeply into the affair.

The Washburn Commission concluded that insufficient water in the boilers precipitated the explosion, despite testimony to the contrary by the *Sultana's* second engineer, Samuel Clemens. Clemens was on watch at the time of the explosion and died soon afterward from the injuries he sustained. He survived long enough to give testimony to the first investigators before he died at the hospital.

Another crew member that survived, Captain George J. Kayton, pilot of the *Sultana*, was also on duty at the time of the explosion. Kayton claimed they were moving along as usual—that they had gotten about seven miles above the city of Memphis, running at the usual rate of speed, or if any difference, not as fast as usual. Suddenly, he saw a flash, and the next thing he knew, he was falling into the water with the wreckage of the pilothouse. He thought he must have been hurled at least forty feet into the air. When he reached the water, he saw flames bursting up from the furnace and enveloping the entire boat.

The most likely scenario pointed to the tubular boilers themselves. Given the unstable nature of the human load on board and the turbulent river flow, it was highly probable that the *Sultana* careened a good deal. With the engine requiring maximum steam pressure to maintain its headway against the heavy flood current, the need to keep sufficient water levels in the boilers was especially critical. It would not have taken too many cycles of red-hot piping suddenly flushed by cold river water to cause a fatigue rupture in one boiler, resulting in two more ruptures.

While the direct cause of the explosion was later determined to be the leaky and poorly repaired steam boiler, there was also reason to believe that allowable working steam pressure was exceeded while attempting to overcome the strong current. The Vicksburg patch job was also suggested as the cause, although the deathbed testimony of engineer Clemens was that there was no loss of pressure in the minutes before the explosion.

It was the investigation and report of J. J. Witzig, the supervising inspector of steamboats, that shed the most light on the cause of the tragedy. He contended that the shoddy repair to the middle larboard boiler at Vicksburg had caused the explosion. The small patch, he reasoned, was too thin to stand the excessive pressure in the boiler on the upriver trip.

Less than a month after the disaster, Brigadier General William Hoffman, Commissary General of Prisoners, investigated the *Sultana* tragedy. His report primarily agreed with the Washburn Commission's findings, except for the number of casualties. Hoffman's investigation reported 69 more fatalities.

A later investigation into the cause of the disaster was conducted by the principal engineer of the Hartford Steam Boiler Inspection Company. The company came into existence in 1866 as a direct result of the *Sultana* explosion. Pat Jennings, principal engineer, determined that three main factors led to the disaster:

   1. The type of metal used in the construction of the boilers—Charcoal Hammered no. 1, which often became brittle with prolonged heating and cooling.

   2. The sediment-laden Mississippi River water used to feed the boilers tended to settle on the bottom of the boilers or clog between the flues and leave hot spots in the metal.

   3. The design of the boilers. The *Sultana* had tubular boilers filled with twenty-four horizontal five-inch flues. Being so closely packed within the boilers, the muddy sediment formed hot pockets and were extremely difficult to clean.

Tubular boilers were discontinued from use on steamboats after two more steamboat explosions occurred shortly after the *Sultana* disaster.

The horror of the *Sultana* tragedy was multiplied by its futility. Headlines in the *Memphis Daily Appeal* screamed: "IT WAS MURDER!" And the newspaper report had a point. There was no military reason requiring or justifying the placement of so many soldiers aboard the *Sultana*. The real cause of the disaster was not only the failure of the patch on the boiler but the sinful conspiracy of greed and incompetence at Vicksburg, which put the quest for profits above the safety of the weary soldiers who thought the horrors of war were behind them forever.

Surprisingly, the *Sultana* disaster received very little coverage in the contemporary media. This omission was partially due to the public's having become somewhat desensitized to death toll numbers during the Civil War, but more specifically, it was due to the assassination of President Abraham Lincoln thirteen days before the *Sultana* explosion. The day before the explosion, Lincoln assassin John Wilkes Booth had been cornered and killed. Measured against these pressing national concerns, the fate of one steamboat paled in comparison. Overshadowed by the death of so monumental an individual, the deaths of the hundreds aboard the *Sultana* received hardly a mention. Still, the system went through the motions.

At the conclusion of the military investigations, Reuben Hatch and Frederick Speed were ordered to appear before court-martial tribunals. The charges against Hatch stemmed from the fact that he had selected the *Sultana* to transport all the prisoners. Speed, because of his temporary replacement of Williams, was deemed to be the officer in direct command of the prisoner transfer and was accused of knowingly loading the ship six times over the legal passenger capacity. After lengthy testimony, a military commission appointed to investigate the tragedy eventually charged Captain Speed with "neglect of duty to the prejudice of good order and military discipline." Speed pled not guilty.

On November 1, 1865, a court was appointed to try Captain Speed at Vicksburg. Although the government called several witnesses to testify, the prosecution failed to compel the appearance of one key witness, Chief Quartermaster Lieutenant Colonel Reuben B. Hatch. A request by the prosecutor to the Secretary of War Edwin M. Stanton to have Hatch arrested and brought to Vicksburg to testify went unanswered.

Hearings resulted in reports that few bothered to read. In an act of retributive justice, just one individual was brought to trial for his part in the matter. In June of 1866, the military court found Captain Frederick Speed guilty on all charges and sentenced him to be dismissed from the Army. The verdict, however, was later reversed by the judge advocate general. Captain Speed was honorably mustered out of service, and no one ever faced official charges. Many officials must have been aware of the condition of the ship and the overcrowding on board, but ultimately no one was ever formally held responsible for the *Sultana* tragedy. Reuben Hatch never stood before a court-martial tribunal. Except for those directly involved, the *Sultana* disaster passed quickly from the headlines.

A group of survivors of the *Sultana* disaster formed the *Sultana Association*, meeting for the first time on December 30, 1885. Sharing a bond after mutually suffering such a tragedy, the members appointed a committee to prepare a memorial and request pensions for the survivors. In 1918, as a member of the *Sultana Association*, James H. Kimberlin expressed disappointment in the failure of Congress to recognize the group's petition:

"Our association twenty-five years ago appointed a monument committee to go before Congress and ask that an appropriation be made for the erection of a suitable monument to those dead martyrs, and every congress has been appealed to, but the committee has as often been met with indifference."

Shortly before his death in 1924, *Sultana Association* member Kimberlin expressed resentment toward his country, when he wrote:

"The men who had endured the torments of a hell on Earth, starved famished from thirst, eaten with vermin, having endured all the indignities insults and abuses possible for an armed bully to bestow upon them, to be so soon forgotten does not speak well for our government or the American people."

On his deathbed, a rebel Confederate agent named Robert Louden confessed the *Sultana* boiler explosion was due to a coal torpedo he placed on the ship. Louden was a Confederate saboteur and mail carrier during the Civil War and was said to be the primary messenger between General Sterling "Old Pap" Price, Confederate regulars, and bushwhackers. Confederate President Jefferson Davis proclaimed Robert Louden as, "the vainest man I ever met."

As a Confederate agent, Louden was involved in the sabotage and sinking of several Union steamboats near St. Louis and claimed to have been responsible for the destruction of the *Sultana*. Louden allegedly confessed his involvement to a man named William Streetor, as having planted a coal torpedo in a coal pile used to fire the *Sultana's* boilers.

Thomas Courtenay

The coal torpedo was invented by a brilliant Confederate spy named Thomas Edgeworth Courtenay. It was a four-pound artillery shell that was cast to resemble a chunk of coal and filled with gunpowder. The outside was coated with soot making it look like the coal typically used to power the boilers. Coal torpedoes were usually hidden in the coal pile and the boiler tender would unwittingly shovel it inside the boiler.

In 1888, an article appeared in a St. Louis newspaper, recounting a conversation with Robert Louden, who claimed his weapon was an explosive device designed as a lump of coal and slipped aboard during the coaling stop outside Memphis. A circumstantial case can put Louden on the scene with motive, opportunity, and the means, but no more than that.

The military's investigations failed to prove Louden's claim and gave no credence to the sabotage theory. Nagging suspicions of sabotage, however, remained.

52

Change

*"And fashion not yourselves like unto this world,
but be ye changed by the renewing of your mind,
that ye may prove what that good,
and acceptable and perfect will of God is."*
— Romans 12:2 GNV

The month of April 1865 nearly caused our nation to implode. After all the events experienced in a divided United States, a singular common denominator emerged from the carnage and ashes. The word that came to the surface was *change*. Opinions and attitudes were shifting. Being forced out of tired habits and imposing better ones upon a population during that historic time was stressful, costly, and destructive. But still, it needed to happen. For many, however, the status quo was much more comfortable.

Ours was a nation divided, from four years of the most brutal and costliest war in terms of blood. An estimated 2% of the population of the United States perished because of the Civil War. That percentage applied to today's population would translate to a staggering 6.64 million lives lost.

The election of 1860 altered the nation and the electoral process. It wasn't simply swearing in a new president. The country elected its first Republican commander-in-chief and launched the two-party election system we have today.

Personal access to the president was forever changed as a result of the Lincoln assassination. During his entire tenure as president, security was minimal at best—lackadaisical at its worst. It seemed anyone and everyone had unfettered and unrestricted access to the most powerful leader of the free world. Just days before his death, Lincoln signed the order to authorize the establishment of the Secret Service. Sadly, this change came less than 80 days after his assassination when the Secret Service was formed on July 5th, 1865.

The treatment of POWs changed after the atrocities of Andersonville came to light. That light shone on the inhumane treatment of our own countrymen as prisoners of this war, in places like Camp Douglas in Illinois and Georgia's Andersonville. The Northern press printed and re-printed sensational stories and drawings of the horrible conditions at Confederate prison camps, enraging the nation.

During the early days of Civil War, a system of paroles and exchanges was used. Paroled prisoners were released to their homes after signing a document pledging not to bear arms until formally exchanged. A simple system was developed with the two opposing sides meeting on a battlefield and exchanging men of equal rank. And then the system went awry.

Accusations of incompetence and confusion about the number of equivalent prisoners coupled with the South's refusal to exchange black prisoners led to a breakdown of the exchange system in mid-1863. After this cessation of the exchange system, the number and size of prison camps increased drastically. The debilitating problems at Andersonville of overcrowding, inadequate food and medicine, shelter, and the lack of sanitation were present in almost all the 150 Civil War military prisons, though not on the same scale.

From the first Geneva Convention in 1864 to Hague Conferences in 1899, 1907, and 1914, international rules of war and universal standards for the treatment of prisoners were developed. Humane and decent treatment of prisoners came to be a right and was not subject to the whim of the captor. The prisoners of war were to be clearly recognized as victims of events and not criminals.

Americans were faced with a first. The murder of a sitting president and the aftermath of a nationwide manhunt for those responsible. With the careless and wholesale sacrifice of recently released POWs—sick, injured, and weary citizens were bartered over and forfeited their safe transportation for greed and personal profit. And as another slap in the former POWs faces, the investigations into the *Sultana* tragedy laid a large part of the blame on the victims themselves.

Through these tragedies there was a redeeming consequence. The product of these tests of humanity, human endurance, and resolve, change finally came about. The way that citizens of a common nation interacted with each other shifted.

By 1865, Northerners and Southerners recognized the United States was embarking on a second American Revolution. The revolution was not the war itself. The Civil War, for all its vast influences thrust upon a fractured nation—the conquest of the Confederacy, the abolishment of slavery, and the creation of a powerful federal government—had only created the conditions *for* the revolution.

The revolution would be legally contained in the Thirteenth, Fourteenth, and Fifteenth Amendments to the Constitution, and the legislation that enabled them. It guaranteed the fundamental rights belonging to every man as a free man: the right to make contracts, to sue in court, and to be sure the state would protect their property and person. The revolution forever transformed the relations of individual citizens to the federal government.

What the federal government sought to do was re-unite the States and create a homogeneous citizenry where the basic rights and liberties of all citizens were the same, no matter where you were in the United States. The federal government would guarantee and enforce those rights. It would not eliminate discrimination, however—women still could not vote—but it did outlaw discrimination based on race and previous conditions of servitude.

The world that mourned Lincoln, the society that seemed so triumphant, was itself vanishing, as surely as the South it had vanquished. In fighting a war against treason and slavery, they ended the old plantation system, prohibited slavery, and settled the question about the nature of the Union. But in winning the war, they set into motion the beginning of an industrial revolution and were accelerating toward a goal that would transform the North. The tempered and benevolent attitude Lincoln expressed in his desire to welcome the seceded States back into the Union only lasted until his passing. The Johnson administration took a more castigating approach toward the former Confederacy, exhibiting a determined initiative to punish those deemed actively responsible for the rebellion. Johnson's position favoring States rights above Federal assistance impeded Southern reconstruction by withholding resources and prolonging the suffering. As a result, the industrial growth of the South was stunted, lagging far behind their Northern brethren.

This new nation of free labor and small producers would partially endure over much of the Midwest into the late nineteenth century, but it was fading fast. It would endure more as an ideal, an iconic representation of the United States. The future was an industrial one, an urban America the people in April 1865 never imagined. The homogenous citizenry they hoped for would not happen. But how the Civil War produced a country no one could envision in 1865, is the story of the late nineteenth century.

A multitude of individuals and their families were forever scarred by these historical events—the war, prison confinement, surrender, the assassination, and the *Sultana* disaster. People like Epp McIntosh, Robert Sneden, and John McElroy, along with many more, tried to reassemble the broken pieces of the American mosaic and salvage what was left of their lives. And for many, the rest of their lives would be a challenging second act. History tells us Americans have always confronted challenges with stamina and determination, and a resolve to persist and endure.

53

Epidemic and Extradition

> *"For the Lord shall judge his people,*
> *and repent towards his servants;*
> *when he seeth that their power is gone*
> *and none shut up in hold or left abroad."*
> —Deuteronomy 32:36, The Soldier's Pocket Bible

During their confinement at Fort Jefferson, inmates faced yet another hardship. An unforeseen enemy, a yellow fever epidemic, swept through the Dry Tortugas from August until November 1867, infecting both inmates and guards indiscriminately. When the only staff doctor succumbed to the disease, inmates Dr. Samuel Mudd and Ned Spangler provided treatment to those infected.

Michael O'Laughlen

Michael O'Laughlen died there from yellow fever on September 23rd, 1867. When Dr. Mudd became sick with yellow fever himself, he was treated by Spangler.

On March 2nd, 1869, three weeks after President Johnson pardoned Dr. Samuel Mudd and on his last day in office, Johnson also pardoned Edmund Spangler and Samuel Arnold after serving four years of a life sentence.

After arriving back home, Spangler went to work at the Holliday Street Theater in Baltimore for his old boss, John T. Ford, the former owner of Ford's Theater. When the Holliday Street Theater burned down in 1873, Spangler accepted an offer to live at Dr. Mudd's farm in Bryantown, Maryland.

Dr. and Mrs. Mudd gave Spangler five acres of land to farm. In addition to farming, Spangler performed carpentry chores in the surrounding area. In his final years, he converted to Catholicism and died on February 7th, 1875, at the age of forty-nine.

Edmund "Ned" Spangler

Samuel Arnold returned to his home in Maryland and moved into his father's house, where he lived quietly and out of the public eye for more than thirty years. Arnold died at the age of seventy-two on September 21st, 1906. The only co-conspirator who survived him was John Surratt, Jr.

Samuel Arnold

John Surratt, Jr. was in Elmira, New York when he learned of the Lincoln assassination. He avoided arrest by immediately fleeing to Montreal, Canada, arriving on April 17th, 1865, just two days after Lincoln's death. He then went to St. Liboire, just outside Montreal where a Catholic priest, Father Charles Boucher, gave him sanctuary. Surratt remained there while his mother Mary was arrested, tried, and hanged in Washington for conspiracy.

Aided by ex-Confederate agents Beverly Tucker and Edwin Lee, Surratt disguised himself and booked passage under the aliases "Walters or Watson". He then steamed across the Atlantic to Europe, landing in Liverpool, England in September, where he lodged in the oratory at the Church of the Holy Cross. Surratt would later serve for a time in the Ninth Company of the Pontifical Zouaves, in the Papal States, under the alias," John Watson".

During Surratt's service, he was recognized by an old acquaintance, Henri Beaumont de Sainte-Marie. In an effort to collect the reward for his capture, Sainte-Marie reported Surratt's whereabouts to papal officials and the U.S. minister in Rome, Rufus King. Surratt was arrested, but before he could be delivered to American authorities, he made another daring escape.

While being temporarily confined at Velletri Prison and walking under guard along the edge of an overlook, Surratt glanced over the cliff where he saw jagged rocks thirty feet below. Before guards could restrain him, he grabbed the handrail and jumped over the side, tumbling to the bottom of the pit. The pit contained the waste dump of the prison—a massive pile of garbage and human excrement broke his fall. Surratt escaped to Alexandria, Egypt but was arrested and extradited to face charges of his involvement in the Lincoln assassination conspiracy.

Unlike his mother and the other conspirators, John Surratt, Jr. was tried by a Maryland civilian court, not a military commission. The first witness in the trial took the stand on June 17th, 1867, two years and two months after Lincoln's death. Surratt's lead attorney, Joseph Bradley, conceded Surratt's involvement in the plot to kidnap the president but denied any participation in the murder plot. The star witness for the prosecution and Surratt's former roommate, Louis Weichmann, was labeled a "perjurer" and all attempts were made by the defense to discredit and defame him. When Surratt was asked about the testimony given by Weichmann, he stated:

John Surratt, Jr. wearing Papal Zouave uniform prior to extradiction back to the United States

> "That man's testimony from beginning to end was outrageously false. He lied, lied; lied from the time he took the witness stand until he left it. During the three days he was on the stand he did not dare look me in the face...I am convinced that if he was on his deathbed, he would send for me and ask my forgiveness for the ruin and trouble he has caused me."

The statute of limitations had run out on all charges except for murder. After two months of testimony, eight jurors voted not guilty, four voted guilty. A mistrial was declared, and Surratt was released on $25,000 bail. He would not face trial again.

Surratt tried to farm tobacco and then taught at the Rockville Female Academy. In 1870, as one of the last surviving members of the conspiracy, Surratt began a much-heralded public lecture tour. On December 6th at a small courthouse in Rockville, Maryland, in a 75-minute speech, Surratt admitted his involvement in the scheme to kidnap Lincoln. He maintained that he knew nothing of the assassination plot, however, and reiterated that he was in Elmira, New York at the time.

In 1872, Surratt married Mary Victorine Hunter, a second cousin of Francis Scott Key. The couple lived in Baltimore and had seven children. Sometime after 1872, he was hired by the Baltimore Steam Packet Company. He rose to freight auditor and, ultimately, treasurer of the company. Surratt retired from the steamship line in 1914 and died of pneumonia in 1916, at the age of seventy-two. John Surratt, Jr. was buried in Baltimore in New Cathedral Cemetery.

In his later years, Louis Weichmann moved to Anderson, Indiana, where he opened a business school. One of his brothers, a Catholic priest, and two of his sisters had moved and settled there. Because of some lingering doubt as to the truth and motives of his testimony, Weichmann became a controversial and somewhat ostracized figure by many. The fact that Mary Surratt was the first woman tried and executed for a capital crime by the federal government caused a backlash against him. There also were strong anti-Catholic elements that attempted to link Lincoln's death to a Catholic conspiracy.

Weichmann spent the rest of his life defending himself from accusations of being a false witness. He testified both at the trials in 1865 prosecuting the conspirators, and in the 1867 trial of John

Surratt, Jr. Weichmann regularly corresponded with judges and other officials involved in both trials, where these letters contain affirmations of Weichmann's integrity and acknowledge the truthfulness of his testimony.

Louis Weichmann

Partially because of this, he swore out a deathbed affidavit, reaffirming that all his testimony concerning Abraham Lincoln's assassination was totally and completely true. When Weichmann realized that he was about to die, he asked his sisters, Mrs Charles O'Crowley and Miss Tillie Wiechmann to take down the following statement, which he signed:

"June 2, 1902; This is to certify that every word I gave in evidence at the assassination trial was absolutely true; and now I am about to die and with love I recommend myself to all truth-loving people."

He died a few days later, on June 5, 1902, in Anderson, Indiana, and is buried there at St. Mary's Cemetery. Despite his using the spelling of Weichmann at the conspiracy trial as "ei", in all his official correspondence, and as the author of his book, *A True History of the Assassination of Abraham Lincoln and the Conspiracy of 1865,* the original family spelling of Wiechmann appears on his tombstone.

54

Madness

"But they shall prevail no longer: for their madness shall be evident unto all men, as theirs also was." —2 Timothy 3:9 GNV

After the Lincoln assassination, Major Henry Rathbone blamed himself for not preventing Lincoln's death. Weeks after that tragic April night, Clara Harris posed for famed Civil War photographer Mathew Brady. In the photo, Clara wore the dress she had worn on the night the president was assassinated—still stained with blood. Clara kept the bloodied white dress, unable to bring herself to wash or destroy it. Not knowing what else to do with it, she eventually stored it in the back of a closet in the family's summer home near Albany, New York. She hoped to forget it.

On April 14th, 1866, exactly one year after Lincoln's assassination, Clara awoke in the night to the sound of low laughter emitting from the closet containing the dress. This eerie occurrence was repeated a year later, witnessed by a guest staying in the same room. After experiencing what she claimed was a visit from Lincoln's ghost, Clara had the closet bricked in and the dress was closed off from the world—entombed, but not forgotten.

Henry and Clara were married on July 11th, 1867. This union produced three children: Henry, Gerald, and Clara Pauline.

Every year on the anniversary of Lincoln's assassination, journalists would contact the couple with questions about Lincoln's death, furthering Rathbone's feelings of guilt. Clara later wrote to a friend:

Henry Rathbone and Clara Harris

"I understand his distress...in every hotel we're in, as soon as people get wind of our presence, we feel ourselves become objects of morbid scrutiny.... Whenever we were in the dining room, we began to feel like zoo animals. Henry...imagines that the whispering is more pointed and malicious than it can possibly be."

Rathbone resigned from the Army in 1870, having risen to the rank of brevet colonel. After his resignation, he struggled to find and keep a job due to his mental instability. He became convinced that Clara was being unfaithful. He also resented the attention she paid their children and reportedly threatened his wife on several occasions after suspecting that she was going to divorce him and take the children.

Despite Rathbone's mental instability, President Chester Arthur appointed Rathbone as the U.S. Consul to the Province of Hanover in 1882. The family relocated to Germany where Rathbone's mental health continued to decline. He became depressed, and some people called him erratic. His marriage to Clara also suffered more and tension permeated their home much of the time. Henry's depression deepened and he was genuinely convinced that Clara was leaving him and taking the kids.

Clara Rathbone in the white satin dress.

The day before Christmas Eve on December 23rd, 1883, Henry Rathbone attacked his family in a fit of madness. He fatally shot Clara in the head and then attempted to kill the children, but a groundskeeper prevented him from doing so. Rathbone then stabbed himself five times in the chest in an attempted suicide. Blaming his crime on an intruder, Rathbone was charged with murder and declared insane by doctors.

Dr. Pope, who attended to his wounds following Lincoln's assassination, stated:

"He never was thoroughly himself after that night...I have no hesitation in affirming that the dreaded tragedy, which preyed upon his nervous and *impressionable temperament for many years, laid the seeds of that homicidal mania."*

After Henry murdered his wife, the Rathbone children were sent back to America to live with their uncle, William Harris in New York. Clara was interred in a German cemetery and Henry was institutionalized in a German asylum in Hildesheim for the criminally insane. He spent the remainder of his life battling paranoid delusions and seeking treatments for other physical problems including constant headaches.

In 1910, eldest son Henry Riggs Rathbone removed the bricks from the closet and had the dress destroyed, reportedly claiming that it had cursed the family long enough. The dress was later the subject of the 1929 book *The White Satin Dress*, by Mary Raymond Shipman Andrews.

After a long and painful deterioration of his health and mental status, Henry Rathbone died at age seventy-four in the German asylum on August 14th, 1911. He was subsequently buried alongside Clara.

Henry Riggs Rathbone

In 1952, in accordance with the cemetery's policy of unvisited graves, the couple's bodies were exhumed and cremated.

Thomas P. "Boston" Corbett

Moved by his role in killing Booth, the Kansas Legislature appointed Boston Corbett assistant doorkeeper for the Kansas House of Representatives in Topeka in 1887. He was proud of his position and took it seriously, wearing his army holster and pistol on the job. By then, however, delusions and paranoia dogged Boston Corbett. He feared irate former Confederates would assassinate him. During a session of the legislature, Corbett overheard a comment he considered blasphemous. At one point, outraged and convinced his fellow court officers were conspiring against him, Corbett brandished his pistol and cleared them from the Statehouse.

Corbett was subsequently arrested, declared insane, and committed to the state hospital in Topeka. In May 1888, while walking on the grounds with other patients, Corbett saw a horse hitched near the entrance and used it to make his escape. He rode south to Neodesha, Kansas, stayed with a friend for a couple of days, then said he was leaving for Mexico.

To this day, no one knows what happened to him. Some theorize he perished in a small cabin in the woods in the Great Hinckley Fire in Minnesota in 1894. A few years later, a man claiming to be Corbett surfaced trying to collect his pension. He was found to be an impostor. No further official record of Boston Corbett exists.

55

The Angel and the Bad Men

> "...and they shall come unto judgement,
> and sentence shall be given upon them,
> and the righteous shall be justified,
> and the wicked condemned,"
> — Deuteronomy 25:1 GNV

With no employment or any place to go after the war, Henry Wirz, along with his wife and daughter, were living in his officer's cabin at the now-deserted Andersonville Prison. He was under the impression that as a former soldier, he was protected by the rules of war, and was therefore not accountable for the brutalities committed at Andersonville. He was mistaken.

On May 7th, 1865, authorities arrested Wirz and transported him to Washington, D. C., where a military tribunal placed him on trial for war crimes. His trial began in August of 1865 and lasted two months. He refused to implicate Confederate President Jefferson

Davis for the atrocities committed at Andersonville in exchange for his exoneration. Wirz's defense council, Louis Frederick Schade, urged his client to cooperate, by testifying as requested in implicating Davis as the one responsible, to which Wirz responded:

> "Mr. Schade, you know that I have always told you that I do not know anything about Jefferson Davis. He had no connection with me as to what was done at Andersonville. If I knew anything about him, I would not become a traitor against him, or anybody else, even to save my life."

Wirz was charged with gross mismanagement, intentional neglect, and deliberate cruelty. National reporting, especially in the Northern press, was relentless in their condemnation. Articles, photographs, and drawings were printed and reprinted, which depicted the Andersonville commandant as the epitome of evil, and in the process, legitimized their historical perspective as unvarnished truth. Though Henry Wirz did demonstrate indifference toward Andersonville's prisoners, he was, in part, a scapegoat, and some evidence against him was fabricated.

Among the 160 witnesses summoned to testify during the Wirz trial were Fathers Hamilton and Whelan, and a former Andersonville prisoner named Boston Corbett.

By far the most damaging testimony against Wirz was that of Felix De la Baume. De la Baume was the only witness who identified a victim by name who was alleged to have been directly murdered by Wirz.

At the trial, De la Baume, a skilled orator, so inspired and impressed the tribunal commission he was given a written commendation signed by all the members regarding his testimony. Additionally, they gave him a position in the Department of the Interior before the Wirz trial ended. Claiming to be a French descendant of Lafayette,

De la Baume was discovered after Wirz's sentencing to actually be Felix Oeser, born in Saxony, Prussia. Oeser lied during testimony to conceal the fact he was a former member of the New York Volunteers who had deserted during the war. Eleven days after the hanging of Henry Wirz, his true identity was discovered and Oeser admitted to perjuring himself during his testimony. Oeser subsequently vanished into obscurity.

Gallows for the Henry Wirz execution. Note the spectators in the trees.

Forty-one-year-old Captain Henry Wirz was one of only three men tried, convicted, and executed for war crimes during the Civil War. The other two were Confederate guerrillas Champ Ferguson, who was tried and hanged in Nashville, and Henry C. Magruder of Louisville, Kentucky. Henry Wirz was hanged at 10:32 a.m. on

November 10th, 1865, at the Old Capitol Prison in Washington D.C.. Just before he was executed, the officer in charge of the execution, Major George B. Russell, expressed sympathy towards Wirz grimly stating, "I have my orders." Wirz calmly replied, "I know what orders are, Major. I am being hanged for obeying them."

In his final correspondence on the morning of his execution, Wirz wrote:

"My life is demanded as an atonement. I am willing to give it, and hope that after a while, I will be judged differently from what I am now."

Henry Wirz's neck did not break from the fall, and the crowd of 200 spectators guarded by 120 soldiers watched as he writhed and slowly strangled to death. There were a few spasmodic convulsions of the chest, a slight movement of the extremities, and all was over. When it was known in the street that Wirz was hanged, the Union soldiers sent up a loud ringing cheer.

Andersonville Prison ceased to exist in May of 1865. During the fourteen months the prison existed, more than 45,000 Union Solders were confined there. Of these, almost 13,000 died from disease, poor sanitation, malnutrition, overcrowding, murder, or exposure to the elements.

The prisoners would never forget the priest, Father Peter Whelan. When they returned home and wrote their memoirs, Father Whelan and his work were often recalled. Some mentioned that he had brought clothing, food, and money from Savannah. One added, "Without a doubt, he was the means of saving hundreds of lives." Another described Whelan's ministering to the sick: "All creeds, color, and nationalities were alike to him…He was indeed the Good Samaritan."

On March 10th, 1866, Father Whelan became ill with a severe attack of "congestion of the lungs", most likely a result of his exposure to the sickness in Andersonville. Before this outbreak, he had written to Secretary of War Edwin Stanton, asking for $400 to pay back his loan from Henry Horne, used to procure bread for the prisoners of Andersonville. By this time, Horne, who was very sick himself, needed the money.

Stanton replied late in October, asking for sworn vouchers and bills of purchase for the wheat flour. The priest replied to Stanton to keep the money because he had, "neither the health nor the strength…to run over Georgia to hunt up vouchers and bills of purchase." Unable to make any headway, the priest informed the Secretary that the "good God" had provided him with another way to repay this debt.

Because of his worsening lung condition, his doctors had recommended that Father Whelan go north to escape the humid air. His friends in Savannah provided him with the necessary funds to make the trip to New York.

Instead, the priest informed Secretary Stanton that, preferring justice to health, Whelan used the travel funds given him to refund the money loaned by Mr. Henry Horne.

When his health improved slightly, Whelan became pastor of St. Patrick's in Savannah and served there until 1868. He was never his former self, however. The cathedral register in Savannah shows that Whelan administered his last baptism on January 15th, 1871.

Two weeks later his imminent death was announced. The priest received the sacraments and died a little after five o'clock on the evening of Monday, February 6th, 1871, at the age of sixty-nine.

The Savannah Evening News described the funeral procession four days later as the longest ever seen in the city and added that seldom was so large a gathering of people found in the streets of Savannah. Eighty-six carriages and buggies escorted the body through the crowded avenues to the Catholic cemetery. People from all over the city turned out to bid farewell to this beloved priest, including many non-Catholics.

Col. Reuben B. Hatch

Chief Quartermaster Colonel Reuben Hatch repeatedly ignored subpoenas to appear in ensuing inquiries and tribunals, likely again benefiting from political connections. With Speed's exoneration, the military closed the books on the *Sultana* tragedy. In the end, no one was held responsible. The *Sultana* tragedy was the worst maritime disaster in the history of the United States, with initially more casualties attributed to it than the ill-fated and more renowned sinking of the *Titanic*.

One report to Secretary of War, Edwin Stanton, concluded that overcrowding should be written off as an extenuating circumstance needed during the war. The explosion of three boilers was the most immediate cause of the *Sultana* disaster. But of all the men who deserved blame for the extent of the tragedy, none were more culpable than Colonel Reuben Hatch.

On June 3rd, 1865, after the report of his incompetence from months earlier was finally approved, Reuben Hatch was relieved of his duties as Chief Quartermaster of the Department of the Mississippi. A few weeks later, he boarded the northbound steamer *Atlantic*, carrying $14,490 in government money. During the voyage, the safe of the *Atlantic* was robbed. The thief was caught before the boat reached St. Louis, and all the money

Illinois Secretary of State
Ozias M. Hatch

was recovered, except for more than $8,500 in government funds that Hatch claimed he had placed in the safe. He was found to have violated military regulations by removing the funds from the Department and was held personally liable for the loss of the money. Thus, Hatch's career ended as it began—in controversy. Hatch died in 1871, having escaped justice due to his numerous highly placed patrons, including two presidents and his brother, the Illinois Secretary of State.

Epilogue

*"What power have I that I should endure?
Or what is mine end, if I should prolong my life?"*
—Job 6:11 GNV

After the war, John McElroy made his way to Ottawa, Ohio, where he worked in a drugstore and studied pharmacology. There he met the daughter of the pharmacy's owner, Elsie Pomeroy. They were married in 1866 and later had two children. The McElroy family moved to Chicago where he worked as a newspaper reporter and editorial writer for *The Inter-Ocean*. Political satirist David R. Locke remembered McElroy, and in 1874 hired him as the editor of the Ohio newspaper, *The Toledo Blade*.

In 1879, McElroy wrote, "Andersonville: A Story of Rebel Military Prisons", a non-fiction work based on his experiences during his fifteen-month incarceration. It quickly became a bestseller and remained popular for the next twenty years. He had thought that most people reading his work would deny it was true, and that he would be accused of hatred of the South. But he couldn't have been more mistaken. The horrible spectacle of Andersonville would soon be confirmed by more than 3,000 letters of support and encouragement from survivors, asserting that it was indeed an accurate account.

In 1884, he relocated from Toledo to Washington, D. C. to become editor and co-owner of the newspaper *The National Tribune* John McElroy died at age 83, on October 12, 1929. He is buried at Arlington National Cemetery in Arlington, Virginia.

Robert Knox Sneden

Altogether, Robert Knox Sneden had sketched scenes of prison life in all the facilities where he was incarcerated: Andersonville, Savannah, and Millen in Georgia; and in Florence and Charleston in South Carolina.

After the Civil War, Sneden returned to Brooklyn, where he had been already declared dead or missing. Sneden made a number of his war sketches into watercolors, leaving a legacy of close to 1,000 watercolors, drawings, sketches, maps, and diagrams.

Sneden contributed some of them to the *Battles and Leaders of the Civil War*, a series of articles published between 1884 and 1887 in *The Century Magazine*, and then re-issued them as a four-volume set of books. Crippled from his time in Andersonville, Sneden never married and devoted the rest of his life to preserving the Civil War memory. In 1918, Sneden died in the New York State Soldiers' and Sailors' Home at age 86. Sneden's extensive collection of documents and drawings, however, would not be re-discovered for over one hundred years since they were last published.

In 1994, an art dealer approached the Virginia Historical Society about a Civil War archive that for many years had languished in a Connecticut bank vault. Robert Sneden's great-great-nephew also transferred through purchase, Sneden's diary and watercolors, close to 5,000 pages of the diary entries and memoirs, and nearly 500 watercolors and maps. According to the Virginia Historical Society, it was, "the largest collection of American Civil War soldier art ever produced". With very few photographs taken of Civil War POW life, documentary-style images created by Robert Knox Sneden are considered important historical records.

Eppenetus (Epp) W. McIntosh of the 14th Illinois Infantry had served honorably, been captured by the enemy, endured confinement at Andersonville Prison, and survived the *Sultana* disaster. Epp had indeed survived all this but consequently, was left a shell of a man from his horrors. He had been wounded at least three times in battle, twice in the left shoulder and once in the right foot.

Eppenetus McIntosh displaying his musical instruments.

Returning to Illinois upon his recovery furlough, he married a local girl named Elizabeth "Lizzie" Holmes in 1867. Epp stayed gone from home for prolonged periods of time but was around long enough to father three boys. His prison confinement likely triggered a behavior in him known as the "wandering jones."

Epp was accused of faking his disability, even though he received none of the money from it. Charged with falsifying statements on his disability application by the family doctor, Epp responded with accusations of an adulterous affair going on between the doctor and his wife Lizzie. Pension records and letters about an ongoing fight with his wife Lizzie illustrate Epp's continued struggle. Lizzie McIntosh had him declared incompetent in 1888, claiming his military pension for herself and the children. Epp's only income after that was from his street performances about his life in Andersonville Prison and surviving the *Sultana* disaster. He played music, sang songs, and supplemented his income by selling songbooks of his compositions and cards with a depiction of himself as an emaciated soldier, entitled "The Living Skeleton" —imploring audiences to "help an old vet."

Epp's wife Lizzie died in 1916, and suddenly Epp was declared competent and capable of handling his own finances again. In the 1920s, he was a passenger in a train wreck. He had left his seat to go to the bathroom and miraculously avoided being killed in the crash. Epp was next to the door of the railway car and escaped the subsequent fire. He lost his guitar but was able to save his banjo. So it was Epp and his banjo, on the road entertaining people.

Relatives and descendants of Eppenetus McIntosh described him as a colorful and interesting character who enjoyed embellishing factual stories with tall tales. Blending absolute truths with unbelievable adventures shaped the narrative of his life's story. Documented evidence such as census and pension records exist proving his service during the Civil War, his capture and confinement as a prisoner of war at Andersonville, his parole at Vicksburg, and his survival of the *Sultana* disaster. Whether or not Epp was ever actually Lincoln's office boy or if they ever met is still up for debate and his claim concerning his wife's indiscretions with the family physician is questionable. Either way, Epp lived an amazing and eventful life full of pain, heartache, joy, and triumph.

Epp finally succumbed to Parkinson's disease in July of 1927. He was aged 83 years and eight months. Eppenetus Washington McIntosh is buried in the Leavenworth National Cemetery, Leavenworth, Kansas.

"But above all things have fervent love among you: for love shall cover the multitude of sins." —1 Peter 4:8 GNV

Acknowledgements

I would like to thank the many people who have assisted me in the creation of this book. Without them, it would never have been possible. First and foremost, I would like to thank my Lord and personal savior Jesus Christ for the many blessings bestowed upon me – among them the health and faculties that allow the creation of this work you now hold.

A heartfelt "thank you" to my wife and the love of my life, Lesa. You have shown me love and strength and nourished and encouraged me in so many ways. Honey, you're the greatest.

Thanks to my son Alex, of whom I am exceedingly proud. An accomplished young man who can find humor in doing all those things that annoy his mother.

Thanks to my grandparents, Tom & Maggie, Dick & Ida Bea. Thanks to my parents, David & Ruth, and my brothers Bruce & Tom. "Oh, the stories we could tell!"

Thanks to my "brothers from other mothers", the old "Hill Estate Gang" in Franklin, who played "cops and robbers" at Fort Granger all those unforgettable days of our youth. You know who you are. You have all molded and shaped me with your presence. I love you all.

I would like to acknowledge my alma mater, The Franklin High School Class of '76.

A well-deserved thank you and a humble tip of my cap to my editor and guiding light, Kathy Rhodes, who steered me away from the obstacles and pitfalls of maintaining an accurate timeline, verb tense consistency, sentence structure, and those pesky redundancies. You believed in the work, kept me on track, and made the process less painful than it probably could have been.

I would be remiss if I didn't pay tribute to the resources on the Sultana disaster that motivated and informed me: Jerry O. Potter's superb book, *The Sultana Tragedy*; the inspiring and excellent *Disaster on the Mississippi* by Gene Salecker; the original and groundbreaking *Loss of the Sultana and Reminiscences of Survivors* by Chester D. Berry; Rosalind O'Neal the preeminent outspoken docent and cheerleader for the *Sultana Disaster Museum* in Marion, Arkansas. You left us too soon, Roz.

Thanks are in order and a huge shout out to the definitive and masterful work exploring the Lincoln assassination, *American Brutus: John Wilkes Booth and the Lincoln Conspiracies*, by Michael W. Kauffman. On the same subject, I would like to also acknowledge excellent sources, *Blood on the Moon: The Assassination of Abraham Lincoln*, by Edward Steers, Jr., and *Manhunt: The 12-Day Chase for Lincoln's Killer*, by James L. Swanson.

I would like to humbly thank the members of The Williamson County Writer's Group. This group was a Godsend to a Greenhorn writer like me. They showed a lot of patience and encouragement throughout the process of making the manuscript better than it was. We shared many Saturday mornings and quite a few laughs at the Williamson County Public Library in historic Franklin, Tennessee. The following members offered their invaluable and generous critiques, input, and vision:

George Spain (*our very own Mark Twain emeritus*), Alan Christman, Cindy King, Ralph Chumbley, Bill Woods, Chris Rosland, Eddie Moth, Ed Triggs, Aaron Broudy, Lee Gerhard, Sandy Zeigler, Kelly DeVerter, and Pam Hertzog. A wonderfully talented bunch with sharp eyes and even sharper pencils. If I have missed anyone, dear friends and gentle readers, blame it on my questionable memory.

The staff at the Williamson County Public Library was very supportive of me personally and of the Williamson County Writer's Group. I would like to express my gratitude to the empress of the Library's Special Collections Section, Marcia Fraser. Marcia generously offered her time and assistance every time I asked. Your patience and support were appreciated more than you'll ever know. Thank you, Paige Hurley, for your problem-solving prowess and technical wizardry.

Thanks to the staff at the Brentwood Library in Brentwood, Tennessee for being an excellent research source. The Roundtable discussions at the historic Carnton House and visits to the celebrated Lotz House Museum were also inspirational in the creation of this book.

Thank you to the staff of the National Park Service of Andersonville, Shiloh, Appomattox, The Surrattsville Tavern & Inn (the knowledgeable guide Coby Treadway in particular), and Ford's Theatre. The rangers and guides were invaluable to my research. Thank you all.

Phillip Anthony Perry
Williamson County, Tennessee

References

Berry, Chester D. (1892). *Loss of the Sultana and Reminiscences of Survivors*

Bonds, Russell S. (2009). *War Like the Thunderbolt: The Battle and Burning of Atlanta*

Browne, Francis Fisher (1886). *The Every-day Life of Abraham Lincoln: A Narrative and Descriptive Biography with Pen-pictures and Personal Recollections by Those Who Knew Him*

Burnett, William G. (2014). *The Prison Camp at Andersonville*

Carwardine, Richard (2006). *Lincoln: A Life of Purpose and Power*

Catton, Bruce (1953). *A Stillness at Appomattox*

Chamlee, Jr., Roy Z. (1990). *Lincoln's Assassins: A Complete Account of Their Capture, Trial, and Punishment*

Chernow, Ron (2017). *Grant*

Clarke, Asia Booth (1996). Alford, Terry (ed.). *John Wilkes Booth: A Sister's Memoir*

Colton, J. H. (1861). *National Geographic Atlas of the Civil War*

Commanger, Henry Steele (1950). *The Blue And The Gray – Two Volumes In One*

Cox, Jacob D. (January 30, 2003). *The March to the Sea/Franklin and Nashville*

Crook, William H. (1907). *Lincoln's Last Day: New Facts Now Told for the First Time*

Davis, Jefferson (1890). *Andersonville and Other War-Prisons*

Doherty, Edward P. (1890). *Pursuit and Death of John Wilkes Booth, Century Magazine XXXIX* (January 1890)

Donald, David Herbert (1995). *Lincoln*

Goodrich, Thomas (2005). *The Darkest Dawn: Lincoln, Booth, and the Great American Tragedy*

Goodwin, Doris Kearns (2005). *Team of Rivals: The Political Genius of Abraham Lincoln*

Grant, Ulysses S. (1885). *The Personal Memoirs of Ulysses S. Grant*

Grant, Ulysses S. (1990). *Memoirs and Selected Letters*

Grimsley, Mark (2007). *The Hard Hand of War: Union Military Policy towards Southern Civilians, 1861-1865*

Halkim, Joy (2002). *War, Terrible War 1855-1865*

Hartranft, John F.; Steers, Edward; and Holzer, Harold (2009). *The Lincoln Assassination Conspirators: Their Confinement and Execution, As Recorded in the Letterbook of John Frederick Hartranft*

Hatch, Frederick (2011). *Protecting President Lincoln: The Security Effort, the Thwarted Plots, and the Disaster at Ford's Theatre*

Hirshson, Stanley P. (1998). *The White Tecumseh: A Biography of William T. Sherman*

Holden-Reid, Brian (2020). *The Scourge of War: The Life of William Tecumseh Sherman*

Huffman, Alan (2009). *Sultana: Surviving the Civil War, Prison, and the Worst Maritime Disaster in American History*

Jacobson, Eric A., and Richard A. Rupp (2007). *For Cause & for Country: A Study of the Affair at Spring Hill and the Battle of Franklin*

Jameson, W. C. (2013). *John Wilkes Booth: Beyond the Grave*

Johnson, Byron Berkley (1914). *Abraham Lincoln and Boston Corbett: With Personal Recollections of Each*

Johnson, B. B. (1914). *John Wilkes Booth and Jefferson Davis, a True Story of Their Capture*

Jones, Madison (1997). *Nashville 1864 – The Dying of the Light*

Kauffman, Michael W. (2004). *American Brutus: John Wilkes Booth and the Lincoln Conspiracies*

Kellogg, Robert H. (1865). *Life and Death in Rebel Prisons*

Kennett, Lee B. (2002). *Sherman: A Soldier's Life*

Kubicek, Earl C, (1981). *"The Case of the Mad Hatter"*
Kunhardt, Jr., Philip (1983). *A New Birth of Freedom*
Kunhardt, Philip B.; Kunhardt, Peter W. (2008). *Looking for Lincoln: The Making of an American Icon*
Lash, J. N. (2003). *A politician turned general: The Civil War career of Stephen Augustus Hurlbut*
Leale, Charles (1909). *Lincoln's Last Hours*
Lewis, Lloyd B. (1932). *Sherman: Fighting Prophet*
Loux, Arthur F. (2014). *John Wilkes Booth: Day by Day*
Martelle, Scott (2015). *The Madman and the Assassin: The Strange Life of Boston Corbett, the Man Who Killed John Wilkes Booth*
Marszalek, John F. (1993). *Sherman: A Soldier's Passion for Order*
McElroy, John (1879). *Andersonville: A Story of Rebel Military Prisons*
McElroy, John (1865). *This was Andersonville*
McPherson, James M. (2008). *Tried by War: Abraham Lincoln as Commander in Chief*
Mudd, Nettie (1906). *The Life of Dr. Samuel A. Mudd*
National Park Service (2017) *Pamphlet Andersonville*
O'Neal, Rosalind Reynolds (2021). *Curator: The Sultana Disaster Museum (personal interview)*
O'Reilly, Bill (2011). *Killing Lincoln: The Shocking Assassination that Changed America Forever*
Page, James Madison & Haley, M. J. (1908). *The True Story of Andersonville Prison*
Potter, Jerry O. (1992). *The Sultana Tragedy: America's Greatest Maritime Disaster*
Ransom, John (1881). *John Ransom's Andersonville Diary*
Ransom, John L. (2017). *Andersonville Diary, Escape, and List of the Dead: With Name, Co., Regiment, Date of Death and No. of Grave in Cemetery*
Ripple, Ezra Hoyt (1996). *Dancing Along the Deadline*
Salecker, Gene (1996). *Disaster on the Mississippi: The Sultana Explosion, April 27, 1865*
Sanger, Donald B.; Hay, Thomas Robson (1952). *James Longstreet: I. Soldier II. Politician, Officeholder, and Writer*

Segars, J. H. (1995). *Andersonville: The Southern Perspective*

Shaara, Michael (1974). *The Killer Angels*

Shaara, Michael (1998). *Gods and Generals*

Sherman, William T. (1875). *Memoirs of General William T. Sherman*

Smith, Gene (1992). *American Gothic: The Story of America's Legendary Theatrical Familt, Junius, Edwin, and John Wilkes Booth*

Sneden, Robert Knox (1832-1918). *Civil War Maps, Library of Congress*

Sneden, Robert Knox (2000). *Eye of the Storm: A Civil War Odyssey*

Steers, Jr., Edward (2001). *Blood on the Moon: The Assassination of Abraham Lincoln*

Steers, Jr., Edward (2010). *The Lincoln Assassination Encyclopedia*

Steinhorst, Stephanie & Barr, Chris (2022). *The Prison Camp at Andersonville*

Stephens, Caleb *(2014). Worst Seat in the House: Henry Rathbone's Front Row View of the Lincoln Assassination*

Stern, Philip Van Doren (1939). *The Man Who Killed Lincoln*

Stevenson, R. Randolph (1876). *The Southern Side of Andersonville Prison*

Swanson, James L. (2006). *Manhunt: The 12-Day Chase for Lincoln's Killer*

Talcott, Sebastian V. (2001). *Genealogical Notes of New York and New England Families*

Tidwell, William A. (1995). *April '65*

The Trial of Henry Wirz, 40th Congress, 2nd Session, House Executive Document 23 (Washington, 1868)

Trindal, Elizabeth Steger (1996). *Mary Surratt: An American Tragedy*

Virginia Historical Society (2000). *Eye of the Storm: The Civil War Drawings of Robert Knox Sneden*

Wade, Hall (1998). *One Man's Lincoln*

Walker, Dale L.; Jakes, John (1997). *Legends and Lies: Great Mysteries of the American West*

Watkins, Sam R. (1882). *Co. Aytch: A Confederate Memoir of the Civil War*

Weichmann, Louis J. (1975). *A True History of the Assassination of Abraham Lincoln and the Conspiracy of 1865*

Wert, Jeffrey D. (1993). *General James Longstreet: The Confederacy's Most Controversial Soldier – A Biography*

Wheeler, Richard (1989). *Witness to Appomattox*

Wilson, Robert (2021). *Dignity in Defeat: Mathew Brady's Photos of Robert E. Lee*

Winik, Jay (2001). *April 1865: The Month That Saved America*

Woodworth, Steven E. (1990). *Jefferson Davis and His Generals: The Failure of Confederate Command in the West*. University Press of Kansas, Lawrence, KS.

PERIODICALS, WEBSITES, & PERSONAL INTERVIEWS

amp.dispatch.com/amp/23150334007 (2022)

archaeology.org/exclusives/articles/1504-camp-lawton-robert-knox-sneden. (2021)

Annales de la Propagation de la Foi, Report of the Diocese of Savannah, vol. 37 (1893): 397 – 401 (trans. Andrew Smith, O.S.B.

"Andersonville, 150 Years Ago." History. Accessed August 28, 2022. https://www.history.com/news/andersonville-150-years-ago.

"Andersonville Prison of the Civil War." Legends of America. Accessed August 28, 2022. https://www.legendsofamerica.com/andersonville-prison-georgia/.

Boyd (D.F), mss. [manuscripts] in possession of Walter L. Fleming, Nashville, TN".

Clara Barton and Andersonville. National Park Service, (retrieved January 30, 2016). Andersonville, GA.

Collected Works of Abraham Lincoln. Volume 8. Lincoln, Abraham, 1809-1865.

Conti, Gerald (June 1984). *"Seeing the Elephant."* Civil War Times Illustrated.

Cox, Jacob D. (January 30, 2003). *The March to the Sea/Franklin and Nashville*. Civilwarhome.com. Retrieved July 19, 2012.

Crook, William H. (1907). *Lincoln's Last Day: New Facts Now Told for the First Time*. Compiled and written down by Margarita S. Gerry, Harper's Monthly Magazine no. 115, Sept. 1907. 523.

Daily National Republican Washington, D.C. 11 April 1865, 2nd edition, 2:4 *Evening Star* (retrieved 2021).

Dattel, Eugene R. (2008). https://www.mshistorynow.mdah.ms.gov/issue/cotton-and-the-civil-war.

Ely, John Clark (March 24, 1865). Journal Entry, upon exiting Andersonville Prison.

Exchange in a letter between William Tecumseh Sherman and Professor David F. Boyd, December 24, 1860.

Hank Harvey, *"The Sinking of the Sultana"* (Toledo: *Toledo Magazine*, October 27, 1996). Accessed on Wikipedia April 27, 2015.

Harper's Weekly, May 13 edition, 1865.

Hawes, Lilla M., ed., *"Charles Olmstead Memoirs, pt. 6" Georgia Historical Quarterly* 44 (March 1960).

History of Bloomington, History of Bloomington City Website, archived February 13, 2008.

HistoryNet.com (2017) *Sultana: A Tragic Postscript to the Civil War* Historynet.com/laws-war-trial-thomas-knox.

Historynet.com/laws-war-trial-thomas-knox. This article appears in the Summer 2017 issue (Vol. 29, No. 4) of *MHQ—The Quarterly Journal of Military History* with the headline: *The Trial of Thomas Knox*.

Horne, Mrs. Richard of Kathleen, Georgia. Personal Notes and correspondence.

Jennings, Pat (2015). *What Happened to the Sultana?* https://www.nationalboard.org/SiteDocuments/General%20Meeting/Jennings.pdf.

"Lieber Code". Oxford Public International Law. Retrieved November 9, 2017.

Lincolnconspirators.com/*Jett-Ruggles-Bainbridge*. (2021)

Morcom, Richard (October 1970). *"They All Loved Lucy."* American History Magazine. Archived from the original 2010.

The New York Times (April 22, 1916). *John H. Surratt Dead! The Last of the Alleged Conspirators in the Lincoln Assassination*. Retrieved November 14, 2020. p. 11.

New York Times (July 30, 1896). *John Wilkes Booth's Last Days*

New York Times (May 7, 1888). *The Sultana's Destroyer. A Mystery of the War Claimed to be Solved*

O'Neal, Rosalind: Docent of the Sultana Disaster Museum (personal interview).

Savannah Daily News-Herald, (June 4, 1866).

Savannah Morning News (December 18, 1885).

Savannah Morning News (March 15, 1959).

"Soldier Details: Wirz, Henry, General and Staff Officers, Non-Regimental Enlisted Men, CSA." Civil War Soldiers and Sailors Database. Accessed September 12, 2022. https://www.nps.gov/civilwar/search-soldiers.htm.

Steinhorst, Stephanie and Barr, Chris, *The Prison Camp at Andersonville* (Based on the original text by William G. Burnett). Accessed September 12, 2022. http://link.coweta.ga.us/portal/The-prison-camp-at-Andersonville-text-by/fKPU5neCq2U/.

suspectunusual.livejournal.com (2022)

Treadway, Coby, Historian, Educator, & Tour Guide – National Park Service, Surrattsville Inn & Tavern, personal interview.

Walker, Dale (2005). *The Mad Hatter*. American Cowboy Magazine, September Issue. 12 (3): 82.

Wamsley, Erin J. (retrieved 2022). Department of Psychology and Program in Neuroscience. Furman University, Greenville, SC. (https://pubmed.ncbi.nlm.nih.gov/30091247/).

Washington Evening Star (December 7, 1870). *The Text of John Surratt's Lecture at Rockville, Maryland*. Retrieved August 30, 2011.

Wilson, Robert (2013). *Dignity in Defeat: Why Robert E. Lee Sat for Photographer Mathew Brady So Soon After Appomattox*. From MHQ: The Quarterly Journal of Military History (Vol. 26, Issue 1). World History Group, LLC.

Wilson, Robert (2021). *Dignity in Defeat: Mathew Brady's Photos of Robert E. Lee*. HistoryNet Retrieved from https://www.historynet.com/dignity-in-defeat-mathew-bradys-photos-of-robert-e-lee/.

https://famous-trials.com/lincoln/2157-commissionorder

https://famous-trials.com/lincoln/2154-marysurratt

https://www.historynet.com/george-mcclellan/.

https://www.georgiaencyclopedia.org/articles/history-archaeology/civil-war-industry-and-manufacturing/.

https://virginiahistory.org/learn/how-did-slaves-support-confederacy.

https://historycollection.com/slavery-in-the-confederate-states-army/21/.

https://www.shermanhouse.org/Sherman-Family-History.html.

https://www.mchistory.org/research/biographies/allin-james.

https://suspectunusual.livejournal.com/4315.html.

https://www.jstor.org/stable/25701281.

https://yesteryearsnews.wordpress.com/tag/eppetenus-mcintosh/

https://military-history.fandom.com/wiki/President_Lincoln%27s_75,000_volunteers.

https://www.washingtonpost.com/lifestyle/kidspost/drummer-boys-played-important-roles-in-the-civil-war-and-some-became-soldiers/2012/01/31/gIQA3cKzRR_story.html.

https://www.thoughtco.com/civil-war-drummer-boys-1773732.

http://www.civilwararchive.com/Unreghst/unilinf1.htm.

https://www.evangelizationstation.com/htm_html/Vocation%20Links/priest_of_andersonville.htm.

https://www.irishgeorgia.com/Whelan.

https://praoh.org/fr-peter-whelan-angel-andersonville/.

https://historycollection.com/the-life-of-a-prisoner-at-camp-sumter-during-the-civil-war/7/.

http://www.jstor.org/stable/25701281; Stevens, R. A., & Tharp, B. (2010). *Incredible Stories of Uncle Epp: Soldier, POW, Survivor, Minstrel, and Lincoln's Office Boy*. Journal of the Illinois State Historical Society (1998-), 103(2),.

https://en.wikipedia.org/wiki/Camp_Lawton_(Georgia).

http://www.abrahamlincolnonline.org/lincoln/speeches/speed.htm (retrieved 2021).

U.S. Library of Congress website on Lincoln's second inauguration-
https://www.loc.gov/resource/msspin.pin2202/?st=gallery.

https://www.measuringworth.com/dollarvaluetoday/?amount=10000&from=1864#.

http://thelincolnlog.org/Results.aspx?type=CalendarMonth&year=1865&month=4.

https://living-in-history.org/2020/12/07/the-surprising-reason-the-lincolns-owned-a-rebel-flag/.

https://www.history.com/this-day-in-history/lincoln-dreams-about-a-presidential-assassination.

https://www.dailymail.co.uk/news/article-2086848/Check-President-Abraham-Lincoln-wrote-day-killed-discovered-bank-vault.html (retrieved 2022).

https://historynewsnetwork.org/article/159117.

https://www.loc.gov/resource/rbpe.20405900/?st=text.

https://www.abrahamlincolnsclassroom.org/abraham-lincolns-contemporaries/abraham-lincoln-and-william-h-seward/.

https://npsfrsp.wordpress.com/2011/04/20/brutus%e2%80%99-judas-willie-jett-part-1/.

https://lincolnconspirators.com/2015/01/15/retracing-the-steps-of-the-16th-new-york/.

https://www.nytimes.com/1865/04/21/archives/the-murderer-of-mr-lincoln-extraordinary-letter-of-john-wilkes.html.

https://www.usni.org/magazines/naval-history-magazine/2009/august/death-river.

https://www.washingtonpost.com/history/2020/02/02/jefferson-davis-trial-impeachment/.

https://www.washingtonpost.com/local/four-people-were-hanged-for-lincolns-assassination--and-it-was-caught-on-camera/2015/07/03/377614d4-1905-11e5-ab92-c75ae6ab94b5_story.html.

http://civilwaref.blogspot.com/2013/04/the-explosion-of-sultana-april-27-1865.html.

https://www.prisonersofeternity.com/blog/sultana-tragedy-on-the-mississippi/.

https://worldhistoryproject.org/1864/1/confederate-secret-service-manufactures-coal-torpedoes.

https://timesmachine.nytimes.com/timesmachine/1888/05/07/103173226.pdf.

https://constitution.congress.gov/constitution/amendment.

yesteryearsnews.wordpress.com/tag/eppenetus-mcintosh

PHILLIP ANTHONY PERRY

Notes and Resources

Prologue

The information in this section comes primarily from an old book by Rev. Chester D. Berry, published in 1892, twenty-seven years after the disaster, titled Loss of the Sultana and Reminiscences of Survivors. Some information comes from an author interview in 2021 with Rosiland Reynolds O'Neal, docent of the Sultana Disaster Museum.

The stench rising on the smoke: Jerry O. Potter, *The Sultana Tragedy—America's Greatest Maritime Disaster* (New Orleans: Pelican, 1992), pp. 107-112. Chester D. Berry, *Loss of the Sultana and Reminiscences of Survivors* (Lansing, Michigan: Darius D Thorp, 1892), p. xix-xx.

The remainder of the sidewheel paddleboat: Chester D. Berry, *Loss of the Sultana and Reminiscences of Survivors* (Lansing, Michigan: Darius D. Thorp, 1892), p. xiv, 9.

The vessel, rudderless and swirling: Ibid., p. 9.

The drummer boy from Springfield: Ibid., p. 253.

The drummer stripped himself of all his clothes: Ibid.

Later, bodies would be found in treetops: Hank Harvey, "The Sinking of the Sultana" (Toledo: *Toledo Magazine*, October 27, 1996). Accessed on Wikipedia April 27, 2015. https://en.wikipedia.org/wiki/Sultana_(steamboat)#cite_note-Harvey,_Hank_1996,_Pages_3,6-11.

Chapter 1

How he wound up here: Robert Knox Sneden, *Eye of the Storm: A Civil War Odyssey* (New York: The Free Press, 2000), p. 149.

Robert Sneden's satchel was now full: Ibid., p. 143.

Bleeding and brushing through the thickets of briers: This paragraph and the four that follow imagine a likely scenario of worn and frazzled soldiers living and marching closely together.

He sat atop a mare: Sneden, *Eye of the Storm*, pp. 146-147.

That evening, as the V Corps: Ibid., p. 146.

As the sun set, he watched: Ibid., p. 147.

Later, he walked outside in the darkness: Ibid., p. 148.

He awakened to a whisper in his ear: Ibid., p. 149.

"Be silent, or I'll blow a hole through you.": Ibid., p. 149.

"Get into your clothes right smart. Mosby wants you.": Ibid., p. 149.

Now, wide-eyed and suddenly sick: Ibid., p. 149.

November 27th, Confederate Rangers: Ibid., p. 149.

Robert Sneden served as a prisoner of war: Ibid., pp. 168, 190.

They were loaded onto crowded cattle cars: John McElroy, *Andersonville: A Story of Rebel Military Prisons* (Zinc Read, 2022). Sneden, *Eye of the Storm*, pp. 192-202.

The prisoners got very little subsistence: Sneden, *Eye of the Storm*, pp. 194-202.

When the train arrived at the depot in Andersonville: J. H. Segars, *Andersonville: The Southern Perspective* (Gretna, Louisiana: Pelican, 1995), p. 124.

These detachments were then subdivided: Ibid., p. 124.

The commandant of the prison was General John Henry Winder: Ezra Hoyt Ripple, *Dancing Along the Deadline* (Novato, California: Presidio Press, 1996), p. 43.

John Henry Winder's features seemed to illustrate: John McElroy and Roy Meredith, *This Was Andersonville* (New York: Bonanza Books, 1957), pp. 10-12.

Chapter 2

It was amazing how quickly humanity: William G. Burnett, *The Prison Camp at Andersonville* (Steinhorst & Barr, 2014), p. 16.

A makeshift market had gradually developed: Ibid., pp. 18-19.

In one journal entry, he quoted: J. H. Segars, *Andersonville: The Southern Perspective* (Gretna, Louisiana: Pelican, 1995), p. 148.

In a journal entry dated July 27, 1864: Ripple, *Dancing Along the Deadline*, p. 45.

After Robert Sneden entered the gates of Andersonville: Burnett, *The Prison Camp at Andersonville*, p. 11.

Robert had somehow managed to keep his distance: Ibid., p. 22.

The growing POW population in the Confederate capital: "Andersonville, 150 Years Ago." History. Accessed August 28, 2022. https://www.history.com/news/andersonville-150-years-ago

"I would respectfully suggest that the city of Richmond": Burnett, *The Prison Camp at Andersonville*, p. 5.

The city of Richmond was pushed to the brink: Ibid., p. 5.

The selected site was chosen: Ibid., pp. 5-6.

It was a family affair concerning the site selection: Ibid., p. 11.

For weeks on end, slaves labored: Ibid., pp. 6-7.

The Union soldiers imprisoned there lived: Ibid., p. 11.

Thousands more prisoners came and milled: Ibid., p. 13.

Many of the men had rags for clothes: Ibid., p. 13.

As a measure to keep the prisoners away from the stockade walls: Ibid., p. 11.

The rebel guards situated in towers atop the wall: "Andersonville Prison of the Civil War." Legends of America. Accessed August 28, 2022. https://www.legendsofamerica.com/andersonville-prison-georgia/

He offered prisoners a twelve-hour head start: Ripple, *Dancing Along the Deadline*, pp. 16-17.

He often used intimidation and brutality: "Andersonville Prison of the Civil War."

The habitually disobedient prisoners: Segars, *Andersonville: The Southern Perspective*, p. 122.

When the ration cart was not in use doling out meager rations: Sneden, *Eye of the Storm*, p. 218.

In a May 25, 1864, report sent to his uncle: Burnett, *The Prison Camp at Andersonville*, p. 12.

In Andersonville, 6,721 prisoners died: Segars, *Andersonville: The Southern Perspective*, pp. 29-30.

By Robert's calculations, each prisoner was allotted: Sneden, *Eye of the Storm*, p. 227.

By the end of the war, 45,613 Union prisoners: Burnett, *The Prison Camp at Andersonville*, p. 34.

Chapter 3

To a newcomer, the stench: Robert Knox Sneden, *Eye of the Storm: A Civil War Odyssey* (New York: The Free Press, 2000), p. 204.

Today was already hot and muggy: Ibid., p. 203.

After recovering from wounds received: "Soldier Details: Wirz, Henry, General and Staff Officers, Non-Regimental Enlisted Men, CSA." Civil War Soldiers and Sailors Database. Accessed September 12, 2022. https://www.nps.gov/civilwar/search-soldiers.htm

In this remote location with meager supplies: Sneden, *Eye of the Storm*, p. 202.

Prisoners and guards alike suffered: J. H. Segars, *Andersonville: The Southern Perspective* (Gretna, Louisiana: Pelican, 1995), p. 84.

"God help you, I cannot: Ibid., pp. 74, 93.

For many, Andersonville was likely: Ibid., p. 128.

Captain Wirz fancied himself a great leader: Stephanie Steinhorst and Chris Barr, *The Prison Camp at Andersonville* (Based on original text by William G. Burnett). Accessed September 12, 2022.

After repeated correspondence by Confederate Commissioner: Segars, *Andersonville: The Southern Perspective*, pp. 42-44.

Additionally, if those numbers: Ibid., pp. 47-48, 75-77.

Chapter 4

George Brinton McClellan: https://www.historynet.com/george-mcclellan/.

In contrast, Lincoln strongly supported: McPherson, James M. (2008). *Tried by*

War: Abraham Lincoln as Commander in Chief. Penguin Books. New York, NY pp. 231 – 250.

Northern support was wavering: Ibid., p. 653.

It was in this setting: Holden-Reid, Brian (2020). *The Scourge of War: The Life of William Tecumseh Sherman.* Oxford University Press. New York, NY p. 330.

"Made in Atlanta": https://www.georgiaencyclopedia.org/articles/history-archaeology/civil-war-industry-and-manufacturing/

The destruction of Atlanta: https://virginiahistory.org/learn/how-did-slaves-support-confederacy

using slave labor: https://historycollection.com/slavery-in-the-confederate-states-army/21/

Part of the success: Marszalek, John F. (1993). *Sherman: A Soldier's Passion for Order.* The Free Press. New York, NY p. 260.

He proclaimed: Simpson & Berlin (1999), *Telegram W.T. Sherman to Gen. Ulysses S. Grant*, October 9, 1864, reproduced in p. 731.

Mary Sherman had no choice: Holden-Reid, Brian (2020). *The Scourge of War: The Life of William Tecumseh Sherman.* Oxford University Press. New York, NY p. 21.

"Cump" Sherman: Walsh, George (2005). *Whip the Rebellion.* Forge Books. p. 32.

These tragic circumstances: Marszalek, John F. (1993). *Sherman: A Soldier's Passion for Order.* The Free Press. New York, NY pp. 1 – 6.

The Sherman family legacy: https://www.shermanhouse.org/Sherman-Family-History.html

Burdened with anxiety: Holden-Reid, Brian (2020) *The Scourge of War: The Life of William Tecumseh Sherman*, Oxford University Press. New York, NY p. 24.

He entered the service: Lewis, Lloyd B. (1932). *Sherman: Fighting Prophet*, University of Nebraska Press, Lincoln, NE. p. 138.

Long before the Civil War: Ibid., p. 138.; attributed to "Boyd (D.F), mss. [manuscripts] in possession of Walter L. Fleming, Nashville, TN".

You people of the South: Exchange in a letter between William Tecumseh Sherman and Professor David F. Boyd, December 24, 1860.

Cump Sherman continued: Marszalek, John F. (1993). *Sherman: A Soldier's Passion for Order*. The Free Press. New York, NY pp. 46 – 47.

He then spent a month: Holden-Reid, Brian (2020) *The Scourge of War: The Life of William Tecumseh Sherman*, Oxford University Press. New York, NY p. 24.

was of infinite use: Lewis, Lloyd B. (1932). *Sherman: Fighting Prophet*, University of Nebraska Press, Lincoln, NE p. 138.

It would be over this same ground: Hirshson, Stanley P. (1998). *The White Tecumseh: A Biography of William T. Sherman*, Wiley Publishing. Hoboken, NJ p. 21.

When Cump returned to Moultrie: Marszalek, John F. (1993). *Sherman: A Soldier's Passion for Order*. The Free Press. New York, NY pp. 48 – 50.

After they married: Ibid., pp. 93 – 110.

He then became a lawyer: Ibid., pp. 115, 120, 121.

In January 1861: Sherman, William Tecumseh (1890). https://archive.org/details/personalmemoirso6947sher. *Personal Memoirs of Gen. W.T. Sherman*. Vol. 1. New York: Charles L. Webster & Co. Sherman (1890), letter by Sherman to Gov. Thomas O. Moore, Jan. 18, 1861, reproduced in pp. 183 – 184.

On no earthly account: Marszalek, John F. (1993). *Sherman: A Soldier's Passion for Order*. The Free Press. New York, NY pp. 137 – 138.

When war broke out: Hirshson, Stanley P. (1998). *The White Tecumseh: A Biography of William T. Sherman*, Wiley Publishing. Hoboken, NJ pp. 95 – 105.

Most of his requests: Kennett, Lee B. (2002). *Sherman: A Soldier's Life*, Harper Perennial Publishing. New York, NY pp. 127 – 149.

Sherman was labeled: Marszalek, John F. (1993). *Sherman: A Soldier's Passion for Order*. The Free Press. New York, NY pp. 154 – 167.

Sherman's exasperation: Ibid., pp. 167 – 170.

The press appeared to Sherman: Ibid., p. 211.

After a disastrous outcome: Historynet.com/laws-war-trial-thomas-knox.

Sherman responded by charging Knox: Historynet.com/laws-war-trial-thomas-knox. This article appears in the Summer 2017 issue (Vol. 29, No. 4) of MHQ—The Quarterly Journal of Military History with the headline: *The Trial of Thomas Knox*.

Thomas Knox escaped the noose: Marszalek, John F. (1993). *Sherman: A Soldier's Passion for Order*. The Free Press. New York, NY pp. 211 – 213, 216.

Chapter 5

When Weichmann graduated: Weichmann, Louis J. (1975). *A True History of the Assassination of Abraham Lincoln and the Conspiracy of 1865*. Borzoi Book published by Alfred A. Knopf, New York. pp. 12 -13.

Born in Baltimore: Ibid., p. 12.

Young Weichmann and Father Waldron: Ibid., p. 12.

The studies at St. Charles: Ibid., p. 14.

Weichmann's first impression: Ibid., p. 14.

The rigorous study regimen: Ibid., p. 14.

By the spring of 1862: Ibid., p. 14.

Weichmann's reasons for leaving: Ibid., p. 16.

It was suspected that John Surratt: Steers, Edward Jr. (2001). *Blood on the Moon: The Assassination of Abraham Lincoln*. University Press of Kentucky, Lexington, KY p 138.

Father Waldron encouraged Weichmann: Weichmann, Louis J. (1975). *A True History of the Assassination of Abraham Lincoln and the Conspiracy of 1865*. Borzoi Book published by Alfred A. Knopf, New York. pp. 16 – 17.

Among his earliest callers: Ibid., p. 18.

On that line lay Surrattsville: Ibid., p. 19.

The road was slightly guarded: Ibid., p. 21.

The Surratt home: Ibid., p. 19.

In addition to the Surrattsville farmhouse: Steers, Edward Jr. (2001). *Blood on the Moon: The Assassination of Abraham Lincoln*. University Press of Kentucky Lexington, KY p. 138.

When they arrived: Weichmann, Louis J. (1975). *A True History of the Assassination of Abraham Lincoln and the Conspiracy of 1865*. Borzoi Book published by Alfred A. Knopf, New York. pp. 19 – 20.

After he mustered in: Steers, Edward Jr. (2001). *Blood on the Moon: The*

Assassination of Abraham Lincoln. University Press of Kentucky, Lexington, KY p. 138.

Miss Anna Surratt: Weichmann, Louis J. (1975). *A True History of the Assassination of Abraham Lincoln and the Conspiracy of 1865.* Borzoi Book published by Alfred A. Knopf, New York. p. 20.

Her maiden name was Jenkins: Ibid., p. 21.

The Surratt country home: Steers, Edward Jr. (2001). *Blood on the Moon: The Assassination of Abraham Lincoln.* University Press of Kentucky, Lexington, KY p. 138.

Mary and John were known: Weichmann, Louis J. (1975). *A True History of the Assassination of Abraham Lincoln and the Conspiracy of 1865.* Borzoi Book published by Alfred A. Knopf, New York. p. 21.

The morning after Louis Weichmann's arrival: Ibid., p. 22.

On the Monday morning after Easter: Ibid., p. 22.

Returning to his post at the school: Ibid., p. 25.

In January 1864, the wheel of fortune: Ibid., p. 25 – 26.

Louis Weichmann and John Surratt: Ibid., p. 27.

The city residence would become a boardinghouse: Steers, Edward Jr. (2001). *Blood on the Moon: The Assassination of Abraham Lincoln.* University Press of Kentucky, Lexington, KY p. 139.

Chapter 6

Originally, the area of Illinois: http://www.downtownbloomington.org/content.php?section=history. *History of Bloomington City Website,* https://web.archive.org/web/20080213033750/http:/www.downtownbloomington.org/content.php? archived February 13, 2008.

James Allin: https://www.mchistory.org/research/biographies/allin-james

Eppenetus Washington McIntosh: https://suspectunusual.livejournal.com/4315.html.; https://www.jstor.org/stable/25701281.

Today's adventure for Epp: https://yesteryearsnews.wordpress.com/tag/eppetenus-mcintosh/

Boys, train up right: https://yesteryearsnews.wordpress.com/tag/eppetenus-mcintosh/

Epp eventually became a Union drummer: https://military-history.fandom.com/wiki/President_Lincoln%27s_75,000_volunteers

he beat the roll that called for volunteers: https://suspectunusual.livejournal.com/4315.html.

He wanted to "see the elephant.": Conti, Gerald (June 1984). "Seeing the Elephant." *Civil War Times Illustrated*.

The regiment was always busy: https://www.washingtonpost.com/lifestyle/kidspost/drummer-boys-played-important-roles-in-the-civil-war-and-some-became-soldiers/2012/01/31/gIQA3cKzRR_story.html; https://www.thoughtco.com/civil-war-drummer-boys-1773732

The regiment proceeded to Memphis: Lash, J. N. (2003). *A politician turned general: The Civil War career of Stephen Augustus Hurlbut*. Kent State University Press, Kent, OH pp. 100 – 101.

But before the regiment reached Corinth: http://www.civilwararchive.com/Unreghst/unilinf1.htm.

Epp McIntosh was cited: https://suspectunusual.livejournal.com/4315.html

Confederate General John Bell Hood's Army: Woodworth, Steven E. (1990). *Jefferson Davis and His Generals: The Failure of Confederate Command in the West*. University Press of Kansas, Lawrence, KS p. 276.

General Hood indicated: Kennedy, Frances H., ed. (1998) *The Civil War Battlefield Guide*. 2nd ed. Houghton Mifflin Co. Boston, MA p. 390.

In the month of October 1864: Horan, Pat (Archived from http://www.realclearhistory.com/historiat/2014/11/12/sherman_unleashes_total_war_on_confederacy-comments.html the original on 2 April 2015). *Sherman Unleashes Total War on Confederacy Real Clear History*; https://suspectunusual.livejournal.com/4315.html

Inside the stockade: Sneden, Robert Knox (2000). *Eye of the Storm*, The Free Press, New York, NY p. 224.

Tent poles, fuel, and other things: Ibid., p. 221, 224.

As if on cue: Segars, J. H. (2001). *Andersonville: The Southern Perspective*, Pelican Publishing Co. Gretna, LA p. 58.

Most of the Raiders: McElroy, John (1957). *This Was Andersonville*, Bonanza Books, New York. pp. 73 – 77.

They were given a wide berth: Sneden, Robert Knox (2000). *Eye of the Storm*, The Free Press, New York, NY. p. 222.

The new prisoners: Ransom, John L. (1881). *John Ransom's Andersonville Diary*. Auburn, NY p. 76.

which were not to be bought for less than fifty dollars each: Sneden, Robert Knox (2000). *Eye of the Storm*, The Free Press, New York, NY p. 224.

The rubber blankets were prized in Andersonville: Ibid., p. 220.

Chapter 7

What Father Hamilton saw: https://www.evangelizationstation.com/htm_html/Vocation%20Links/priest_of_andersonville.html

Father Whelan had distinguished himself: *Savannah Morning News*, December 18, 1385.

He volunteered to remain: https://www.irishgeorgia.com/Whelan

A year later he received: https://praoh.org/fr-peter-whelan-angel-andersonville/

Irish-born Catholic priest: Sheeran, Reverend James B. (1960) *Confederate Chaplain: A War Journal*, The Bruce Publishing Co., Milwaukee, WI pp. 750 – 752.

One day Father Whelan: Ibid., pp. 705 – 752.

On another day, Father Whelan: Hawes, Lilla M., ed., "Charles Olmstead Memoirs, pt. 6" *Georgia Historical Quarterly 44* (March 1960); pp. 189 – 90.

A week after Father Whelan's arrival at Andersonville: https://historycollection.com/the-life-of-a-prisoner-at-camp-sumter-during-the-civil-war/7/

Bishop Verot wrote: Chipman, Norton Parker (1911). *The Tragedy of Andersonville: Trial of Captain Henry Wirz, the Prison Keeper*, Blair-Murdoch Co., San Francisco, CA pp.197 – 201; Annales de la Propagation de la Foi, Report of the Diocese of Savannah, vol. 37 (1893): 397 – 401 (trans. Andrew Smith, O.S.B.)

Father Whelan ministered: https://historycollection.com/the-life-of-a-prisoner-at-camp-sumter-during-the-civil-war/7/

Whelan's duties were performed: Sneden, Robert Knox (2000). *Eye of the Storm*, The Free Press, New York, NY pp. 228 – 229.

Into this daily nightmare: *The Trial of Henry Wirz, 40th Congress, 2nd Session, House Executive Document 23*, (Washington, 1868) pp. 426 – 31.

He worked days: George Robbins, ed., *Diary of Rev. Henry P. Clavreul*, (Waterbury, Ct., 1910), pp. 5 – 16.

Father Whelan was joined: Ibid., pp. 6, 12.

As the number of prisoners grew: Ibid., pp. 6, 12.

But before he left Andersonville Prison: *Savannah Daily News-Herald*, June 4, 1866.

With this, he went to the town of Americus: *The Trial of Henry Wirz, 40th Congress, 2nd Session, House Executive Document 23*, (Washington, 1868) pp. 662 – 63.

The prisoners referred to it as "Whelan's bread.": notes of Mrs. Richard Horne of Kathleen, Georgia.

"I found the stockade extremely filthy: *The Trial of Henry Wirz, 40th Congress, 2nd Session, House Executive Document 23*, (Washington, 1868) pp. 287 – 90.

Most nights, Father Whelan: George Robbins, ed., *Diary of Rev. Henry P. Clavreul*, (Waterbury, Ct., 1910), pp. 5-16.

Chapter 8

Historians have theorized that the mental issues: Walker, Dale L.; Jakes, John (1997). *Legends and Lies: Great Mysteries of the American West*. Tom Doherty Associates, Publisher, New York. p. 159.

After working as a hatter in Troy: *Harper's Weekly*, May 13, 1865.

He was reported to be a proficient hatter: Johnson, Byron Berkley (1914). *Abraham Lincoln and Boston Corbett: With Personal Recollections of Each*; B. B. Johnson, *John Wilkes Booth and Jefferson Davis, a True Story of Their Capture*. Waltham, MA pp. 45 – 46.

Corbett quickly earned a reputation: Jameson, W. C. (2013). *John Wilkes Booth: Beyond the Grave*. Taylor Trade Publishing, Lanham, MD p. 128.

two prostitutes approached and propositioned him: Walker, Dale L.; Jakes, John (1997). *Legends and Lies: Great Mysteries of the American West*. Tom Doherty Associates, Publisher, New York. p. 159.

Corbett's eccentric behavior: Ibid., 160 – 161.

Butterfield found no humor: Ibid., p. 161.

Due to his continued disruptive behavior: Jameson, W. C. (2013). *John Wilkes Booth: Beyond the Grave*. Taylor Trade Publishing, Lanham, MD p. 129.

Corbett was captured by Confederate Colonel John S. Mosby's men: Walker, Dale L.; Jakes, John (1997). *Legends and Lies: Great Mysteries of the American West*. Tom Doherty Associates, Publisher, New York. p. 161.

Chapter 9

They were Army deserters: McElroy, John (1879). *This Was Andersonville*. Bonanza Books, New York. pp. 73 – 74.

"fresh fish": Ibid., p. 74.

The Raiders were an organized force: Sneden, Robert Knox (2000). *Eye of the Storm*, The Free Press. New York. pp. 222, 235.

Raiders were feared and thought an invincible: Ibid., pp. 222, 235.

At last, driven by desperation: McElroy, John L. (1957). *Andersonville: A Story of Rebel Military Prisons*, D.R. Locke Publisher. Toledo, OH pp. 220 – 222.

Tensions soon mounted in Andersonville: Sneden, Robert Knox (2000). *Eye of the Storm*, The Free Press. New York. p. 236.

Chapter 10

But physically, they weren't healthy enough: Sneden, Robert Knox (2000). *Eye of the Storm*, The Free Press. New York. p. 237.

The Raiders formed up along the south side: Ibid., p. 238.

The louder their war cries became: Ibid., p. 239.

Evidence, witnesses, and proof: Ibid., p. 241

Except for the scheduled execution: Ibid., p. 241 – 242.

Three strong men stood ready: Ibid., p. 243.

"Prisoners . . . I return to you dese men: Ibid., p. 243.

Chapter 11

it rained for twenty-one consecutive days: Ransom, John L. (1963). *John Ransom's Andersonville Diary*, Paul S. Eriksson, Publisher. Middlebury, VT pp. 87, 90.

those poor fellows who were without any shelter: Ripple, Ezra Hoyt (1996). *Dancing on the Deadline*. Presidio Press, Novato, CA p. 23.

It consisted of two heavy vertical timbers: McElroy, John L. (1879). *This Was Andersonville*, Bonanza Books, New York. p. 88.

At the appropriate moment, the barrels would be snatched by ropes: McElroy, John L. (1957). *Andersonville: A Story of Rebel Military Prisons*, D.R. Locke Publisher. Toledo, OH pp. 242 – 243.

Among the prisoners: Ibid., pp. 242 – 243.

Outside the stockade: McElroy, John L. (1879). *This Was Andersonville*, Bonanza Books, New York. p. 89.

One of the condemned Raiders screamed: Sneden, Robert Knox (2000). *Eye of the Storm*, The Free Press. New York. p. 244.

"That's about the size of it: Ibid., p. 244.

"All stop now; let the priest talk: Ibid., p. 244.

Father Peter Whelan stopped reading: McElroy, John L. (1957). *Andersonville: A Story of Rebel Military Prisons*, D.R. Locke Publisher. Toledo, OH p. 247.

Upon understanding his words, the crowd shouted: McElroy, John L. (1879). *This Was Andersonville*, Bonanza Books, New York. p. 89.

Father Whelan could no longer be heard: McElroy, John L. (1957). *Andersonville: A Story of Rebel Military Prisons*, D.R. Locke Publisher. Toledo, OH p. 249.

Then one of the condemned men, "Mosby" Collins: McElroy, John L. (1879). *This Was Andersonville*, Bonanza Books, New York. p. 91.

Patrick Delaney admonished Collins: Sneden, Robert Knox (2000). *Eye of the Storm*, The Free Press. New York. p. 244.

Sergeant Key took out his pocket watch: Ibid., p. 245.

He continued, "If oive hurted: McElroy, John L. (1879). *This Was Andersonville*, Bonanza Books, New York. p. 91.

After the pause, Sergeant Key: Sneden, Robert Knox (2000). *Eye of the Storm*, The Free Press. New York. p. 245.

General William Tecumseh Sherman: Horan, Pat (archived April 2, 2015, retrieved from the original on March 28, 2015). *"Sherman Unleashes Total War on Confederacy"*. Real Clear History.

One hundred miles north of Andersonville: Jacobson, Eric A., and Richard A. Lupp (2007). *For Cause & for Country: A Study of the Affair at Spring Hill and the Battle of Franklin*. O'More Publishing, Franklin, TN pp. 29 – 32.

Sherman determined to leave behind him a wasteland: Grimsley, Mark (2007). *The Hard Hand of War: Union Military Policy towards Southern Civilians*, 1861-1865, Report by Maj. Gen. W.T. Sherman, January 1, 1865, Cambridge University Press, quoted in p. 200.

After he took Atlanta: Bonds, Russell S. (2009). *War Like the Thunderbolt: The Battle and Burning of Atlanta*. Westholme Publishing, Yardley, PA pp. 337 – 334.

leave the churches and private homes unscathed: Marszalek, John F. (1993). *Sherman: A Soldier's Passion for Order*, The Free Press, New York, NY p. 303.

Armed with recent census maps: Ibid., p. 301.

Atlanta burned: Ibid., p. 299 – 301.

Sergeant Key raised his right hand: Sneden, Robert Knox (2000). *Eye of the Storm*, The Free Press. New York. p. 245.

After the meal sack was removed: Ibid., p. 245.

"We'll soon show you where you are: Ibid., p. 245.

While the other five dangled and squirmed: Ibid., p. 245.

Only one of the six died of a broken neck: Ibid., p. 246.

After the execution, McElroy, Sneden, and Corbett: Ibid., p. 246.

Chapter 12

The ration cart creaked into the square: Sneden, Robert Knox (2000). *Eye of the Storm*, The Free Press. New York. p. 246 – 247.

They shoveled red Georgia clay directly over the corpses: Ibid., p. 246.

the burial plots would be carefully marked: *Clara Barton and Andersonville*. National Park Service, (retrieved January 30, 2016). Andersonville, GA.

Prayers and moaning continued day and night: Sneden, Robert Knox (2000). *Eye of the Storm*, The Free Press, New York, NY p. 249.

The reign of terror from the Raiders: McElroy, John (1957). *This Was Andersonville*, Bonanza Books, New York. p. 94.

Robert returned to his shebang: Sneden, Robert Knox (2000). *Eye of the Storm*, The Free Press, New York, NY p. 239.

The dugout pit where he lived: Ibid., p. 249.

Dead and dying men lay all around: McElroy, John L. (1957). *Andersonville: A Story of Rebel Military Prisons*, D.R. Locke Publisher. Toledo, OH p. 214.

They died all hours of the night and day: Sneden, Robert Knox (2000). *Eye of the Storm*, The Free Press, New York, NY pp. 249, 253.

Capable ones carried or dragged the weaker ones: Ibid., pp. 249, 251.

Weichmann became a boarder at Mrs. Surratt's boardinghouse: Weichmann, Louis J. (1975). *A True History of the Assassination of Abraham Lincoln and the Conspiracy of 1865*, Alfred A. Knopf, Publisher. New York. p. 28.

On the day he moved in: Ibid., p. 28.

Shortly after Weichmann became a boarder: Ibid., p. 28.

The day before Christmas Eve: Ibid., p. 32.

"John, someone is calling you,": Ibid., p. 32.

"Why, Doctor, how do you do?": Ibid., p. 32.

Such was the name that Weichmann heard: Ibid., p. 32.

"...In dress, he was faultless.": Ibid., p. 32.

Weichmann shook hands with Dr. Mudd and Mr. Boone: Steers, Edward Jr. (2001). *Blood on the Moon: The Assassination of Abraham Lincoln*, The University Press of Kentucky, Lexington, KY p. 78.

When they arrived at room number 84: Weichmann, Louis J. (1975). *A True*

History of the Assassination of Abraham Lincoln and the Conspiracy of 1865, Alfred A. Knopf, Publisher. New York. p. 33.

"I hope you will excuse us: Ibid., p. 33.

Boone made similar apologies: Ibid., pp. 33 – 34

On the return home that night: Ibid., p. 34.

A month prior, on November 25: Kunhardt, Jr., Philip (1983). *A New Birth of Freedom*. Published by Little, Brown. Boston, MA pp. 342 – 43.

In major cities, crowds of adoring fans: Smith, Gene (1992) *American Gothic: The Story of America's Legendary Theatrical Family, Junius, Edwin, and John Wilkes Booth*. Simon & Schuster, New York. p. 105.

Robert Sneden watched a column of prisoners march: Sneden, Robert Knox (2000). *Eye of the Storm*, The Free Press, New York, NY p. 255.

After inquiries, Robert learned: Ibid., p. 255.

This revelation dashed all hope: Ibid., p. 255.

Sherman's actions would kill hundreds more: Ibid., p. 256.

Robert Sneden was informed by his captors: Ibid., p. 257.

War news coming through: Ibid., p. 255.

Robert concealed all his drawings, maps, and journal writings: Ibid., pp. 257 – 258.

Guards marched him to the station: Ibid., pp. 258 – 259.

Robert and his comrades were loaded onto rail cars again: Ibid., pp. 259 – 260.

On October 4, 1864, Epp's luck ran out: http://www.jstor.org/stable/25701281; Stevens, R. A., & Tharp, B. (2010). *Incredible Stories of Uncle Epp: Soldier, POW, Survivor, Minstrel, and Lincoln's Office Boy*. Journal of the Illinois State Historical Society (1998-), 103(2), pp. 143 – 44.

As prisoners of war, they were marched across Georgia: Ibid., pp. 144, 146.

Epp remained at Andersonville Prison: Ibid., p. 144.

Chapter 13

Robert Sneden, along with a few hundred fellow prisoners: Sneden, Robert Knox (2000). *Eye of the Storm*, The Free Press, New York, NY pp. 260 – 61.

Camp Lawton, or Millen Prison: https://en.wikipedia.org/wiki/Camp_Lawton_(Georgia)

When Robert walked into Millen Prison: Sneden, Robert Knox (2000). *Eye of the Storm*, The Free Press, New York, NY pp. 260 – 61.

He stood close to a fire: Ibid., p. 264.

A guard escorted Robert outside the gates: Ibid., pp. 259 – 260.

It turned out to be General John Henry Winder's headquarters: Ibid., pp. 259 – 260.

Robert was offered a written parole: Ibid., p. 264.

"It's my business to run away, and your business to try to catch me.": Ibid., p. 264.

Winder had his provost marshal read: Ibid., pp. 264 – 265.

The provost marshal was an older man: Ibid., p. 265.

"Is that scarecrow really a provost?": Ibid., p. 265.

Robert and caught his hand, passing along a secret Masonic sign: Ibid., p. 265.

"What do you call a Yankee?": Ibid., p. 266.

"I don't belong to either.": Ibid., p. 266.

he would not attempt to escape, lest he be shot trying: Ibid., p. 267.

Dr. White led him to a tent: Ibid., p. 267

He quickly stripped: Ibid., p. 268.

Four days later, three prisoners froze to death: Ibid., p. 271.

Robert marched with Dr. White and his group to the railroad depot: Ibid., p. 272.

rebel officers were lying all around in drunken slumber: Ibid., p. 273.

Robert was confident that freedom: Ibid., p. 278.

Captain Stubbs was a cripple: Ibid., pp. 282, 286.

By the time Stubbs was released four days later: Ibid., pp. 286 – 287.

Chapter 14

Robert trudged on alone, walking the railroad tracks for two and a half miles: Sneden, Robert Knox (2000). *Eye of the Storm*, The Free Press, New York, NY p. 287.

Robert Sneden was officially exchanged at Charleston: Ibid., p. 290.

Varuna neared the coast at Cape Hatteras: Ibid., p. 292.

The ship's bell sounded the alarm: Ibid., p. 294.

Before reaching Chesapeake Bay: Ibid., p. 294.

Robert finally arrived at the port in Washington, DC: Ibid., p. 295.

Robert Knox Sneden was "found alive.": Ibid., p. 297.

Chapter 15

Abraham Lincoln was weary: Winik, Jay (2001). *April 1865: The Month That Saved America*, HarperCollins Publishing. New York, NY pp. 29 – 30, 39.

"until every drop of blood drawn with the lash: U.S. Library of Congress website on Lincoln's second inauguration; https://www.loc.gov/resource/msspin.pin2202/?st=gallery.

"What an excellent chance I had, if I wished, to kill the president on Inauguration Day!": Swanson, James L. (2006). *Manhunt: The 12-Day Chase for Lincoln's Killer*. HarperCollins, New York, NY p. 4.

Abraham Lincoln had expressed his own disgust: Browne, Francis Fisher (1886). *The Every-day Life of Abraham Lincoln: A Narrative and Descriptive Biography with Pen-pictures and Personal Recollections by Those Who Knew Him*. N. D. Thompson Publishing. New York. p. 153.

"How can anyone who abhors the oppression of Negroes: http://www.abrahamlincolnonline.org/lincoln/speeches/speed.htm (retrieved 2021).

Chapter 16

Lewis Powell stared at the Baltimore sidewalk: Weichmann, Louis J. (1975). *A True History of the Assassination of Abraham Lincoln and the Conspiracy of 1865*, Alfred A. Knopf, Publisher. New York. p. 83.

British Shakespearean actor Junius Brutus Booth, Sr.: Smith, Gene (1992). *American Gothic: the story of America's legendary theatrical family, Junius, Edwin, and John Wilkes Booth*. Simon & Schuster, New York. p. 23.

John Wilkes Booth made his stage debut in 1855 at age seventeen: Kauffman, Michael W. (2004). *American Brutus: John Wilkes Booth and the Lincoln Conspiracies*. Random House, New York p. 95.

Booth later honed his craft: Weichmann, Louis J. (1975). *A True History of the Assassination of Abraham Lincoln and the Conspiracy of 1865*, Alfred A. Knopf, Publisher. New York. p. 42.

By the end of the Civil War: https://www.measuringworth.com/dollarvaluetoday/?amount=10000&from=1864

"That man's appearance, his pedigree: Clarke, Asia Booth (1996). Alford, Terry (ed.). *John Wilkes Booth: A Sister's Memoir*. University Press of Mississippi, Jackson, MS p. 88.

In the audience that night was a young Florida soldier: Weichmann, Louis J. (1975). *A True History of the Assassination of Abraham Lincoln and the Conspiracy of 1865*, Alfred A. Knopf, Publisher. New York. p. 40.

As a member of Mosby's Rangers: Ibid., p. 80.

Powell portrayed himself as a refugee: Ibid., p. 82.

Lewis Powell's role in the presidential assassination plot: Ibid., pp. 82 – 83.

Powell swore he was from Fauquier County: Ibid., pp. 82 – 83.

"Booth, I want bread—I am starving.": Ibid., p. 83.

"I will give you as much money as you want: Ibid., p. 83.

When Booth was convinced that Powell was fully indoctrinated: Kunhardt, Philip B.; Kunhardt, Peter W. (2008). *Looking for Lincoln: The Making of an American Icon*. Alfred A. Knopf. New York. p. 204.

Chapter 17

At the Surratt boardinghouse: Weichmann, Louis J. (1975). *A True History of the Assassination of Abraham Lincoln and the Conspiracy of 1865*, Alfred A. Knopf, Publisher. New York. p. 84.

"The gentleman would like to have some supper: Ibid., p. 84.

"I am from Baltimore: Ibid., p. 85.

On the afternoon of March 16: Ibid., p. 101.

John is gone away.": Ibid., p. 101.

Anna became suddenly agitated: Ibid., p. 101.

"What's the matter?": Ibid., p. 102.

Surratt waved the pistol around: Ibid., p. 102.

"Hallo, you here? I did not see you.": Ibid., p. 102.

Booth then signaled Powell and Surratt: Ibid., pp. 102 – 103.

This mistress—a petite, sensual, red-headed prostitute: Swanson, James L. (2006). *Manhunt: The 12-Day Chase for Lincoln's Killer*, HarperCollins. New York. p. 149.

While a clerk at the War Department: Weichmann, Louis J. (1975). *A True History of the Assassination of Abraham Lincoln and the Conspiracy of 1865*, Alfred A. Knopf, Publisher. New York. p. 103.

"What's the matter, John?: Ibid., p. 105.

"Queer preacher: Ibid., p. 97.

"I would like to talk privately with Mr. Surratt.": Ibid., p. 97.

Mary told him to think nothing of it: Ibid., p. 98.

John Wilkes Booth had taken on the financial responsibilities: Ibid., p. 108.

Later, Booth held a meeting at the Lichau House: Ibid., pp. 111, 113.

Chapter 18

The three men—Herold, Surratt, Atzerodt: Weichmann, Louis J. (1975). *A True History of the Assassination of Abraham Lincoln and the Conspiracy of 1865*, Alfred A. Knopf, Publisher. New York. p. 118.

Upon hearing Lloyd's reluctance: Steers, Jr., Edward (2001). *Blood on the Moon: The Assassination of Abraham Lincoln*. The University Press of Kentucky, Lexington, KY p. 139.

The scheme was supposed to go like this: Weichmann, Louis J. (1975). *A True History of the Assassination of Abraham Lincoln and the Conspiracy of 1865*, Alfred A. Knopf, Publisher. New York. p. 119.

The Sultana was licensed to operate: Potter, Jerry O. (1992). *The Sultana Tragedy: America's Greatest Maritime Disaster*, Pelican Publishing Co., Gretna, LA p. 5.

Mason had married well: Ibid., p. 6.

Mason occasionally raced other Mississippi riverboat operators: Salecker, Gene (1996). *Disaster on the Mississippi: The Sultana Explosion, April 27, 1865*, Naval

Institute Press, Annapolis, MD p. 11; Confirmed by Rosalind O'Neal: Docent of the Sultana Disaster Museum.

The Sultana, built in Cincinnati in early 1863: Salecker, Gene (1996). *Disaster on the Mississippi: The Sultana Explosion, April 27, 1865*, Naval Institute Press, Annapolis, MD p. 3.

John Litherbury Shipyard on Front Street: Ibid., p. 4.

With a legal carrying capacity of 376 people: Ibid., p. 9.

Four decks proud: Ibid., p. 1.

The Sultana boasted a bar for men and a Ladies Lounge: Ibid., p. 2.

Above the promenade deck: Ibid., p. 11.

"Sherman neckties,": Cox, Jacob D. (January 30, 2003). *The March to the Sea/ Franklin and Nashville*. Civilwarhome.com. Retrieved July 19, 2012.

Chapter 19

The three architects of Union victory: Winik, Jay (2001). *April 1865: The Month That Saved America*. HarperCollins, New York. p. 66.

Grant and Sherman assured the president: Ibid., p. 67.

On March 29, President Lincoln: Ibid., p. 69.

Lieutenant Colonel Horace Porter wrote: Donald, David Herbert (1995). *Lincoln*. Simon & Schuster, New York. p. 568.

"Good-bye, gentlemen, God bless you all!": Winik, Jay (2001). *April 1865: The Month That Saved America*. HarperCollins, New York. p. 69.

Chapter 20

Let the thing be pressed.": Winik, Jay (2001). *April 1865: The Month That Saved America*, HarperCollins, New York. p. 138.

General Grant and his Union Army advanced to Farmville: Ibid., p. 140.

James Longstreet had been a poor student academically: Wert, Jeffrey D. (1993). *General James Longstreet: The Confederacy's Most Controversial Soldier – A Biography*. Simon & Schuster, New York. pp. 26 – 29, 30 – 32.

Longstreet met his future first wife Maria Louisa Garland: Ibid., p. 34.

Reports suggest that Longstreet served as Grant's best man: Chernow, Ron (2017).

Grant. Penguin Press, London p. 872; Sanger, Donald B.; Hay, Thomas Robson (1952). *James Longstreet: I. Soldier II. Politician, Officeholder, and Writer.* Louisiana State University Press, Baton Rouge, LA p. 13.

Longstreet's memoirs reveal: Wert, Jeffrey D. (1993). *General James Longstreet: The Confederacy's Most Controversial Soldier – A Biography.* Simon & Schuster, New York. p. 53.

a scarlet fever epidemic in Richmond claimed: Ibid., p. 97.

Longstreet quietly read Grant's letter: Winik, Jay (2001). *April 1865: The Month That Saved America.* HarperCollins, New York. p. 140.

I have read your note of this date: Ibid., p. 141.

Chapter 21

After leaving Farmville: Winik, Jay (2001). *April 1865: The Month That Saved America.* HarperCollins, New York. p. 143.

One of General Grant's aides: Ibid., pp. 144 – 145.

General John Gordon, in command of the Second Corps: Ibid., p. 144.

A message to Lee from Gordon: Ibid., p. 145.

Now, Lee couldn't go forward, backward, or sideways: Ibid., p. 145.

I would rather die a thousand deaths: Ibid., p. 169.

General James Longstreet advised Lee: Wert, Jeffrey D. (1993). *General James Longstreet: The Confederacy's Most Controversial Soldier -A Biography.* Simon & Schuster. New York. p. 403.

Lee felt the tragedy of war: Winik, Jay (2001). *April 1865: The Month That Saved America.* HarperCollins, New York. p. 183 – 84.

Lee presented himself to the Union commander: Wheeler, Richard (1989). *Witness to Appomattox.* Harper & Row, Publishers. New York pp. 217 – 18.

Chapter 22

What little conversation exchanged: Winik, Jay (2001). *April 1865: The Month That Saved America.* HarperCollins, New York. p. 184.

"bare and cheerless place,": Ibid., p. 183.

Following a brief inspection: Ibid., p. 184.

Selecting the McLean house as the surrender site gave credence: Halkim, Joy (2002). *War, Terrible War 1855-1865*, Oxford University Press, New York.

The contrast between the two generals was remarkable: Wheeler, Richard (1989). *Witness to Appomattox*, Harper & Row, Publishers. New York. pp. 225 – 26.

"I met you once before, General Lee: Winik, Jay (2001). *April 1865: The Month That Saved America*. HarperCollins, New York. p. 185.

I have never been able to recall a single feature.": Ibid., p. 185.

Lee cordially continued: Ibid., p. 185.

"The terms I propose are those stated substantially in my letter of yesterday: Ibid., p. 185.

"Those are about the conditions I expected: Ibid., p. 185.

General Lee quietly contemplated the gravity of the discussion: Ibid., p. 185.

"Very well, I will write them out.": Ibid., p. 186.

Chapter 23

The order book passed from Grant's hand to Lee's: Winik, Jay (2001). *April 1865: The Month That Saved America*. HarperCollins, New York. p. 186.

General Lee pushed aside candlesticks: Ibid., p. 186.

In accordance with the substance of my letter to you of the 8th instant: Ibid., pp. 186 – 87.

Lee's expression brightened: Ibid., pp. 187 – 88.

"This will have a very happy effect: Ibid., p. 188.

"Unless you have some suggestions to make: Ibid., p. 188.

"This will have the best possible effect upon the men,": Ibid., p. 189.

Lee admitted to Grant his dilemma concerning foodstuffs: Ibid., p. 189.

"Plenty. An abundance, I assure you.": Ibid., p. 189.

"I am glad to see one real American here.": Ibid., pp. 189 – 90.

"We are all Americans.": Ibid., p. 190.

Chapter 24

With ink copies of the surrender agreement completed and signed: Winik, Jay (2001). *April 1865: The Month That Saved America*. HarperCollins, New York. p. 190.

"General Lee surrendered the Army of Northern Virginia: Ibid., p. 191.

General Lee ended his day by speaking to a crowd of weeping soldiers: Ibid., p. 192.

Lee was acutely aware of his power: Wilson, Robert (2013). *Dignity in Defeat: Why Robert E. Lee Sat for Photographer Mathew Brady So Soon After Appomattox*. From MHQ: The Quarterly Journal of Military History (Vol. 26, Issue 1). World History Group, LLC p. 22.

News of General Lee's surrender at Appomattox reached John Wilkes Booth: Stern, Philip Van Doren (1939). *The Man Who Killed Lincoln*. Published by Jonathan Cape, London, England p. 20.

President Lincoln was in a cheerful mood: Wade, Hall (1998). *One Man's Lincoln*. Kentucky Humanities Council, Inc. Lexington, KY p. 70.

Lincoln wrote in his journal: Grafton, John (1991). Dover Thrift Editions, *Great Speeches Abraham Lincoln*. Dover Publications p. 109.

The president returned to Washington, still suffering from insomnia but otherwise in excellent health: Crook, William H. (1907). *Lincoln's Last Day: New Facts Now Told for the First Time*. Compiled and written down by Margarita S. Gerry, *Harper's Monthly Magazine no. 115*, Sept. 1907. 523.

Seward and his family had planned to go out for a pleasure ride: Kauffman, Michael W. (2004). *American Brutus: John Wilkes Booth and the Lincoln Conspiracies*. New York: Random House p. 203.

"I think we are near the end at last.": Donald, David Herbert (1995). *Lincoln*. Simon & Schuster, New York. p. 581.

"Speech! Speech!": Browne, Francis F. (1897). *The Every-day Life of Abraham Lincoln*. N.D. Thompson Publishing Co., St. Louis, MO pp. 694 – 95.

Chapter 25

former POW Epp McIntosh rode a train across Four-Mile Bridge: http://www.jstor.org/stable/25701281; Stevens, R. A., & Tharp, B. (2010). *Incredible Stories of Uncle Epp: Soldier, POW, Survivor, Minstrel, and Lincoln's Office Boy*. Journal of the Illinois State Historical Society (1998-), 103(2), pp. 146 – 47.; https://yesteryearsnews.wordpress.com/tag/epetenus-mcintosh/

the band play "Dixie," since Union forces had "fairly captured it.": Donald, David Herbert (1995). *Lincoln*. Simon & Schuster, New York. p. 581.

Crowds serenaded the president throughout the day: Daily National Republican, Washington, D.C. 11 April 1865, 2nd edition, 2:4 *Evening Star* (retrieved 2021).

"Tad wants some flags.": Crook, William H. (1907). *Lincoln's Last Day: New Facts Now Told for the First Time*. Compiled and written down by Margarita S. Gerry, Harper's Monthly Magazine no. 115, Sept. 1907. 523.

John Wilkes Booth again visited Surratt House: Weichmann, Louis J. (1975). *A True History of the Assassination of Abraham Lincoln and of the Conspiracy of 1865*. Alfred A. Knopf, Publisher. New York. p. 131.

"I'm done playing: Ibid., p. 131.

Mary Surratt asked Weichmann: Steers, Jr., Edward (2001). *Blood on the Moon: The Assassination of Abraham Lincoln*. The University Press of Kentucky, Lexington, KY p. 139.

Chapter 26

A flurry of activity came rushing at Lincoln as soon as he awoke: Carwardine, Richard (2006). *Lincoln: A Life of Purpose and Power*. Alfred A. Knopf, New York. p. 223.

The president consulted with General Benjamin Butler: http://thelincolnlog.org/Results.aspx?type=CalendarMonth&year=1865&month=4

"Allow the bearer, W. H. Lamon: *Collected Works of Abraham Lincoln*. Volume 8. Lincoln, Abraham, 1809-1865.

The chief topic was the cotton industry: Dattel, Eugene R. (2008). https://www.mshistorynow.mdah.ms.gov/issue/cotton-and-the-civil-war

A young and boisterous Tad Lincoln got caught up in the moment: https://living-in-history.org/2020/12/07/the-surprising-reason-the-lincolns-owned-a-rebel-flag/

That is the last speech he will ever make.": Swanson, James L. (2006). *Manhunt: The 12-Day Chase for Lincoln's Killer*. HarperCollins Publishers, New York. p. 6.

Booth answered, "I have sold my horse and buggy: Weichmann, Louis J. (1975). *A True History of the Assassination of Abraham Lincoln and of the Conspiracy of 1865*. Alfred A. Knopf, Publisher. New York. p. 133.

"No, they are mine," replied Booth: Ibid., p. 133.

Mary Surratt leaned out of the buggy: Ibid., pp. 133 – 34.

I'm afraid the house might be searched.": Ibid., p. 134.

"Get them out ready—they will be wanted soon.": Steers, Jr., Edward (2001). *Blood on the Moon: The Assassination of Abraham Lincoln*. The University Press of Kentucky, Lexington, KY p. 110.

He noticed the dark circles under his eyes: Swanson, James L. (2006). *Manhunt: The 12-Day Chase for Lincoln's Killer*. HarperCollins Publishers, New York. pp. 15 – 16.

Chapter 27

Private William Fies, 64th Ohio Volunteer Infantry: Berry, Chester D. (2005). *Loss of the Sultana and Reminiscences of Survivors*. The University of Tennessee Press, Knoxville, TN pp. 124 – 33.

At Camp Fisk, William Fies, William Lugenbeal, and Epp McIntosh: Ibid., pp. 124 – 33.

It was in that bewitching hour: Wamsley, Erin J. (retrieved 2022). *Department of Psychology and Program in Neuroscience*. Furman University, Greenville, SC; https://pubmed.ncbi.nlm.nih.gov/30091247/

although it was only a dream, I have been strangely annoyed by it ever since.": https://www.history.com/this-day-in-history/lincoln-dreams-about-a-presidential-assassination

Washington DC was in the mood to celebrate: Swanson, James L. (2006). *Manhunt: The 12-Day Chase for Lincoln's Killer*. HarperCollins Publishers, New York. p. 9.

Abraham Lincoln wrote a check to Self for $800.00: https://www.dailymail.co.uk/

news/article-2086848/Check-President-Abraham-Lincoln-wrote-day-killed-discovered-bank-vault.html (retrieved 2022).

Captain Speed volunteered to act in absentia during Williams's absence: Potter, Jerry O. (1992). *The Sultana Tragedy: America's Greatest Maritime Disaster*. Pelican Publishing Co., Gretna, LA pp. 29 – 30.

On April 13, 1865, Speed took over Williams's job: Ibid., p. 30.

At first light, the Cairo newspaper The War Eagle: Salecker, Gene Eric (1996). *Disaster on the Mississippi: The Sultana Explosion, April 27, 1865*. Naval Institute Press, Annapolis, MD pp. 27 – 28.

Chapter 28

a dapper John Wilkes Booth entered the hotel dining room: Weichmann, Louis J. (1975). *A True History of the Assassination of Abraham Lincoln and of the Conspiracy of 1865*. Alfred A. Knopf, Publisher. New York p. 135.

His secret fiancée, Lucy "Bessie" Hale: Morcom, Richard (October 1970). "They All Loved Lucy." *American History Magazine*. Archived from the original 2010.

Booth fell captive to Bessie's beauty and charm at first sight: Weichmann, Louis J. (1975). *A True History of the Assassination of Abraham Lincoln and of the Conspiracy of 1865*. Alfred A. Knopf, Publisher. New York p. 135.

"Here comes the handsomest man in the United States.": Ibid., p. 136.

"What's on tonight?": Ibid., p. 136.

"I hope they are not going to do like the Romans: Ibid., p. 136.

Immediately, he became noticeably distracted: Ibid., p. 136.

"Suppose Lincoln was killed: Ibid., p. 138.

Davy Herold and George Atzerodt went to Naylor's stables: Ibid., p. 142.

Herold returned at 4:15 p.m. and retrieved the horse: Ibid., p. 142.

Grillo said, "What's the matter? You are walking lame.": Ibid., p. 143.

"You ain't going to kill anybody with that.": Ibid., p. 143.

That same afternoon, Harry Ford sent two employees: Ibid., p. 144.

"The president is going to be here tonight.": Ibid., p. 144.

To Rhodes, it looked like the improvised wood slat would indeed secure the box: Ibid., p. 145.

Sergeant John Clark Ely recorded in his diary: Huffman, Alan (2009). *Sultana*. HarperCollins, New York p. 171.

Union General William T. Sherman received a communique: Winik, Jay (2001). *April 1865: The Month That Saved America*, HarperCollins Publishing. New York. p. 291.

President Abraham Lincoln had watched a performance by Booth: Steers, Jr., Edward (2001). *Blood on the Moon: The Assassination of Abraham Lincoln*. The University Press of Kentucky. Lexington, KY pp. 106 – 107.

Satisfied, Booth went directly from Ford's Theatre to Pumphrey's livery stable: Ibid., p. 109.

James W. Pumphrey was an acquaintance: Ibid., p. 109.

Booth got a swift, little bay mare: Swanson, James L. (2006). *Manhunt: The 12-Day Chase for Lincoln's Killer*. HarperCollins, New York p. 36.

Mrs. Mary J. Anderson and Mrs. Mary A. Turner: Weichmann, Louis J. (1975). *A True History of the Assassination of Abraham Lincoln and of the Conspiracy of 1865*. Alfred A. Knopf, Publisher. New York p. 139.

What Greenback Saloon barkeeper James P. Ferguson saw: Swanson, James L. (2006). *Manhunt: The 12-Day Chase for Lincoln's Killer*. HarperCollins, New York p. 38.

Booth remarked to Maddox, "See what a fine horse I have got: Weichmann, Louis J. (1975). *A True History of the Assassination of Abraham Lincoln and of the Conspiracy of 1865*. Alfred A. Knopf, Publisher. New York p. 139.

"Great God! I have no longer a country!": Swanson, James L. (2006). *Manhunt: The 12-Day Chase for Lincoln's Killer*. HarperCollins, New York p. 17.

"John, how nervous you are! What is the matter?": Weichmann, Louis J. (1975). *A True History of the Assassination of Abraham Lincoln and of the Conspiracy of 1865*. Alfred A. Knopf, Publisher. New York p. 140.

At that moment, an open carriage carrying General Grant: Ibid., p. 140.

"Why, Johnny, there goes Grant: Steers, Jr., Edward (2001). *Blood on the Moon: The Assassination of Abraham Lincoln*. The University Press of Kentucky. Lexington, KY p. 112.

The curiosity of the rider did not elude Mrs. Grant: Ibid., p. 112.

Here he is again riding after us.": Weichmann, Louis J. (1975). *A True History of the Assassination of Abraham Lincoln and of the Conspiracy of 1865*. Alfred A. Knopf, Publisher. New York p. 140.

Lewis Powell ordered an early dinner: Ibid., p. 142.

Chapter 29

Captain Robert Todd Lincoln arrived in Washington: Swanson, James L. (2006). *Manhunt: The 12-Day Chase for Lincoln's Killer*. HarperCollins, New York p. 13.

Lincoln went for a short drive with General Ulysses S. Grant: Steers, Jr., Edward (2001). *Blood on the Moon: The Assassination of Abraham Lincoln*. The University Press of Kentucky. Lexington, KY p. 98.

On March 23rd, the president and the first lady visited General Grant's military headquarters at City Point: Ibid., p. 97.

When the two wives arrived on the scene: Ibid., p. 97.

Mary and Julia arrived just in time to see Mary Ord riding next to the president: Ibid., p. 97.

Mary Lincoln screamed: Ibid., p. 97.

Eckert respectfully declined the president's theater invitation: Ibid., p. 105.

At about 10 a.m., Governor Thomas Swann of Maryland and Senator John Creswell: Ibid., p. 98 – 99.

"moving with great rapidity toward a dark and indefinite shore": Swanson, James L. (2006). *Manhunt: The 12-Day Chase for Lincoln's Killer*. HarperCollins, New York p. 13.

"I never saw Mr. Lincoln more cheerful and happy: Steers, Jr., Edward (2001). *Blood on the Moon: The Assassination of Abraham Lincoln*. The University Press of Kentucky. Lexington, KY p. 95.

Later that afternoon, Mrs. Nancy Bushrod: https://historynewsnetwork.org/article/159117

Chapter 30

Mary Lincoln suggested they cancel their theater plans: Steers, Jr., Edward (2001). *Blood on the Moon: The Assassination of Abraham Lincoln*. The University Press of Kentucky. Lexington, KY p. 95.

"Well," said Lincoln, "when you have got an elephant by the hind leg: Goodwin, Doris Kearns (2005). *Team of Rivals: The Political Genius of Abraham Lincoln*. Simon & Schuster, New York pp. 732 – 33.

Chapter 31

Booth called out to Ned Spangler: Weichmann, Louis J. (1975). *A True History of the Assassination of Abraham Lincoln and of the Conspiracy of 1865*. Alfred A. Knopf, Publisher. New York pp. 149 – 50.

Once inside, Booth grabbed the iron ring: Steers, Jr., Edward (2001). *Blood on the Moon: The Assassination of Abraham Lincoln*. The University Press of Kentucky. Lexington, KY p. 114.

Booth slipped into the outer hallway of the theater: Swanson, James L. (2006). *Manhunt: The 12-Day Chase for Lincoln's Killer*. HarperCollins, New York pp. 38 – 39.

During Act 3, Scene 2 of the play: Steers, Jr., Edward (2001). *Blood on the Moon: The Assassination of Abraham Lincoln*. The University Press of Kentucky. Lexington, KY p. 118.

"Sic Semper Tyrannis!" (Thus always with tyrants!): Swanson, James L. (2006). *Manhunt: The 12-Day Chase for Lincoln's Killer*. HarperCollins, New York p. 48.

Booth passed between actors Laura Keene and William J. Ferguson: Ibid., p. 62.

At that moment, Major Stewart burst through the backstage door and spotted Booth: Ibid., pp. 63 – 64.

Many in the audience recognized the assassin: Steers, Jr., Edward (2001). *Blood on the Moon: The Assassination of Abraham Lincoln*. The University Press of Kentucky. Lexington, KY p. 118.

Chapter 32

The frozen theater crowd watched: Kauffman, Michael W. (2004). *American Brutus: John Wilkes Booth and the Lincoln Conspiracies*. Random House, New York. p. 8.

Major Henry Rathbone noted that Lincoln had not changed positions: Steers, Jr., Edward (2001). *Blood on the Moon: The Assassination of Abraham Lincoln*. University Press of Kentucky. Lexington, KY pp. 120 – 21.

Rathbone could hear people on the other side of the door pressing against it: Ibid. pp. 120 – 21.

Upon the first look at Lincoln, Dr. Leale thought the president was dead: Swanson, James L. (2006). *Manhunt: The 12-Day Chase for Lincoln's Killer*. HarperCollins, New York. pp. 71 – 72.

"While kneeling on the floor over his head: Leale, M.D., Charles (1909). *Lincoln's Last Hours*. The Estate of Charles Augustus Leale, New York p. 5.

they decided to move the president to a boardinghouse across the street—the Petersen House: Swanson, James L. (2006). *Manhunt: The 12-Day Chase for Lincoln's Killer*. HarperCollins, New York. pp. 107 – 108.

"Oh! My husband's blood!": Ibid., pp. 108 – 109.

Chapter 33

David Herold escorted Lewis Powell to Secretary Seward's residence: Swanson, James L. (2006). *Manhunt: The 12-Day Chase for Lincoln's Killer*. HarperCollins, New York. p. 52.

Powell pushed past him and began mounting the stairs: Ibid., pp. 54 – 57.

With Frederick dispatched, Powell drew his knife: Ibid., pp. 57 – 58.

"I'm mad! I'm mad!": Ibid., p. 60.

Dr. G. W. Pope was called to attend to the wounded Major Henry Rathbone: Kauffman, Michael W. (2004). *American Brutus: John Wilkes Booth and the Lincoln Conspiracies*. Random House, New York. p. 37.

Robert Todd Lincoln and the president's personal secretary John Hay:

Weichmann, Louis J. (1975). *A True History of the Assassination of Abraham Lincoln and the Conspiracy of 1865.* Alfred A. Knopf, New York. p. 157.

Booth galloped toward a bridge: Steers, Jr., Edward (2001). *Blood on the Moon: The Assassination of Abraham Lincoln.* University Press of Kentucky. Lexington, KY p. 143.

"We have killed President Lincoln and Secretary Seward!": Ibid., pp. 142 – 143.

Chapter 34

"rode sixty miles that night, with the bones of my leg tearing the flesh at every jump.": Weichmann, Louis J. (1975). *A True History of the Assassination of Abraham Lincoln and the Conspiracy of 1865.* Alfred A. Knopf, New York. p. 209.

Mudd hurriedly returned home and ordered Booth and Herold off his property: Ibid., pp. 32 – 34.

"Now he belongs to the ages.": Steers, Jr., Edward (2001). *Blood on the Moon: The Assassination of Abraham Lincoln.* University Press of Kentucky. Lexington, KY p. 134.

Chapter 35

"Along a ride of less than a mile: Wilson, Robert (2021). *Dignity in Defeat: Mathew Brady's Photos of Robert E. Lee.* ; HistoryNet Retrieved from https://www.historynet.com/dignity-in-defeat-mathew-bradys-photos-of-robert-e-lee/

Lee struggled through the crowd of well-wishers: Ibid.

"I thought that to be the time for the historical picture.": Ibid.

Brady posed the officers beneath the overhang: Ibid.

But Lee had a fine sense of history: Ibid.

The results were an undeniably iconic portrait: Ibid.

In the wake of Lincoln's death: Ibid.

Ulysses Grant wrote in his memoirs: Ibid.

Chapter 36

After leaving Dr. Mudd's farm before daylight: Swanson, James L. (2006). *Manhunt: The 12-Day Chase for Lincoln's Killer.* HarperCollins, New York. p. 163.

Cox, unwilling to let them stay: Steers, Jr., Edward (2001). *Blood on the Moon: The Assassination of Abraham Lincoln*. University Press of Kentucky. Lexington, KY pp. 159 – 60.

Epp McIntosh and about 340 other prisoners: http://www.jstor.org/stable/25701281; Stevens, R. A., & Tharp, B. (2010). *Incredible Stories of Uncle Epp: Soldier, POW, Survivor, Minstrel, and Lincoln's Office Boy*. Journal of the Illinois State Historical Society (1998-), 103(2), pp. 146 – 47.

"if anyone would have told him how good hardtack: https://yesteryearsnews.wordpress.com/tag/epetenus-mcintosh/

Thomas Jones whistled a secret melody: Swanson, James L. (2006). *Manhunt: The 12-Day Chase for Lincoln's Killer*. HarperCollins, New York. pp. 172, 177.

Sultana shared the devastating news of Lincoln's assassination: Salecker, Gene Eric (1996). *Disaster on the Mississippi: The Sultana Explosion, April 27, 1865*. Naval Institute Press, Annapolis, Md. pp. 28, 32, 33.

Major Henry W. Smith and two detectives, Ely Devoe and William Wermerskirsh: Kauffman, Michael W. (2004). *American Brutus: John Wilkes Booth and the Lincoln Conspiracies*. Random House, New York. p. 264.

"They can walk,": Ibid., p. 265.

"Oh, Mother! To be taken for such a thing!": Ibid., p. 265.

"I guess I have mistaken the house,": Ibid., p. 265.

Smith slowly reached for his pistol. "This is the house. Come in at once.": Ibid., p. 265.

"I came to get directions from Mrs. Surratt: Ibid., p. 265.

"I think you are a spy.": Ibid., p. 266.

"Before God, I do not know this man: Steers, Jr., Edward (2001). *Blood on the Moon: The Assassination of Abraham Lincoln*. University Press of Kentucky. Lexington, KY p. 177.

William Bell, was nervously waiting in a room: Kauffman, Michael W. (2004). *American Brutus: John Wilkes Booth and the Lincoln Conspiracies*. Random House, New York. p. 267.

With Lewis Powell identified: Steers, Jr., Edward (2001). *Blood on the Moon: The Assassination of Abraham Lincoln*. University Press of Kentucky. Lexington, KY p. 177.

The most important prisoners were kept aboard the monitors: Steers, Jr., Edward (2001). *Blood on the Moon: The Assassination of Abraham Lincoln*. University Press of Kentucky. Lexington, KY p. 209.

The April 18th edition of The New York Times reported: https://www.loc.gov/resource/rbpe.20405900/?st=text

After the Sultana docked at Vicksburg: Potter, Jerry O. (1992). *The Sultana Tragedy: America's Greatest Maritime Disaster*. Pelican Publishing Co., Gretna, LA p. 52.

Stanton issued a reward poster: Swanson, James L. (2006). *Manhunt: The 12-Day Chase for Lincoln's Killer*. HarperCollins, New York. pp. 221 – 22.

The poster displayed pictures of all three conspirators: Weichmann, Louis J. (1975). *A True History of the Assassination of Abraham Lincoln and the Conspiracy of 1865*. Alfred A. Knopf, New York. photo p. xiii.

Jones instructed Herold to dispose of the horses at once: Swanson, James L. (2006). *Manhunt: The 12-Day Chase for Lincoln's Killer*. HarperCollins, New York. p. 187.

Chapter 37

"Sultana may be employed as a steamer upon the waters herein specified: Potter, Jerry O. (1992). *The Sultana Tragedy: America's Greatest Maritime Disaster*. Pelican Publishing Co., Gretna, LA p. 43.

"excessive cruelty to prisoners and gross neglect of duty.": Ibid., p. 29.

At dusk, Thomas Jones came back to the makeshift campsite: Swanson, James L. (2006). *Manhunt: The 12-Day Chase for Lincoln's Killer*. HarperCollins, New York. p. 226.

"Darkness favors us.": Ibid., p. 226.

Atzerodt had tried to drink up enough courage: Swanson, James L. (2006). *Manhunt: The 12-Day Chase for Lincoln's Killer*. HarperCollins, New York pp. 78 – 79.

Booth and Herold made landfall and concealed the boat: Ibid., p. 247.

"On Friday, the 21st of April, I went to Mudd's farm again: Edwards, William C. (2012). *The Lincoln Assassination Trial – The Court Transcripts*. University Press of Kentucky, Lexington, KY p. 214.

The Sultana left New Orleans: Salecker, Gene Eric (1996). *Disaster on the Mississippi: The Sultana Explosion, April 27, 1865*. Naval Institute Press, Annapolis, MD p. 35.

Wintringer declared that he would not proceed beyond Vicksburg: Potter, Jerry O. (1992). *The Sultana Tragedy: America's Greatest Maritime Disaster*. Pelican Publishing Co., Gretna, LA p. 49.

President Lincoln's funeral train departed Washington: Steers Jr., Edward (2001). *Blood on the Moon: The Assassination of Abraham Lincoln*. The University Press of Kentucky, Lexington KY p. 279.

Chapter 38

After dusk, Booth and Herold pushed off: Steers Jr., Edward (2001). *Blood on the Moon: The Assassination of Abraham Lincoln*. The University Press of Kentucky, Lexington KY p. 184.

Lewis Powell repeatedly banged his head: Kauffman, Michael W. (2004). *American Brutus: John Wilkes Booth and the Lincoln Conspiracies*. Random House, New York. pp. 329 – 30.

During the third week of April: Potter, Jerry O. (1992). *The Sultana Tragedy: America's Greatest Maritime Disaster*. Pelican Publishing Co., Gretna, LA p. 49.

Captain Speed got angry: Ibid., p. 50.

Epp now weighed eighty-five pounds: http://www.jstor.org/stable/25701281; Stevens, R. A., & Tharp, B. (2010). *Incredible Stories of Uncle Epp: Soldier, POW, Survivor, Minstrel, and Lincoln's Office Boy*. Journal of the Illinois State Historical Society (1998-), 103(2), p. 147.

Epp and about thirteen hundred other: Salecker, Gene Eric (1996). *Disaster on the Mississippi: The Sultana Explosion, April 27, 1865*. Naval Institute Press, Annapolis, MD p. 75.

Booth and Herold touched down in Gambo Creek: Weichmann, Louis J. (1975). *A True History of the Assassination of Abraham Lincoln and the Conspiracy of 1865*. Alfred A. Knopf, Publisher, New York. p. 196.

Dr. Stuart gave them food and whiskey: Steers Jr., Edward (2001). *Blood on the Moon: The Assassination of Abraham Lincoln*. The University Press of Kentucky, Lexington KY p. 186.

The Sultana, in need of repairs, was docked at Vicksburg: Potter, Jerry O. (1992). *The Sultana Tragedy: America's Greatest Maritime Disaster*. Pelican Publishing Co., Gretna, LA p. 56.

Captain Speed, aware that the rolls of only three hundred: Ibid., p. 52.

Chapter 39

$5 per enlisted man and $10 per officer: Potter, Jerry O. (1992). *The Sultana Tragedy: America's Greatest Maritime Disaster*. Pelican Publishing Co., Gretna, LA p. 45.

Reuben Hatch had managed to keep his job: Salecker, Gene Eric (1996). *Disaster on the Mississippi: The Sultana Explosion, April 27, 1865*. Naval Institute Press, Annapolis, MD pp. 29 – 30.

Captain Frederick Speed felt pressure: Potter, Jerry O. (1992). *The Sultana Tragedy: America's Greatest Maritime Disaster*. Pelican Publishing Co., Gretna, LA p. 53.

Captain Speed reported to Major General Dana: Ibid., p. 56.

Lieutenant William Tillinghast, stood to make money: Salecker, Gene Eric (1996). *Disaster on the Mississippi: The Sultana Explosion, April 27, 1865*. Naval Institute Press, Annapolis, MD p. 196.

Henry Ames departed Vicksburg on April 22nd, carrying 1,315 soldiers: Ibid., p. 69.

Chapter 40

A local boilermaker, R. G. Taylor: Salecker, Gene Eric (1996). *Disaster on the Mississippi: The Sultana Explosion, April 27, 1865*. Naval Institute Press, Annapolis, MD p. 40.

Kerns had tried in vain to convince Speed: Potter, Jerry O. (1992). *The Sultana*

Tragedy: America's Greatest Maritime Disaster. Pelican Publishing Co., Gretna, LA pp. 57, 59.

By then, the Sultana already exceeded her carrying capacity: Huffman, Alan (2009). *Sultana*. HarperCollins, New York. p. 230.

"[No,] they can all go on one boat.": Potter, Jerry O. (1992). *The Sultana Tragedy: America's Greatest Maritime Disaster*. Pelican Publishing Co., Gretna, LA p. 62.

"interpose his influence and have part of the prisoners go on the Pauline Carroll.": Ibid., p. 62.

Pauline Carroll steamed away from Vicksburg with a total of seventeen passengers: Ibid., p. 67.

Dr. Kemble's actions: Ibid., p. 63.

Fidler complained to Mason: Ibid., pp. 65, 67.

Chapter 41

"packed on the boat like damned hogs.": Potter, Jerry O. (1992). *The Sultana Tragedy: America's Greatest Maritime Disaster*. Pelican Publishing Co., Gretna, LA p. 68.

Mason protested any further loading: Salecker, Gene Eric (1996). *Disaster on the Mississippi: The Sultana Explosion, April 27, 1865*. Naval Institute Press, Annapolis, MD p. 59.

While the exact number of people: Salecker, Gene Eric (1996). Ibid., p. 63.

Booth and Herold arrived at the William Lucas farm: Swanson, James L. (2006). *Manhunt: The 12-Hour Chase for Lincoln's Killer*. HarperCollins, New York. pp. 262 – 65.

The next morning, Lucas' son: Steers Jr., Edward (2001). *Blood on the Moon: The Assassination of Abraham Lincoln*. The University Press of Kentucky, Lexington, KY p. 187.

Chapter 42

"The president is dead: https://www.abrahamlincolnsclassroom.org/abraham-lincolns-contemporaries/abraham-lincoln-and-william-h-seward/

Frances would ever get over the shock: Ibid.

Next door to Secretary Seward's home: Steers Jr., Edward (2001). *Blood on the Moon: The Assassination of Abraham Lincoln*. The University Press of Kentucky, Lexington, KY p. 128.

General Augur had been assigned the task: Ibid., p. 196.

Lieutenant Doherty sat on a bench: Weichmann, Louis J. (1975). *A True History of the Assassination of Abraham Lincoln and the Conspiracy of 1865*. Alfred A. Knopf, Publisher, New York. pp. 202 – 03.

Moments later, Doherty and the two detectives: Ibid., p. 203.

Doherty showed everyone in the company a photograph: Steers Jr., Edward (2001). *Blood on the Moon: The Assassination of Abraham Lincoln*. The University Press of Kentucky, Lexington, KY p. 196.

This being accomplished and no trace found: Kauffman, Michael W. (2004). *American Brutus: John Wilkes Booth and the Lincoln Conspiracies*. Random House, New York. p. 311.

"Willie", as he was known: https://npsfrsp.wordpress.com/2011/04/20/brutus%e2%80%99-judas-willie-jett-part-1/

By his own account: Ibid.

Herold attempted to curry favor and assistance with Willie and his associates: Swanson, James L. (2006). *Manhunt: The 12-Hour Chase for Lincoln's Killer*. HarperCollins, New York. pp. 272 – 73.

"I suppose you have been told who I am?": Ibid., p. 274.

"Yes, I am John Wilkes Booth, the slayer of Abraham Lincoln: Ibid., p. 274.

Jett, Ruggles, and Bainbridge were astonished: Ibid., p. 276.

Ruggles noticed that Booth's wounded leg: Ibid., p. 275 – 76.

"I'm safe in glorious old Virginia, thank God!": Ibid., p. 277.

Herold asked Willie to help find a place for Booth: Ibid., p. 277.

Richard H. Garrett's place: Ibid., p. 278.

"If they don't kill me, I'll kill myself.": Kauffman, Michael W. (2004). *American Brutus: John Wilkes Booth and the Lincoln Conspiracies*. Random House, New York. p. 309.

"Here is a wounded Confederate soldier: Swanson, James L. (2006). *Manhunt: The 12-Hour Chase for Lincoln's Killer*. HarperCollins, New York. p. 279.

"Yes, I certainly will,": Ibid., p. 279.

"Coming like cattle across an open field were scores of men who were nothing but skin and bones: Ely, John Clark (March 24, 1865). *Journal Entry, upon exiting Andersonville Prison.*

Chapter 43

more than six times the Sultana's legal limit: Huffman, Alan (2009). *Sultana*. HarperCollins, New York. p. 183.

the greatest trip ever made on the western waters,": Salecker, Gene Eric (1996). *Disaster on the Mississippi: The Sultana Explosion, April 27, 1865*. Naval Institute Press, Annapolis, MD p. 65.

"something like a flock of sheep or a drove of hogs.": Ibid., p. 66.

At 9 p.m., the Sultana slowly backed away from the wharf: Potter, Jerry O. (1992). *The Sultana Tragedy: America's Greatest Maritime Disaster*. Pelican Publishing Co., Gretna, LA p. 71.

Dr. Ashton had neither seen nor heard anything: https://lincolnconspirators.com/2015/01/15/retracing-the-steps-of-the-16th-new-york/.

When they arrived at the Rappahannock River: Ibid.

Luther Baker, Everton Conger, and four troopers: Ibid.

Up until this time, Doherty and the other: Ibid.

While Conger slept, Luther Baker: Ibid.

Doherty's detachment met some Negro men: Ibid.

William Rollins confessed he had seen Booth: Weichmann, Louis J. (1975). *A True History of the Assassination of Abraham Lincoln and the Conspiracy of 1865*. Alfred A. Knopf, Publisher, New York. pp. 203 – 04.

Mr. Rollins informed Doherty that the two men: Swanson, James L. (2006). *Manhunt: The 12-Day Chase for Lincoln's Killer*. HarperCollins, New York. p. 299.

Rollins refused them the use of his small boat: Ibid., p. 299.

Rollins said, that three Confederate soldiers came up: Ibid., p. 302.

When Conger returned with four comrades: Ibid., p. 302.

Doherty met a Black man on horseback: Ibid., p. 303.

Chapter 44

In the hours before the standoff: Swanson, James L. (2006). *Manhunt: The 12-Hour Chase for Lincoln's Killer*. HarperCollins, New York. p. 305.

The first night, Richard Garrett had been hospitable toward Booth: Ibid., p. 308.

"Where do you think you're sleeping?": Ibid., p. 308.

"We'll sleep there then," said Herold: Ibid., p. 309.

"We had better lock those men up.": Ibid., p. 310.

The detachment arrived in Bowling Green: Ibid., p. 311.

In Bowling Green, the detachment found out that Jett was sleeping in the Star Hotel: Ibid., p. 311.

Mrs. Gouldman opened the door: Steers Jr., Edward (2001). *Blood on the Moon: The Assassination of Abraham Lincoln*. The University Press of Kentucky, Lexington KY p. 199.

Mrs. Gouldman reluctantly showed them upstairs: Swanson, James L. (2006). *Manhunt: The 12-Hour Chase for Lincoln's Killer*. HarperCollins, New York. p. 312.

Baker and Doherty had scarcely left the room: Ibid., p. 312.

William J. Gambrel, warned that if the passengers: Potter, Jerry O. (1992). *The Sultana Tragedy: America's Greatest Maritime Disaster*. Pelican Publishing Co., Gretna, LA p. 74.

Bankes snapped his now iconic image: Ibid., p. 74.

One of its passengers, Epp McIntosh: Salecker, Gene Eric (1996). *Disaster on the Mississippi: The Sultana Explosion, April 27, 1865*. Naval Institute Press, Annapolis, MD pp. 75 – 76.

"Very fine day, still upward we go.": Huffman, Alan (2009). *Sultana*. HarperCollins, New York. p. 230.

The steamship arrived in Memphis that evening: Potter, Jerry O. (1992). *The Sultana Tragedy: America's Greatest Maritime Disaster*. Pelican Publishing Co., Gretna, LA p. 75.

"go higher than a kite.": Salecker, Gene Eric (1996). *Disaster on the Mississippi: The Sultana Explosion, April 27, 1865*. Naval Institute Press. Annapolis, MD p. 49.

Henry Ames sailed without him: Salecker, Gene Eric (1996). Ibid., pp. 75 – 76.

While the Sultana was at the Memphis docks: Potter, Jerry O. (1992). *The Sultana Tragedy: America's Greatest Maritime Disaster*. Pelican Publishing Co., Gretna, LA pp. 68, 74.

Chapter 45

All was quiet on the Garrett farm: Swanson, James L. (2006). *Manhunt: The 12-Day Chase for Lincoln's Killer*. HarperCollins, New York. p. 316.

Booth and Herold were fast asleep in the tobacco barn: Ibid., p. 316.

"We went right up to the barn door and tried to get out,": Ibid., p. 316.

Booth and Herold then went to the back of the barn: Ibid., p. 317.

When the search party reached the gate to the Garrett farm: Ibid., p. 314.

"I know nothing about any men being here.": Ibid., p. 318.

"Bring in a lariat rope here: Ibid., p. 318.

"Don't hurt the old man. He is scared: Ibid., p. 319.

"Maybe they will go off thinking we are not here.": Kauffman, Michael W. (2004). *American Brutus: John Wilkes Booth and the Lincoln Conspiracies*. Random House, New York. p. 316.

Conger heard someone moving around inside: Weichmann, Louis J. (1975). *A True History of the Assassination of Abraham Lincoln and the Conspiracy of 1865*. Alfred A. Knopf, Publisher, New York. p. 205.

"You must go into the barn and get the arms from those men.": Swanson, James L. (2006). *Manhunt: The 12-Day Chase for Lincoln's Killer*. HarperCollins, New York. p. 319.

"They know you, and you can go in.": Kauffman, Michael W. (2004). *American Brutus: John Wilkes Booth and the Lincoln Conspiracies*. Random House, New York. p. 316.

Garrett nervously told them, "The barn is surrounded: Swanson, James L. (2006). *Manhunt: The 12-Day Chase for Lincoln's Killer*. HarperCollins, New York. p. 320.

Herold told Booth, "I'm willing to surrender.": Ibid., p. 321.

"For whom do you take me?": Ibid., p. 322.

"But we know who you are. You had better come out at once.": Weichmann, Louis J. (1975). *A True History of the Assassination of Abraham Lincoln and the Conspiracy of 1865.* Alfred A. Knopf, Publisher, New York. p. 206.

"It doesn't make any difference. Come out.": Swanson, James L. (2006). *Manhunt: The 12-Day Chase for Lincoln's Killer.* HarperCollins, New York. p. 324.

"Oh Captain! There is a man here who wants to surrender awful bad.": Ibid., p. 324.

draw your men up fifty paces off and give me a chance": Weichmann, Louis J. (1975). *A True History of the Assassination of Abraham Lincoln and the Conspiracy of 1865.* Alfred A. Knopf, Publisher, New York. p. 206.

"Well, my brave boys, prepare me a stretcher: Ibid., p. 207.

Booth replied, "I own all the arms: Ibid., pp. 205 – 06.

On his crutch, Booth at first moved toward the fire: Ibid., p. 207.

Chapter 46

Corbett fired his Colt revolver through the crack: Martelle, Scott (2015). *The Madman and the Assassin: The Strange Life of Boston Corbett, the Man Who Killed John Wilkes Booth.* Chicago Review Press. Chicago, IL p. 103.

Booth went down: Swanson, James L. (2006). *Manhunt: The 12-Day Chase for Lincoln's Killer.* HarperCollins, New York. pp. 337 – 339.

Conger initially thought Booth had shot himself: Jameson, W. C. (2013). *John Wilkes Booth: Beyond the Grave.* Taylor Trade Publishing, Lanham, MD p. 135.

Corbett replied, "Providence directed me: Swanson, James L. (2006). *Manhunt: The 12-Day Chase for Lincoln's Killer.* HarperCollins, New York. p. 340.

Did Jett betray me?": Ibid., p. 341.

Booth gasped, "Useless, useless!": Goodrich, Thomas (2005). *The Darkest Dawn: Lincoln, Booth, and the Great American Tragedy.* Indiana University Press, Bloomington, IN pp. 227 – 228.

"Tell my mother I died for my country.": Weichmann, Louis J. (1975). *A True*

History of the Assassination of Abraham Lincoln and the Conspiracy of 1865. Alfred A. Knopf, Publisher, New York. p. 208.

A soldier was sent to Port Royal for a physician: Swanson, James L. (2006). *Manhunt: The 12-Day Chase for Lincoln's Killer.* HarperCollins, New York. p. 348.

Booth had on his person a diary: Weichmann, Louis J. (1975). *A True History of the Assassination of Abraham Lincoln and the Conspiracy of 1865.* Alfred A. Knopf, Publisher, New York. pp. 209, 211.

"For four long years I have waited: https://www.nytimes.com/1865/04/21/archives/the-murderer-of-mr-lincoln-extraordinary-letter-of-john-wilkes.html

In the aftermath, Richard Garrett petitioned the federal government: Swanson, James L. (2006). *Manhunt: The 12-Day Chase for Lincoln's Killer.* HarperCollins, New York. p. 359.

Chapter 47

By 2 a.m., the Sultana was only a few miles north of Memphis: Salecker, Gene Eric (1996). *Disaster on the Mississippi: The Sultana Explosion, April 27, 1865.* Naval Institute Press, Annapolis, MD p. 78.

"a hundred earthquakes.": Potter, Jerry O. (1992). *The Sultana Tragedy: America's Greatest Maritime Disaster.* Pelican Publishing Co., Gretna, LA p. 81.

The twin smokestacks shuddered and then toppled: Salecker, Gene Eric (1996). *Disaster on the Mississippi: The Sultana Explosion, April 27, 1865.* Naval Institute Press, Annapolis, MD p. 83.

"I saw men, while attempting to escape: Berry, Chester D. 1892). *Loss of the Sultana and Reminiscences of Survivors.* Originally published: D.D. Thorp, printer, Lansing, MI p. 32.

The Mississippi River for a mile around: Potter, Jerry O. (1992). *The Sultana Tragedy: America's Greatest Maritime Disaster.* Pelican Publishing Co., Gretna, LA p. 96.

Hundreds died within the first minute: Salecker, Gene Eric (1996). *Disaster on the Mississippi: The Sultana Explosion, April 27, 1865.* Naval Institute Press, Annapolis, MD pp. 84 – 85.

Confusion and pandemonium ensued: Potter, Jerry O. (1992). *The Sultana Tragedy: America's Greatest Maritime Disaster*. Pelican Publishing Co., Gretna, LA p. 95.

Husbands threw their wives into the river: Salecker, Gene Eric (1996). *Disaster on the Mississippi: The Sultana Explosion, April 27, 1865*. Naval Institute Press, Annapolis, MD p. 153.

Lieutenant Harvey Annis paid for a private cabin: Potter, Jerry O. (1992). *The Sultana Tragedy: America's Greatest Maritime Disaster*. Pelican Publishing Co., Gretna, LA pp. 99 – 100.

Many drowned in the freezing waters: Ibid., pp. 106, 108.

Survivors clung desperately to the bow and stern: Ibid., pp. 96 – 97.

The mule finally gave up.": https://www.usni.org/magazines/naval-history-magazine/2009/august/death-river.

"he was saved by an alligator.": Salecker, Gene Eric (1996). *Disaster on the Mississippi: The Sultana Explosion, April 27, 1865*. Naval Institute Press, Annapolis, MD p. 97.

A military courier boat, the General Boynton: Ibid., p. 173.

USS Grosbeak, a river gunboat, saw the flash of light and heard the explosion: Potter, Jerry O. (1992). *The Sultana Tragedy: America's Greatest Maritime Disaster*. Pelican Publishing Co., Gretna, LA p. 105.

Chapter 48

One of the first boats on the scene was the southbound steamer Bostonia II: Salecker, Gene Eric (1996). *Disaster on the Mississippi: The Sultana Explosion, April 27, 1865*. Naval Institute Press, Annapolis, MD p. 136.

Yawls, skiffs, and every available small boat: Ibid., p. 140.

Lieutenant James Berry of the Essex: Huffman, Alan (2009). *Sultana*. HarperCollins, New York. p. 215.

We cannot hold out any longer!": Potter, Jerry O. (1992). *The Sultana Tragedy: America's Greatest Maritime Disaster*. Pelican Publishing Co., Gretna, LA p. 111.

Captain Mason did his part responsibly: Salecker, Gene Eric (1996). *Disaster on the*

Mississippi: The Sultana Explosion, April 27, 1865. Naval Institute Press, Annapolis, MD p. 107.

"top heavy and consequently inclined to careen over from side to side.": Potter, Jerry O. (1992). *The Sultana Tragedy: America's Greatest Maritime Disaster*. Pelican Publishing Co., Gretna, LA pp. 134, 149.

Their bodies were never found: Ibid., p. 131

The burning mass of what had been the Sultana: Huffman, Alan (2009). Sultana. HarperCollins, New York. pp. 221 – 222.

Fogleman's residence was converted into a temporary hospital: Salecker, Gene Eric (1996). *Disaster on the Mississippi: The Sultana Explosion, April 27, 1865*. Naval Institute Press, Annapolis, MD p. 164.

Chapter 49

plucked from the tops of trees along the Arkansas shore: Huffman, Alan (2009). *Sultana*. HarperCollins, New York. p. 218.

most of them were relieved by death in a few hours.": Salecker, Gene Eric (1996). *Disaster on the Mississippi: The Sultana Explosion, April 27, 1865*. Naval Institute Press, Annapolis, MD p. 177.

Both the military's estimate of 1,238 and the Customs Department's figure of 1,547: Ibid., p. 206.

Hoffman concluded that "the shipment of so large a number of troops: Potter, Jerry O. (1992). *The Sultana Tragedy: America's Greatest Maritime Disaster*. Pelican Publishing Co., Gretna, LA p. 150.

His report also pointed a finger of guilt at Brigadier General Morgan L. Smith: Ibid., p. 152.

disaster was rumored to be an act of sabotage: Ibid., p. 154.

Reuben Hatch never appeared before the court-martial tribunal: Ibid., pp. 32 – 34.

Secretary Hatch, along with Illinois Governor Richard Yates and Jesse K. Dubois: Ibid., p. 36.

"totally unfit" to discharge the duties of that post: Salecker, Gene Eric (1996).

Disaster on the Mississippi: The Sultana Explosion, April 27, 1865. Naval Institute Press, Annapolis, MD pp. 30, 197.

Chapter 50

The leaders for the prosecution were John A. Bingham, Joseph Holt, and Henry Lawrence Burnett: Weichmann, Louis J. (1975). *A True History of the Assassination of Abraham Lincoln and the Conspiracy of 1865*. Alfred A. Knopf, Publisher, New York. pp. 235 – 237.

President Johnson offered a $100,000 reward: https://www.washingtonpost.com/history/2020/02/02/jefferson-davis-trial-impeachment/

Mary Surratt was charged with aiding, abetting, concealing, counseling, and harboring her co-defendants: Weichmann, Louis J. (1975). *A True History of the Assassination of Abraham Lincoln and the Conspiracy of 1865*. Alfred A. Knopf, Publisher, New York. p. 242.

the first woman ever to be executed by the federal government: Ibid., p. 243.

Stone described Davy Herold as "a weak, cowardly, foolish miserable boy: Kauffman, Michael W. (2004). *American Brutus: John Wilkes Booth and the Lincoln Conspiracies*. Random House, New York. pp. 364 – 65.

When the verdict was delivered: Steers Jr., Edward (2001). *Blood on the Moon: The Assassination of Abraham Lincoln*. The University Press of Kentucky, Lexington, KY pp. 225 – 26.

Lewis Powell boldly strode tall and erect: Kauffman, Michael W. (2004). *American Brutus: John Wilkes Booth and the Lincoln Conspiracies*. Random House, New York. pp. 372 – 73.

Major General John Frederick Hartranft read the execution order: Ibid., p. 373.

On Lewis Powell's behalf, the Reverend Dr. Abram Dunn Gillette: Ibid., p. 374.

"Mrs. Surratt is innocent: Kunhardt, Philip B.; Kunhardt, Peter W. (2008). *Looking for Lincoln: The Making of an American Icon*. Alfred A. Knopf, New York. pp. 210 – 211.

"I want you to die quick,": Swanson, James L. (2006). *Manhunt: The 12-Day Chase for Lincoln's Killer*. HarperCollins, New York. p. 365.

"You know best, Captain," Powell replied: https://www.washingtonpost.com/local/four-people-were-hanged-for-lincolns-assassination-and-it-was-caught-on-camera/2015/07/03/377614d4-1905-11e5-ab92-c75ae6ab94b5_story.html

"Well, it won't hurt long.": Swanson, James L. and Weinberg, Daniel R. (2008). *Lincoln's Assassins: Their Trial and Execution.* Harper Perennial, New York. p. 365.

"Please don't let me fall.": Kauffman, Michael W. (2004). *American Brutus: John Wilkes Booth and the Lincoln Conspiracies.* Random House, New York. p. 374.

"Gentlemen, take warn—": Ibid., p. 374.

Chapter 51

The official cause of the Sultana explosion: Potter, Jerry O. (1992). *The Sultana Tragedy: America's Greatest Maritime Disaster.* Pelican Publishing, Gretna, LA p. 141.

Captain George J. Kayton, pilot of the Sultana: Salecker, Gene Eric (1996). *Disaster on the Mississippi: The Sultana Explosion, April 27, 1865.* Naval Institute Press, Annapolis MD p. 88.

Sultana careened a good deal: Ibid., p. 81.

While the direct cause of the explosion: Ibid., pp. 80, 191.

It was the investigation and report of J. J. Witzig: Ibid., p. 80.

Less than a month after the disaster: Ibid., pp. 195 – 96.

Pat Jennings, principal engineer, determined that three main factors led to the disaster: Jennings, Pat (2015). What Happened to the Sultana? https://www.nationalboard.org/SiteDocuments/General%20Meeting/Jennings.pdf

"IT WAS MURDER!": http://civilwaref.blogspot.com/2013/04/the-explosion-of-sultana-april-271865.html

"neglect of duty to the prejudice of good order and military discipline.": Potter, Jerry O. (1992). *The Sultana Tragedy: America's Greatest Maritime Disaster.* Pelican Publishing, Gretna, LA p. 160.

Chief Quartermaster Lieutenant Colonel Reuben B. Hatch: Ibid., p. 166.

Captain Frederick Speed guilty on all charges: Salecker, Gene Eric (1996). *Disaster on the Mississippi: The Sultana Explosion, April 27, 1865.* Naval Institute Press, Annapolis MD pp. 200 – 201.

James H. Kimberlin expressed disappointment: Potter, Jerry O. (1992). *The Sultana Tragedy: America's Greatest Maritime Disaster*. Pelican Publishing, Gretna, LA p. 189.

to be so soon forgotten does not speak well for our government or the American people.": Ibid., p. 191.

Robert Louden, on his deathbed confessed: https://www.prisonersofeternity.com/blog/sultana-tragedy-on-the-mississippi/

Confederate spy named Thomas Edgeworth Courtenay: https://worldhistoryproject.org/1864/1/confederate-secret-service-manufactures-coal-torpedoes

In 1888, an article appeared in a St. Louis newspaper: Potter, Jerry O. (1992). *The Sultana Tragedy: America's Greatest Maritime Disaster*. Pelican Publishing Co., Gretna, LA p. 154.

A circumstantial case can put Louden on the scene: https://timesmachine.nytimes.com/timesmachine/1888/05/07/103178226.pdf

Chapter 52

The prisoners of war are to be clearly recognized as victims: "Lieber Code". *Oxford Public International Law*. Retrieved November 9, 2017.

Thirteenth, Fourteenth, and Fifteenth Amendments to the Constitution: https://constitution.congress.gov/constitution/amendment

Chapter 53

A yellow fever epidemic swept through Dry Tortugas: Kauffman Michael W. (2004). *American Brutus: John Wilkes Booth and the Lincoln Conspiracies*. Random House, New York. p. 386.

John Surratt, Jr. was in Elmira, New York: Steers, Jr., Edward (2001). *Blood on the Moon: The Assassination of Abraham Lincoln*. The University Press of Kentucky, Lexington, KY p. 231.

Aided by ex-Confederate agents Beverly Tucker and Edwin Lee: Swanson, James L. (2006). *Manhunt: The 12-Day Chase for Lincoln's Killer*. HarperCollins, New York. p. 375.

Surratt was arrested: Steers, Jr., Edward (2001). *Blood on the Moon: The*

Assassination of Abraham Lincoln. The University Press of Kentucky, Lexington, KY p. 231.

Surratt escaped to Alexandria, Egypt: Swanson, James L. (2006). *Manhunt: The 12-Day Chase for Lincoln's Killer*. HarperCollins, New York. pp. 375 – 376.

When Surratt was asked about the testimony given by Weichmann: Weichmann, Louis J. (1975). *A True History of the Assassination of Abraham Lincoln and the Conspiracy of 1865*. Alfred A. Knopf, Publisher, New York. p. 450.

Surratt was released on $25,000 bail: Loux, Arthur F. (2014). *John Wilkes Booth: Day by Day*. McFarland & Co., Jefferson, NC p. 224.

Surratt admitted his involvement in the scheme: *Washington Evening Star* (December 7, 1870). The Text of John Surratt's Lecture at Rockville, Maryland. Retrieved August 30, 2011.

Surratt married Mary Victorine Hunter: Trindal, Elizabeth Steger (1996). *Mary Surratt: An American Tragedy*. Pelican Publishing Co., Gretna, LA p. 233.

Surratt retired from the steamship line in 1914 and died of pneumonia in 1916: *The New York Times* (April 22, 1916). John H. Surratt Dead! The Last of the Alleged Conspirators in the Lincoln Assassination. Retrieved November 14, 2020. p. 11.

Louis Weichmann moved to Anderson: Chamlee, Jr., Roy Z. (1990). *Lincoln's Assassins: A Complete Account of Their Capture, Trial, and Punishment*. McFarland & Co., Jefferson, NC p. 341.

Weichmann spent the rest of his life defending himself: Weichmann, Louis J. (1975). *A True History of the Assassination of Abraham Lincoln and the Conspiracy of 1865*. Alfred A. Knopf, Publisher, New York. p. 405.

Chapter 54

Major Henry Rathbone blamed himself for not preventing Lincoln's death: Talcott, Sebastian V. (2001). *Genealogical Notes of New York and New England Families*. Heritage Books. p. 637.

"I understand his distress: Hatch, Frederick (2011). *Protecting President Lincoln: The Security Effort, the Thwarted Plots, and the Disaster at Ford's Theatre*. McFarland. p. 161.

Despite Rathbone's mental instability: Steers, Edward (2010). *The Lincoln Assassination Encyclopedia*. HarperCollins. New York. p. 158.

Henry Rathbone attacked his family in a fit of madness: Swanson, James L. (2009). *Manhunt: The 12-Day Chase to Catch Lincoln's Killer*. HarperCollins, New York. p. 372.

"He never was thoroughly himself after that night: Hatch, Frederick (2011). *Protecting President Lincoln: The Security Effort, the Thwarted Plots, and the Disaster at Ford's Theatre*. McFarland. p. 161.

Kansas Legislature appointed Boston Corbett assistant doorkeeper: Goodrich, Thomas (2005). *The Darkest Dawn: Lincoln, Booth, and the Great American Tragedy*. Indiana University Press, Bloomington, IN p. 291.

Corbett was subsequently arrested, declared insane, and committed: Walker, Dale (2005). *The Mad Hatter. American Cowboy Magazine*, September Issue. 12 (3): 82.

He rode south to Neodesha, Kansas: Johnson, Byron Berkley (1914). *Abraham Lincoln and Boston Corbett: With Personal Recollections of Each*; B. B. Johnson, *John Wilkes Booth and Jefferson Davis, a True Story of Their Capture*. p. 51.

No further official record of Boston Corbett exists: Kubicek, Earl C, (1981). *"The Case of the Mad Hatter"*, Lincoln Herald, Volume 83, Lincoln Memorial University Press, Harrogate, TN pp. 708–719.

Chapter 55

Wirz was arrested and brought to Washington: Davis, Jefferson (1890). *Andersonville and Other War-Prisons*. Belford Co., New York.

Wirz was charged: Stevenson, R. Randolph (1876). *The Southern Side of Andersonville Prison*. Turnbull Brothers, Baltimore, MD p. 126.

At the trial, De la Baume was a skilled orator: *"Myth: The Mystery of Felix de la Baume"*. National Park Service. Retrieved June 22, 2015.

Oeser admitted to perjuring himself: Ibid.

"I know what orders are, Major. I am being hanged for obeying them.": Segars, J. H. (1995). *Andersonville: The Southern Perspective*. Pelican Publishing, Gretna, LA p. 166.

"My life is demanded as an atonement: Ibid., p. 166.

Reuben Hatch repeatedly ignored subpoenas: Salecker, Gene Eric (1996). *Disaster on the Mississippi: The Sultana Explosion, April 27, 1865*. Naval Institute Press, Annapolis MD p. 200.

none were more culpable than Colonel Reuben Hatch: Ibid., p. 202.

Hatch's career ended as it began—in controversy: Ibid., p. 198.

Epilogue

John McElroy made his way to Ottawa, Ohio: http://www.online-literature.com/john-mcelroy/

McElroy wrote, "Andersonville: A Story of Rebel Military Prisons": Ibid.

Robert Knox Sneden had sketched scenes of prison life in all the facilities where he was incarcerated: *Publisher description for Images from the Storm: 300 Civil War Images/* written and illustrated by Robert Knox Sneden; edited by Charles F. Bryan, Jr., James C. Kelly, Nelson D. Lankford, Library of Congress.

Sneden contributed some of them to the Battles and Leaders of the Civil War: Robert Knox Sneden (2000). Charles F. Bryan, Nelson D. Lankford (ed.). https://archive.org/details/eyeofstormcivilw00sned, *Eye of the Storm* ,The Free Press. New York.

Epp had indeed survived all this: Stevens, R. A., & Tharp, B. (2010). *Incredible Stories of Uncle Epp: Soldier, POW, Survivor, Minstrel, and Lincoln's Office Boy.* Journal of the Illinois State Historical Society (1998), 103(2), pp. 141 – 164; http://www.jstor.org/stable/25701281; https://yesteryearsnews.wordpress.com/tag/epetenus-mcintosh/

"help an old vet.": Ibid.

Epp was declared competent: Ibid.

Epp lived an amazing and eventful life: Ibid."

Index

13th Amendment, 25, 329
14th & 15th Infantry, Illinois Battalion, 42-43, 88-89, 169, 179
14th Amendment, 329
15th Amendment, 329
15th Illinois Infantry – 59
15th New York Cavalry, 56, 211, 235, 252, 256, 265, 267, 290
1st Georgia Volunteer Regiment, 47
25th Alabama Regiment, 12
55th Georgia Regiment, 12
58th Indiana Infantry, 88
64th Ohio Infantry, 166, 307
Acworth, GA, 43, 76
Alexandria, Egypt, 334
Alexandria, MD, 105
Allatoona Pass, (Bartow County, GA), 43, 76
Allen, Daniel, 295
Allin, James, 40
Americus, GA, 5, 11, 46, 50
Anaconda Plan, 125
Anacostia River/Bridge, 190, 207, 211, 226, 256
Anderson, GA, 11
Anderson, IN, 335-36
Anderson, Mary J., 179
Andersonville, xii, xviii, 6, 9, 11-17, 19, 21-23, 44-50, 56-60, 64, 66, 68, 73-77, 80-81, 124-125, 155, 166, 221-222, 263, 276, 332-333, 347-348, 350-351, 354-357
Andrews, Mary Raymond Shipman, 340
Annapolis, MD (Hospital), 53, 56, 91
Annis, Lt. Harvey & Anna, 296

Appomattox River, 128
Appomattox, VA, 134, 136, 138-139, 149, 165, 182, 185, 219
Aquia Creek, 256
Arlington National Cemetery, 350
Arnold, Isaac, 191
Arnold, Samuel, 110, 115-116, 222, 227, 313-314, 332-333
Arthur, President Chester, 339
Ashmun, George, 190
Ashton, Dr. Horace, 265-266
Atlanta, GA, 25-26, 28, 43, 50, 68-69, 74
Atzerodt, George, (aka Atwood, George; Port Tobacco), 99, 110, 115, 118, 161, 174, 178-179, 190, 222, 232-233, 312-13, 315-17
Augur, General Christopher C., 204, 223, 225
Bainbridge, Absalom R., 258-259, 261-262, 267
Baker, Lafayette, 229, 252-253, 256, 290
Baker, Luther, 265-267, 269, 272, 274, 280-283, 289-290
Baltimore, MD, 32-34, 101-106, 109, 116, 180, 226, 332-35
Bankes, T. W., 275
Baton Rouge, LA, 28
Battle of Allatoona, 76
Battle of Bull Run, 139
Battle of Gettysburg, 104
Battle of Reams Station, First – 257
Battle of Seven Pines, 19, 21
Battle of Shiloh, 42-43
Battle of Stones River, 104
Battles and Leaders of the Civil War, 350

Bean, Carrie, 171
Beantown, MD, 207
Beauregard, General P. G. T., 131
Bell, William, 204, 206, 225-226
Belle Grove, VA, 266
Belle Isle, VA, 10, 44
Belle Memphis, 120
Belle Plain, VA, 256, 289
Bellevue Hospital Medical College, 200
Bennett, James, 176
Benton Barracks (see Camp Benton)
Berry, Lt. James, 301-02
Big Black River, (Vicksburg, MS), 154
Bingham, John A., 311-12
Bliss, Dr. D. W., 206
Bloomington, IL, 39-41, 59, 306
Blue Ridge Mountains, 129
Boor, William, 276
Booth, Asia, 103, 288
Booth, Edwin, 78, 102-103
Booth, John Wilkes, (aka Boone, Mr.; Boyd, James William), xii, 35, 78, 93-94, 98-99, 102-103, 106-107, 109-116, 150, 157, 161-162, 168, 170-174, 177-180, 190, 192-198, 200, 202-203, 207-209, 211-212, 220-222, 227, 229, 232-233, 236, 239-240, 252, 256-262, 266-268, 270-274, 278-291, 317-319, 327, 345
Booth, Junius Brutus, Jr., 78, 102
Booth, Junius Brutus, Sr., 102
Boston, MA, 53
Bostonia II, xvii, 300-301
Boucher, Father Charles, 333
Bowling Green, VA, 261-262, 267-270, 272
Brady, Mathew, 217-219, 337
Brandy Station, Orange County, VA, 3
Branson, Margaret, 105
Brooks, Noah, 156
Brown, Governor Joseph E., 14
Bryantown, MD, 34, 36, 212, 228, 332
Bucked and gagged, 64
Burnett, Henry Lawrence, 311-12
Burroughs, Joseph "Peanut John", 175, 194, 197
Burtle, William, 220-221
Bushrod, Nancy, 186-187
Butler, General Benjamin, 160
Butterfield, General Daniel A., 55
Cahaba Prison, AL, xviii, 155, 166

Cairo, IL, 169, 264, 275, 277, 309
Camp Benton, (aka Benton Barracks, St. Louis, MO), 156, 245, 276
Camp Douglas (Chicago, IL), 327
Camp Duncan (Jacksonville, IL), 42
Camp Fisk, (Vicksburg, MS), 154-156, 166, 176, 221-222, 228-229, 231, 237-240, 244, 249, 262-263
Camp Lawton, (see Millen Prison)
Camp Sumter, (see Andersonville)
Camp Townsend, (Vicksburg, MS), 156, 237
Cape Hatteras, NC, 90
Castle Thunder Prison, (Richmond, VA), 10
Catlett, George Washington, 261
Charles County, MD, 92, 207, 211, 233
Charles Street Theatre, 102
Charleston, SC, 50, 76, 89-90, 350
Chase, Secretary Salmon P., 213
Chattanooga, TN, 26
Chesapeake Bay, (Annapolis, MD), 91
Chickasaw Bayou, (Warren County, MS), 29
Cincinnati, Ohio, 120
City Point, VA, 126-128, 150, 182
Clark, Joseph, 262
Clarke, John Sleeper, 288
Clavreul, Father Henry, 49
Clemens, Samuel, 234, 303, 320-21
Cleydael, (King George County, VA), 239, 266
Clover Hill Tavern, 139
Cobb County, GA, 43
Cobb, Sergeant Silas, 207-208
Cole, Cornelius, 189
Colfax, Schuyler, 182, 189
Collins, William "Mosby", 64, 67-71
Confederate Army of Northern Virginia, 129, 132-133, 135, 137, 144, 146, 149, 165, 257
Conger, Everton, 256-257, 266, 268-269, 272, 274, 279-281, 285
Conway's Ferry (see Port Conway)
Corbett, Sergeant Thomas P. "Boston", 48, 53-56, 71, 74, 76, 91, 235, 253, 256, 272, 279, 283, 286-287, 291, 341, 343
Corinth, MS, 42-43
Courtenay, Thomas Edgeworth – 325
Cox, Samuel, 34, 221

Coyle, John F., (editor, National Intelligencer), 173-174, 178
Creswell, Senator John (Maryland), 185
Culpepper, VA, 48, 56
Curtis, Charles, 64
Custer, General George Armstrong, 134
Dana, Charles, (Assistant Secretary of War), 189
Dana, General Napoleon Jackson Tecumseh, 176, 228, 231, 238-240, 244-245, 250, 307-308
Danville, VA, 129
Davis, CSA President Jefferson, 21, 32, 151, 173, 185, 312, 324, 347-348
Davis, Peregrine, 233
De la Baume, Felix, 343-44
Deadline, 15, 60
Dean, Apollonia, 78, 109
DeBow, Sam, 119
Delaney, Patrick, 63, 67-68
Dent, Julia (see Grant)
Derringer, 111, 195
Devoe, Ely, 223-224
Doherty, Lieutenant Edward P., 235, 252-253, 255-257, 265-269, 272-274, 279-290
Douglas, Stephen A., 32
Dozier, James, 120
Dozier, Rowena M., 120
Dry Tortugas, FL, 314-15, 331
Dubois, Governor Jesse K., 309
Durham, NC, 176
Dykes, Benjamin, 11
Eckert, General Thomas T., 184
Elmira, NY, 314, 333-35
Ely, Lieutenant John Clark, 176, 248, 263, 276
Essex, 301-302
Ewing, Ellen (Sherman), 27-29
Ewing, Thomas, Jr., 313
Ewing, Senator Thomas, Sr., 26-28
Fairfax Court House, VA, 104
Farmville, VA, 128-129, 133
Fauquier County, VA, 105-106
Ferguson, Champ, 344
Ferguson, James P., 179
Ferguson, William J., 196
Fidler, William, 250, 265
Field, Maunsell B., 168
Fies, William, 156, 166, 265, 306

Fitzpatrick, Honora, 78, 108-112, 223
Fletcher, John, 174
Florence County, SC, 86-89, 355
Fogleman, John, 303
Forbes, Charles, 195
Ford, Harry, 172-175
Ford, John T., 332
Ford's Theatre, 78, 102, 109-110, 173, 177-179, 185, 190-194, 211, 226, 332
Forrest, General Nathan Bedford, x, 76
Fort Fisher, (Wilmington, NC), 189
Fort Jefferson, (Key West, FL), 314-15, 331
Fort Monroe, (Hampton Roads, VA), 116, 222
Fort Pulaski, (Savannah, GA), 47
Four-mile Bridge, (Vicksburg, MS), 155-156
Fredericksburg, VA, 257
Freedmen's Bureau, 97
Freeman, Douglas Southall, 217
Fresh fish, 58
Fry, James Barnet, 105
Galvanized Yanks, 91
Gambo Creek, (King George, VA), 239
Gambrel, William J., 119, 264-265, 275, 303
Gardner, Alexander, 157, 315
Garland, General John, 130, 141
Garland, Maria Louisa, 130
Garrett, John, 269-272, 280-282, 284, 289-290
Garrett, Richard H., 260-262, 274, 279-281, 289-291
Garrett, William, 270-272, 282
Gautier's Restaurant, 110
General Boynton, 298
General Orders No. 67, 30
General Orders No. 8, 30
Geneva Convention, 328
Gettysburg Address, 2, 176
Gettysburg, PA, 105
Gillette, Reverend Dr. Abram Dunn, 316
Gleason, Major Daniel H., 112-113, 210-211
Gouldman, Izora, 258, 262, 267
Gordon, General John, 135-137
Grant, General Ulysses S., 29, 75, 97, 126-130, 132-137, 140-147, 149-150, 161, 165, 168, 172-173, 175, 180, 182,

185, 190, 218-219, 231, 243, 292, 314
Grant, Julia (nee Dent), 130, 180, 182-184
Great Hinkley Fire, 341
Greenback Saloon, 179
Griffin, General Charles, 183
Grillo, Scipiano, 174-175
Grover's Theatre, (D.C.), 174, 178
Hale, Senator John P., 112, 171, 182
Hale, Lucy Lambert "Bessie", 99, 112, 171-172, 288
Halleck, General Henry, 43
Hamilton, Reverend William, 46, 50, 343
Hamlin, Vice-President Hannibal, 97
Hanover, Germany, 339
Hansell, Emerick "Bud", 205
Harbin, Thomas, 239
Harris, Clara, 185-186, 188, 191, 199, 201-202, 206, 342-344
Harris, Senator Ira, 186
Harris, Thomas, 312
Harris, William, 340
Hartford Steam Boiler Inspection Company, 321
Hartranft, General John Frederick, 315-316
Hatch, Secretary Ozias M., 308-309, 348
Hatch, Colonel Reuben B., 241-245, 249, 308-309, 327-328, 352-353
Hatchie River, (southwest TN), 42
Hawk, Harry, 191, 195
Hay, John, 207
Helena, AR, 275
Henri Beaumont de Stainte-Marie, 333
Henry Ames, 238-240, 244-245, 275-277
Herndon House, 180, 190
Herold, David, (aka Boyd, David E.), 37-38, 99, 110, 115, 117-118, 161, 174-175, 178-179, 192, 203-206, 208-209, 211-212, 215, 220-222, 229, 232-233, 236, 239-240, 252, 257-262, 266-268, 270-274, 278-290, 312-323
Hildesheim, Germany, 340
Hoffman, General William, 307, 320-321
Holliday Street Theatre, 332
Holmes, Elizabeth "Lizzie", 351-52
Holmes, Mary Ann (nee Booth), 102
Holohan, Eliza, 78, 114
Holohan, John T., 78
Holohan, Mary, 109

Holt, Joseph, 311-12
Hood, General John Bell, x, 43, 44
Hopefield, AR, 277
Horne, Henry, 50, 346
Howard, William H., 184
Howard's Stables, 114, 162
Hughes, John J., 233, 236
Hughesville, MD, 220
Humphreys, General Andrew, 128
Hurlbut, General Stephen A., 42
Hurricane Deck, xviii, 122, 265, 277, 294
Impression Act of 1863, 12
Indiantown, MD, 233, 236
Ingraham, Harry, 303
Irwinville, GA, 312
Iverson, Lt. John, 89
Jacksonville, FL, 104
James River, 216
Jane Shore, 109
Jefferson Barracks, MO, 130
Jenkins, Olivia, 223
Jenkins, Zadoc, 36
Jennings, Pat, 321
Jett, William "Willie" Storke, 257-262, 267, 269, 272-274, 279, 287, 289-290
John Litherbury Shipyard, 120
John S. Ide, 256, 290
Johnson, President Andrew, 97-98, 173, 178, 185, 190, 213, 232, 311-312, 329, 332
Johnston, General Joseph E., xii, 27, 126, 176
Jones, Thomas A., 221-222, 229, 232
Julius Caesar, 78
Kayton, George, 293, 303, 320
Keene, Laura, 191, 196
Kemble, Dr. George S., 249-250
Kennedy, President John F., 193
Kennesaw Mountain, (GA), 27
Kentucky, Cadiz, 20
Kentucky, Hopkinsville, 20
Kentucky, Louisville, 344
Kerns, Captain William, 238, 248-249, 307
Key, Francis Scott, 335
Key West, FL, 315
Key, Sergeant Leroy L., 59, 62, 65-70
Kimberlin, James H., 323-24
King, Dr. Albert F. A., 201
King, Rufus, 333

Kirby, Reverend John, 50
Kirkwood House, 174, 178, 213, 232
Know Nothings, 99-100
Knox, Thomas W., 30
Lady Gay, 248
Lamon, Ward Hill, 160, 167-168, 192
Lancaster, Ohio, 27
Leale, Dr. Charles A., 162, 190-192, 199-202, 206
Leavenworth, KS, 28, 358
Lee, Edwin, 333
Lee, General Custis, 218
Lee, General Robert E., xii, 10, 69, 97, 126-130, 132, 134-137, 140-151, 165, 172, 179, 182, 216-219
Lee, Rob, 219
Lewis, W. J., 119
Libby Prison, (Richmond, VA), 5, 10
Lichau House, (D.C.), 115
Lincoln, Abraham, xii, 24-25, 32, 35, 37, 40-42, 56, 96-100, 110, 115-116, 118, 126-128, 150-153, 156-157, 159-161, 163, 167-168, 173, 177-178, 181-182, 184-191, 195-201, 207, 209, 211-212, 219, 223, 229, 235, 255, 259, 262, 269, 285, 287, 291, 313-314, 317, 319, 327, 332, 334, 338-344, 358
Lincoln, Mary Todd, 151, 182-186, 188-191, 199-202, 213, 235
Lincoln, Robert Todd, 141, 182, 207, 213
Lincoln, Tad, 151
Lincoln, Willie, 235
Live Oak Station, FL, 104
Liverpool, England, 333
Lloyd, John M., 77-78, 118, 162, 208-209, 227, 312
Lloyd's Tavern, 118, 161, 208-209
Locke, David R., 349
Locust Hill, 260
Lodwick, Preston, 120-121
Longstreet, General James, 130-132, 136, 166
Louden, Robert, 329-330
Loudoun County, VA, 258
Louisiana State University (LSU), 28
Lovett, Alexander, 233
Lucas, Charlie, 252
Lucas, William, 240, 252, 271
Luganbeal, William, 166, 298
Lynchburg, VA, 129, 139

Machodoc Creek, 239
Maddox, James L., 179
Madison, President James, 266
Magruder, Henry C., 344
Manassas, VA, 131
Marshall, Charles, 137, 139-140, 146
Marshall, Levin, 20
Mason, James, 21
Mason, Captain James Cass, 119-123, 228-230, 234, 240-241, 243-244, 247-248, 250-251, 274, 303, 324
Matthews, John, 179-180
McClellan, General George Brinton, 24
McClernand, John Alexander, 30
McCulloch, Secretary Hugh, 185
McCullough, Peter "Big Pete", 63
McElroy, John, 6, 9, 61, 71, 335, 354-355
McIntosh, Eppenetus Washington, 40-44, 76-77, 156-157, 166, 221-222, 239, 276-277, 306, 335, 356-358
McIntosh, John Wesley, 40
McIntosh, Joseph, 40
McIntosh, Nancy Beach, 40
McLean, Wilmer, 139-140, 148-149
Meade, General George, 3-4, 128
Memphis Daily Appeal, 322
Memphis, TN, xvii, 27, 42, 231, 239, 275-277, 292-293, 296-299, 303, 306, 310-313, 320, 330
Mercury Nitrate, 53
Metamora, TN, 42
Millen Prison (aka Camp Lawton), 76, 79-80, 85-86, 355
Millington, John W., 211, 235, 253, 256, 279, 285
Mississippi River, xvii, xviii, xix, 27, 119-120, 123, 125-126, 155-156, 228, 230, 264-265, 293, 295-296, 308-309, 326
Mobile, AL, 125
Montgomery Guards, 47
Montreal, Canada, 314, 333
Mosby, General John Singleton, 5, 48, 56, 104, 269
Mosby's Rangers, 104-105, 192, 258
Mouley, John, 179
Moultrie, GA, 28
Mound City, AR, 296, 304
Mudd, Dr. Samuel A., 34, 92-94, 211-212, 220, 228, 233-234, 237,

313-314, 336-337
Mulford, John E., 23
Munn, Andy, 64
Murfreesboro, TN, 104
Nanjemoy Creek, (Charles County, MD), 232, 236
Natchez, MS, 234, 247
National Hotel, 92-93, 161, 170-171, 177-178
National Intelligencer, 173, 178, 180
National Tribune, 350
Naylor's Stables, 174, 229
Neill, Edward D., 185
Neodesha, KS, 341
New Orleans, LA, 119, 123, 169, 223, 228-231, 234, 247, 309
New York Times, 227
New York Herald, 29
New York, NY, 28, 47, 53, 78, 84, 103, 116, 156, 185, 200, 319, 338, 340, 342, 344, 351
Noakville, VA, 105
O'Laughlen, Michael, 110, 115-116, 222, 226-227, 313-314, 332
Odd Fellows Hall, 92
Oeser, Felix (see De le Baume, Felix)
Office Hall, VA, 266
Oglesby, Governor Richard J., 189
Oil business, 106
Olive Branch, 238-240, 244-245
Orange Court House, VA, 267
Ord, General Edward Otho C., 183
Ord, Mary Mercer (nee Thompson), 183-184
Ould, Colonel Robert, 22, 217
Our American Cousin, 172, 190
Paddy's Hen and Chickens, xviii, 293
Parker, Lt. Colonel Ely, 143, 147
Parker, John, 192
Parr, David Preston, 109
Pauline Carroll, 244, 249
Peery, Andrew, 297-298
Pennsylvania College Hospital, 104
Pennsylvania House, 94
Petersburg, VA, 126, 262, 268
Peterson House, (D.C.), 201, 207, 212-213
Peyton, Randolph, Sarah Jane, & Lucy, 260
Philadelphia, PA, 32, 37, 106, 288

Philadelphia Inquirer, 288
Piedmont, VA, 104
Pilothouse, xviii, 122-123, 265, 293-294, 325
Pomeroy, Elsie, 349
Pontifical Zouaves, 333-34
Pope, Dr. G. W., 206, 339
Port Conway, VA, 257-258, 260, 266-267
Port Royal, VA, 104, 260-262, 268-269, 279, 287, 289
Port Tobacco, MD, 256
Porter, Admiral David Dixon, 126-127, 182
Porter, Dr. George L., 290
Porter, Lt. Colonel Horace, 127
Potomac River, 34, 37, 118, 151, 186, 222, 232-233, 236, 256, 316
Powell (aka Paine, Payne, Wood), Lewis Thornton, 99, 101-107, 109-116, 161, 178-180, 190, 192, 202-206, 223-227, 236-237, 313, 315-317
Price, General Sterling "Old Pap", 324
Prince George's County, MD, 34
Promenade Deck, 122
Pumphrey, James W. (Pumphrey's Livery Stable), 177-178, 229
Queensberry, Mrs. Elizabeth Rousby, 239
Raiders, 10, 44-45, 57-60, 62-67, 72-73, 91
Rappahannock River, 257-258, 266-268
Rath, Captain Christian, 310, 316-317
Rathbone, Gerald & Clara Pauline, 338
Rathbone, Major Henry, 185-186, 188, 191, 196, 198-202, 206-207, 259, 342-345
Rathbone, Henry Riggs, 338-340
Raybold, Thomas J., 109
Regulators, 59-63, 68, 70
Rhodes, Theodore, 175-176
Richard III, 102
Richmond, VA, 5, 9-10, 12, 21, 25-26, 44, 75, 102-103, 126, 131, 135, 139, 160, 166, 173, 186, 192, 216-217
Richter, Hartmann, 233
River Queen, 150-151
Roberts, William, 303
Robinson, Sergeant George F., 205
Rollins, William, 267-268, 272

Rosecrans, General William S., 42, 130
Rowena, 120
Rucker, General G. H., 113
Ruggles, Mortimer B., 258-262, 267
Running the gauntlet, 64
Russell, George B., 345
San Francisco, CA, 28, 156
Sarsfield, John, 64
Savannah, GA, 50, 69, 76, 86, 88, 350
Sayler's Creek, VA, 133
Schade, Louis Frederick, 343
Schneider, Joseph, 252
Scott, General Winfield, 141
Seddon, James (CSA Secretary of War), 10-11
See the elephant, 42
Seward, Augustus, 205, 226
Seward, Fanny, 204
Seward, Frances Adeline, 255
Seward, Frederick, 204
Seward, Secretary of State William H., 151-153, 174, 179, 190, 192, 202-203, 205-206, 209, 223, 226-227, 254-255
Sewell, General A. R., 252
Shakespeare, William, xv, 151
Shebangs, 13, 62, 68, 71, 73
Shenandoah Valley, VA, 104
Sheridan, General Philip, 128
Sherman Neckties, 123
Sherman, Ellen, 27-29
Sherman, General William Tecumseh, 25-30, 43-44, 50, 68-69, 74-75, 80, 86, 88, 123, 126-127, 176, 182, 318
Sherman, Mary, 26
Sic Semper Tyrannis, 196
Siege of Corinth, 42-43
Slidell, John, 21
Smith, General Morgan L., 240-241, 245, 249, 307-308
Smith, Henry W., 223-225
Sneden, Robert Knox, 3-6, 9, 15, 17, 61, 71, 73-76, 79, 89, 91, 335, 355-356
Spangler, Edmund "Ned", 175-176, 178-179, 194-195, 199, 226-227, 313-314, 336-337
Spanish Fort, AL, 125
Speed, Captain Frederick, 169, 238, 240-241, 244-245, 248-249, 252, 309, 327-328, 352
Speed, Attorney General James, 311

Speed, Joshua, 100
Springfield, IL, xix, 150, 235
St. Charles Borromeo, (Howard County, VA), 32-33
St. Liboire, (Quebec, Canada), 333
St. Louis, MO, 119-120, 123, 156, 231, 234, 245, 248, 329-330, 353
St. Mary's, (Baltimore, MD), 33, 341
St. Matthews, (Pikeville, MD; Washington, DC), 34
Stanton, Secretary of War Edwin, 97, 113, 128, 149, 157, 168, 184-185, 189, 213, 215, 229, 243, 287, 312, 328, 351-352
Star Hotel (Bowling Green, VA), 262, 267, 272
Star Saloon, (Peter Taltavull's), 174, 178, 192, 194
Stewart, Joseph B., 196-197
Stone, Dr. Robert K., 206-207
Stone, Frederick, 313-314
Stratton, William, 303
Streetor, William, 324
Stuart, Dr. Richard, 239-240
Stubbs, Captain C. F., 86-87
Sultana, 119-123, 169, 223, 228-231, 234, 240, 243-245, 247-252, 263-265, 274-277, 292-293, 295-298, 305-309, 312-314, 317, 324-329, 333, 335, 352-353, 356-358
Sultana Association, 323-24
Surratt, Anna, 35-36, 111-112, 224
Surratt, Isaac, 35-36
Surratt, John Harrison, Jr., 32-38, 77, 91-92, 94, 99, 109-118, 162, 177, 210-211, 222, 229, 312, 314, 337-341
Surratt, John Harrison, Sr., 36
Surratt, Mary (nee Jenkins), 35-37, 77, 107-111, 114, 158, 161-162, 208, 223-225, 237, 312-313, 316-317, 340
Surratt's boardinghouse, 77, 99, 107-108, 112, 115, 172, 192, 206, 211, 223, 318
Surrattsville Tavern, 115, 118, 161-162, 208-209, 312-313
Swann, Governor Thomas, 185
Swann, Oswell, 220
Taft, Dr. Charles S., 201
Tallahassee, FL, 104
Taltavull, Peter (see Star Saloon)
Taylor, R. G., 247-248

Taylor, Walter, 218
Ten Regiment Bill, 42
Terre Haute, IN, 40
Texas Deck, 122, 265, 293
The Atlantic, 353
The Century Magazine, 350
The Inter-Ocean, 349
The Living Skeleton, 221-222, 357
The Marble Heart, 177
The Toledo Blade, 349
The War Eagle, 169
The White Satin Dress, 340
Thompson, Jacob, 189
Thornberg, William A., 119
Thornton, Jim, 260
Tibbett, John, 37
Tillinghast, William, 244
Tinker, Charles A., 168
Titanic, xii, 352
Topeka, KS, 341
Traveller, 136, 149, 216-217
Troy, NY, 53
Tubular Boilers, 121, 265, 321-322
Tucker, Beverly, 333
Turner, Cornelius, 266
Turner, Ella, 112
Turner, Mary A., 179
Turner, William, 11
Usannez, Reverend Anselm, 50
Usher, Secretary John Palmer, 160
USS Grosbeak, 298, 301
USS Saugus, 226-227, 237
USS Tyler, 301
Van Alen, General James Henry, 184
Varuna, 90-91
Velletri Prison, (Rome, Italy), 333
Venice Preserved, 157
Verdi, Dr. T. S., 204
Verot, Bishop Augustin, 47-48
Vicksburg, MS, xix, 27, 154-156, 169, 176, 228-231, 234, 237-241, 243-249, 265, 274, 310, 312-314, 325-328, 357
Virginia, Midland Railroad, 105
Virginia Historical Society, 351
Waldron, Father E.Q.S., 31-34
Walker, General Reuben Lindsay, 134
War Department, 30, 38, 110, 112-113, 123, 158, 184, 189, 210-211, 229, 253, 256

Warrenton, VA, 104
Washburn Commission, 320-321
Washburn, General C. C., 308
Washington (City), DC, 26, 32-38, 55, 77-78, 91, 93-94, 116, 150-151, 155, 159-160, 162, 168, 171, 182, 184, 185, 192, 196, 235, 253, 255, 259, 266, 290, 318, 321, 338, 347, 349, 355
Washington Arsenal, 311, 315, 321
Weichmann, Louis J., 31-38, 77-78, 91-94, 108-116, 157-158, 161-162, 210, 313, 339-340, 341
Welles, (Secretary of the Navy) Gideon, 157, 168
Wells, Henry, 223
Wermerskirsh, William, 223-225
West Building Hospital, 104
West Point Military Academy, 27, 130, 231
Western & Atlantic Railroad, 26, 43
Westfall, J. W., 99
Westmoreland County, VA, 258
Whelan, Father Peter, 47-51, 64-65, 67, 70, 348, 350-352
White Plains, MD, 208
White, Dr. Isaiah H., 84-89
White, Reverend Charles I. (D.D.), 34
Willard Hotel, (D.C.), 174, 253
Williams, Captain George, 169, 231, 240, 244, 307
Williams, General Seth, 129
Winchester, VA, 104
Winder, General John Henry, 6-21, 81-87
Winder, Richard, 11, 16-17
Winder, William Sidney, 11
Winters, Erastus, 265
Wintringer, Nathan, 303
Wirz, Captain Heinrich "Henry" Hartman, 14-22, 59-65, 124-125, 347-350
Withers, William, Jr., 197
Witzig, J. J., 321
Wolfe, Elizabeth (Wirz), 20
Wright, General Horatio Gouverneur, 128
Yellow fever, 331-332
Zekiah Swamp, (Charles Co., MD), 220

About the Author

Phillip Perry grew up playing at the nearby Union Civil War Camp Fort Granger in Historic Franklin, Tennessee, graduating from Franklin High School in 1976. He holds two degrees from Aquinas College in Nashville and is retired from the local power utility after more than 36 years of service. He is a history and movie buff whose hobbies include writing, gardening, martial arts, travel, and music. He and his wife Lesa still reside in Williamson County, Tennessee.

www.ingramcontent.com/pod-product-compliance
Lightning Source LLC
Chambersburg PA
CBHW020335010526
44119CB00002B/64